GARDEN DIY

First published in Great Britain in 2001 by
Hamlyn, a division of Octopus Publishing Group Ltd
2–4 Heron Quays, London E14 4JP

First published in paperback in 2003

ISBN 0 600 60891 3

A CIP catalogue record for this book is available from the British Library

Printed and bound in China

10 9 8 7 6 5 4 3 2 1

Some of the material in this book has been previously published by Hamlyn

NOTE

In describing all the projects in this book, every care has been taken to
recommend the safest methods of working. Before starting any task, you
should be confident that you know what you are doing, and that you
know how to use all tools and equipment safely. The Publishers cannot
accept any legal responsibility or liability for accidents or damage
arising from the use of any items mentioned, or in the carrying out of
any of the projects.

hamlyn

GARDEN DIY

Contents

Introduction

Few of us are entirely happy with the garden we find when we move to a new house. Either it is a completely blank sheet, with a few heaps of builder's rubble and an apology of a lawn, or it bears the marks of a developer's hand, with easy-care but anonymous and impersonal heathers and conifers, or it has been so carefully tended and nurtured by the previous owners that its character is as obviously not 'you' as the wallpaper in the sitting room or the fittings in the bathroom.

Increasingly, television and gardening magazines invite us to 'make over' the garden as we might paint the hall and to impose structures, patterns and plants on our garden that are dictated by garden centres and nurseries and by television gardeners. But gardens aren't so easily or so quickly changed to reflect a new style or a passing fad. Nor is it easy to remove and replace features that have been added with little or no thought to the overall design of the garden and the wishes of the people who will use it.

In the first place, most people have two gardens, an area at the front and one at the back, and each serves completely different purposes. The front garden is the part of the house that everyone can see. There has to be access to the front door and the garage or hardstanding for the car, and screening to provide some privacy has to accord with local bye-laws and regulations about the height and material of fences and walls.

The back garden, on the other hand, is for enjoyment. It is where you can delight in leisurely meals on summer evenings or entertain guests. The patio is for relaxing and cooking barbecues. If you have children, this will be where they can play safely, in view of the kitchen or sitting room window. This may be where you will grow vegetables and fruit for the kitchen or create bizarre topiary shapes from clipped yew.

Gardens evolve slowly. Just as plants develop and change as they mature, so the needs and wishes of a garden's owners will alter. A family with young children will want a different type of garden from someone who is interested in raising particular species of plants. One family might want space to entertain and hold barbecues while another might prefer to have a garden that provides a habitat for a wide range of wildlife. Some families want space to grow their own fruit and vegetables, while others will want to develop a garden that requires less effort to maintain.

Identifying your needs and matching them with a practical programme of change is something that almost every gardener can undertake, and this book contains some easy-to-follow guidelines for starting that process, from assessing your garden and listing the factors that will influence the design to actually building the structures and laying the hard surfacing that will bring the design to fruition.

There are projects here for all aspects of garden design. Individual ideas can be undertaken for small gardens when a single feature, such as an arbour or water feature, will become the focal point of the plot, or they can be combined for larger gardens. Projects can be undertaken over a period of time so that paths, paving and structures, such as greenhouses and sheds, are added as time and funds permit. There are ideas and suggestions for materials and methods that will allow you to develop and build the garden that matches your hopes and needs and that reflects your personality and the requirements of your family. Whether you want a formal garden, with fine York stone paving, or prefer a more informal look, with wooden decking and curved paths and borders, you will find ideas and practical guidance to help you create the garden of your dreams.

PLANNING AND DESIGN

Realizing the potential of your space

The most important part of planning a new garden or improving an existing one is to get to know the site, because the character of a plot is influenced by the shape, the aspect and the views (or lack of them) from various points within the garden. At first sight, the combination of factors in a garden may seem unpromising, but there are no gardens that cannot be improved by thoughtful design and careful planting.

Before and after. A muddy wasteland is transformed into a lush garden.

First steps

Whether your garden is brand new or is full of established beds and borders, the same principles apply to planning and design. First, assess what you have got in terms of the size and shape of the plot. Then you can think about what you really want from your garden and whether you have the time and money to make your dreams come true. Remember that nothing in the garden happens overnight, and you will not wake up next morning to find that your garden has been transformed. Clever planning will, however, make sure that your garden comes together piece by piece.

Size

There is, of course, nothing you can do about the size of your garden, but the only limit that size might impose on your plans is in the number of features that you will be able to include and the number of plants you will be able to grow. If the garden is small, there are a number of ways in which you can utilize the available space more efficiently. Use vertical surfaces to grow climbers and wall shrubs and to support hanging baskets, for example. Raised beds and terraces increase the space available for planting, and containers can be placed on paved areas. A garden that is too large, on the other hand, can be divided into 'rooms' by internal walls, fences and hedges. This has the practical effect of instantly making the garden more manageable. It becomes possible to tackle smaller areas rather than having to tackle the entire garden, which might be daunting, especially if you are a newcomer to gardening.

You help to make a garden appear larger than it is by filling borders with plants with pale flowers and silver-grey foliage, which will have the effect of making the border recede visually. In the same way, a garden can be made to appear smaller by using 'hot' colours – reds and oranges – which make the plants seem closer than they are. A long garden will appear shorter if there are brightly coloured cannas or dahlias in the far border.

If you have a small, triangular plot, resist the temptation to place a focal point at the far end. This will serve to emphasize the lack of length. Instead, put a feature further forwards and frame it with lush planting. It will highlight the width and give the illusion of a lot more garden beyond. A large, brightly coloured urn will reduce the feeling of length, whereas a small, plain statue will emphasize it because smaller features appear to be further away from the viewer.

A path that widens as it goes down the garden will foreshorten the view in a long, narrow garden; conversely, one that tapers in the other direction will give the illusion of length, appearing to disappear into the distance and thereby lengthening a short garden.

Shape

The shape of the garden will affect the design, and the more awkwardly shaped your garden, the more carefully the design must be thought through. You may feel that there is little you can do to alter the shape of your garden, but there is much that can be done to disguise unattractive boundaries and to emphasize the good points.

A triangular or L-shaped garden can offer more design potential than a rectangular one, but perhaps the most difficult shape of all is a square, especially if it is small, as many front gardens are.

A long, narrow area can be divided into contrasting sections with barriers across its width. If you leave a narrow view right down the length of the garden you will create an additional sight-line. Placing an ornamental feature, such as a statue or seat, at the far end will allow you to gain the full benefit from the site's length while the screens will minimize the disadvantages of the shape.

Topography

As well as the overall shape and size of the plot, its topography will play a part in the design. Think twice before levelling slopes in your garden. Perhaps surprisingly, a perfectly level site offers far less exciting design potential than one with interesting, gradual changes. Slopes, banks and variations in level bring opportunities to build terraces, steps, retaining walls or stepped beds. Alterations in level within a garden also make the building of ponds or rock gardens easier.

Shapes and styles

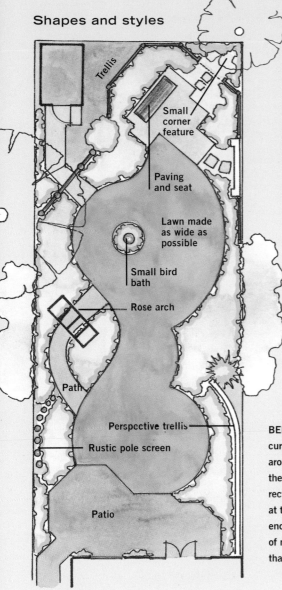

Trellis

Small corner feature

Paving and seat

Lawn made as wide as possible

Small bird bath

Rose arch

Path

Perspective trellis

Rustic pole screen

Patio

LEFT A long, narrow garden can be made to seem more interesting by the use of perspective and by the introduction of features such as paths and hard landscaping. The illusion of secret places and hidden corners invites the visitor to explore this informal garden, which cannot be seen in its entirety from the patio.

RIGHT Corner plots are often difficult to design because they tend to divide into two quite separate areas. The use of the same type of paving unifies this semi-formal area, while at the same time leaving plenty of space for planting, which provides both privacy and, in a town garden, helps to muffle the sound of traffic.

BELOW RIGHT The sweeping curve of the lawn draws the eye around the garden and away from the rather severe lines of the rectangular boundary. Focal points at the sides, rather than at the far end of the garden, have the effect of making the garden appear wider than it actually is.

Brick walls with trellis top

Low raised bed

Slightly higher raised bed

Fence

Garden seat

Brick or block paving

Well 'pump' water feature

Lawn

Outhouse

Random rectangular paving

Wooden beam arch

Sawn timber pergola

Sunny patio

Step up

Low raised bed

Sundial surrounded by brick edged gravel

Lawn

Stepping stones

Seat on brick paving

Compost bin

Wooden beam arch

Trellis

Shed

tree

Access path

Styles

Before you can begin to design you need to decide on the style of garden you want. Town gardens often lend themselves to formal designs because it is easier to incorporate surrounding party walls into a methodical, precise concept. Remember, too, that a town garden will be seen as much from the upper storey windows of your own house as the lower ones, and formal gardens tend to look better from above than informal ones.

Formal gardens generally incorporate geometric shapes – ovals, circles and squares – in the layout, with identical or symmetrical features balancing each other on each side of the garden. Lawns are generally round or square, and ponds will be rectangular and often raised.

If you live in the country and the view beyond your garden is of trees and fields, you are more likely to prefer an informal garden, with winding paths and curved borders. Informal is not the same as disordered, however, and most cottage gardens have defined borders, lawns and paths, even though they will have relaxed edges. The hard landscaping will be of irregularly shaped pavers, and ponds will be kidney-shaped or be designed to attract wildlife to the water's edge.

Assessing the site

Even when you have assessed the shape and size of your garden and have thought about the style of garden you would prefer, there are still several factors to take into account before you can get down to designing your ideal garden.

Climate and microclimate

Climate dictates the kinds of plants you can grow, and this will influence your design. If you have moved to a new area, you can easily find out the average temperature and rainfall, but some gardens are prone to extremes of climate.

Regional climate is influenced by fundamental geographical factors, but microclimates, both natural and artificial, can arise within very small areas. Most cities, for example, are nearly frost free because of the heat that is retained by buildings and released at night. Many tender plants can be kept outside all year round that, in rural areas, would need winter protection.

Although you cannot do much about the weather in your garden, you can do much to mitigate its effects – by erecting windbreaks against icy winds, for example, which will allow you to incorporate a wide range of interesting and delicate plants in your design that wouldn't have been able to survive without the extra shelter.

Soil types

It hardly needs saying that the better the soil in your garden the better will be the plants that you can grow. If your soil is poor and infertile you will have to improve it. However, because soils vary widely in their texture, structure and quality, your first step should be to find out what type of soil you have in your garden.

Most gardeners need know only if their garden is clayey or sandy. Clay soil retains moisture and is often fertile, but it is difficult to work and sticky when wet. In hot,

dry weather, on the other hand it bakes dry, and the surface cracks. Regular digging and the incorporation of well-rotted compost will eventually improve its texture. Sandy soil is easy to work, but it dries out quickly. Incorporating large amounts of well-rotted compost or manure will improve its water-retaining capacity.

Both types of soil will benefit from the addition of organic material, such as garden compost and leaf mould, which will improve the structure and attract beneficial soil-borne organisms.

Acidity and alkalinity

For some gardeners, knowing whether the soil is clayey or sandy is less important than knowing if it is acid or alkaline. If you have alkaline soil you will be unable to grow lime-hating plants such as rhododendrons, camellias, azaleas and some heathers. If the soil is very acid you will find that plants such as dianthus (pinks), some clematis and philadelphus will not thrive.

One of the best ways of checking the soil type in your garden is to see what your neighbours grow. If their gardens are filled

A rough guide to soil types

Soil type	Appearance	Physical qualities	Chemical status
Clay	Soil remains wet in wet weather. Sedges, alder, willow and buttercups are common	Very slow to drain. Small particles, few air spaces. Sticky and greasy if wet; hard and lumpy when dry. Hard to work, easily compacted	Naturally rich in nutrients but these need to be released. Often neutral (pH7) or acidic
Heavy loam	All factors between clay and medium loam		
Medium loam	Roses, shrubs and grasses grow well	Drains moderately fast. Fairly easy to work but can stay waterlogged after rain	Fairly rich in plant food but needs improvement to help release nutrients
Light loam	All factors between medium loam and sandy soil		
Sandy soil	Light in colour. Broom, gorse, Scots pine grow well	Drains quickly. Lots of spaces between large particles. Grainy to feel	Low in nutrients. Often acidic (pH under 5). Loses nutrients easily due to free drainage
Chalk or limestone	Pale or white subsoil. Pieces of chalk may be present in soil. Clematis, viburnum, dogwoods (Cornus) grow well	Sticky when wet (chalk). Gritty to feel (limestone). Usually easy to work	Low in organic matter. Nutrients easily washed away. Alkaline (pH over 7)
Peaty soil	Dark and fibrous. Vegetation smell. Heather, willow, alder do well	Spongy and stays wet after rain	Low in phosphate. Acidic (pH under 7)
Stony soil	Pale, many stones present. Sparse natural vegetation. Rowan often present	Shallow with large amounts of stones and rocks present. Hard to work	Low in nutrients and organic material. Needs regular and heavy feeding
Acid soil	Heather and rhododendrons do well	Variable but often dark in colour	Variable pH under 7
Good loam	Most plants grow well except those that must have acid or alkaline conditions	Friable to touch, good structure and soil life. Brown colour and pleasant smell. Easy to work and fairly free draining	pH of around 6.5. Good balance of nutrients and trace elements

Soil pH

Knowing the degree of acidity or alkalinity of your soil, its pH, is important because it has a direct effect on the type of plants you can grow. A neutral soil is said to have a pH of 7. Soils with a pH lower than that are acid; those with a higher pH are alkaline. Most soils are between 5.5 and 7.5, and many plants will grow in soils in this range. However, ericaceous plants must have acid soil and simply will not thrive in alkaline conditions.

ABOVE Soil-testing kits, available from most garden centres and DIY stores, are a quick and inexpensive way of finding whether your soil is acid or alkaline.

with heathers and rhododendrons, it would be safe to assume that the soil is acid. You can check for yourself with one of the inexpensive soil-testing kits that are available from most garden centres. It is worth testing the soil in several parts of the garden in case there are pockets of acid or alkaline soil or in case the previous owner has treated parts of the garden, and then you should plan to include in your design those plants that suit your soil type.

Short-term treatments are available. You can, for example, increase the alkalinity of soil by adding lime or mushroom compost, but it is unlikely that you will be able to effect long-term change. If you have set your heart on a bed of heathers but find you have alkaline soil, consider building raised beds, which you can fill with the appropriate soil type.

Sun, shade and shelter

The quality of light will have a major influence on your garden design. Heavy shade is usually more of a problem in town gardens than in the countryside because walls, fences and neighbouring buildings cast shadows for at least part of the day. If only a corner of your garden receives sun, it would be sensible to position a seat, patio or greenhouse there.

Shelter within the garden is another important factor for the gardener to consider. Most plants do best in a sheltered site, and ideally your garden should provide a haven in which they can thrive. Wind can be problem because it dehydrates the soil and stunts plant growth. If the site is exposed, build a windbreak, such as an openwork fence, or plant a hedge or a row of shrubs. However, it is crucial that you avoid solid walls, because the wind will eddy over the top of the wall and create a damaging whirlwind effect.

Protection from frost is as important as protection from wind. Even though many plants will survive low winter temperatures, frost in late spring, when blossom and young shoots have appeared, can kill plants. Frost pockets occur in valleys and hollows in the ground, where cold, frosty air sinks and collects beneath walls and dense hedges. Thinning hedges or removing trees and walls can allow the cold air to flow through the garden rather than being trapped.

Existing features

In many ways, it is easy to design a garden when you begin with a bare plot. It is generally more difficult to rework an established garden, but before you dig out the features you find in your garden, do nothing for a year so that you can judge the overall impact in all seasons. Make a note of seasonal bulbs, autumn and winter colour and plants with interesting seedheads, and mark areas that are boggy in winter rains or dry in summer.

Existing planting and built features may not fit into your new design. Before you cut down a large bush or shrub, consider incorporating it into your scheme. Mature plants will be a welcome addition to any new planting that you may have planned. Incorporating hard landscaping and built ornamental features is less of a problem since they can, in most instances, be dismantled and the materials often re-used.

Do not, however, keep features that you do not like and feel will never be part of your design. It is your garden, after all, so make sure that you are happy with everything in it.

ABOVE   A blue picket fence provides an attractive backdrop to a border filled with summer annuals.

Assessing priorities

Many people find that deciding what will go in their garden is the most difficult part of the planning process. There is little point in endlessly doodling on a sheet of paper. Instead, try to define exactly what you want from your garden.

Beginning to plan

The first step in drawing a plan of your garden is to identify the features you want. It is worth drawing up a list of 'must have' and 'would like to have'. If you have young children, for example, you will need somewhere for them to play safely, within sight of the house. If you are thinking of incorporating features that will make life easier when you retire, you might want to

include raised beds or replace large borders with low-maintenance hard landscaping. If you have pets, you will need somewhere secure for them. If members of your family are elderly, you should consider building wide paths, perhaps with a handrail. If you are interested in plants, you will need the greatest possible space for planting and a greenhouse and a cold frame.

It is quite likely that your list will be too long and unrealistic, and the next step is to refine it in the cold light of space, time and money. You might like the idea of having a swimming pool, but lack of space or money might rule it out from the start. Other features, even with a great deal of thought, may be irreconcilable. Children playing ball games on the lawn and large flowerbeds, filled with choice plants are not compatible in a small garden. Football goalposts and greenhouses may not be an ideal combination, although carefully sited trellises and screens might help to overcome this problem.

Make sure you include the 'must have' items on your final list. If you have a large garden you should be able to include many of the things you would like to have as well. The problem may be deciding how much space to assign to each area and how to divide one from another. In a smaller plot, however, you will have to limit yourself to just one or two features, and the less space you have at your disposal the more ingenious your design must be.

Remember that your children will not be children for ever. If you plant a tree in the centre of the lawn on which they tear around playing football, it will be large enough for you to relax in its shade by the time they have moved on to other pursuits. If you create a sandpit for your children, it can be transformed into a small water feature when they are no longer interested in sand castles. A child's wendy house might eventually become an arbour or a garden shed.

LEFT A shady, well-planted patio will be a haven on hot summer days and provide an ideal spot for alfresco dining.

Budgeting and timing

Time and money are the major factors to take into consideration at this stage. So that you do not become disillusioned and to avoid disappointment only plan a garden that you can afford to make in a realistic timescale and that you can afford to maintain.

The joy of gardening is that it suits every pocket. Landscaping a small area with choice materials and lavish, mature plants is expensive. Using inexpensive materials, on the other hand, and propagating as many plants as you can and being prepared to wait is the best way to develop a fine garden on a tight budget. The difference in price between small plants that will take two or three years to achieve maturity and buying full-grown plants is huge. You can also save money by buying long-lasting perennials instead of constantly renewing your displays with annuals and biennials.

Beds can be filled with seed-sown annuals until you can afford more expensive trees and shrubs. Attractive pots can provide a focal point until you can afford the statue or sculpture you have imagined in your original design. Bulbs will produce reliable spring and summer colour and interest until larger, slower growing plants have matured. Containers filled with seasonal plants can be moved around to fill gaps and enliven dull areas while the larger plants are growing.

Drawing up a list

Use the following as a guide to the type of features that you might want to incorporate in your new garden design:

- Patio or barbecue area
- Lawn for recreation or appearance
- Borders for plants
- Greenhouse
- Compost heap
- Vegetable and fruit gardens
- Herb garden
- Summer house
- Shed
- Hardstanding
- Children's play area
- Water feature

ABOVE Vegetable gardens needn't be simply functional. This elegant potager demonstrates how a variety of vegetables can be grown in a decorative fashion.

While the expense of planting can be spread over several years, the cost of the hard landscaping materials cannot. If your design includes a patio and paths or raised beds, using the same materials for all the features will provide a unifying element in the garden. Paths that are a different colour from the stone used for the patio will look odd. Hard materials also age and mellow, and if you delay building one or more features, even if you use the same type of stone, you may have to wait several years before they look similar.

Before deciding on your scheme, check that there are no local bye-laws governing what you can and cannot do. There are regulations in most areas about building against public highways, and you should also be aware of limitations that might be imposed on height. Established trees and watercourses are also subject to local regulations.

Checklist

Every gardener has practical considerations for the design of their garden. Answer the following questions before planning your new garden:

What type of garden do you have?
- [ ] Type of soil
- [ ] Shade

What do you want to do in your garden?
- [ ] Entertain
- [ ] Have barbecues
- [ ] Grow plants
- [ ] Grow vegetables
- [ ] Grow herbs
- [ ] Encourage nature
- [ ] Play games
- [ ] Relax
- [ ] Sunbathe
- [ ] Retire

What do you want to have in the garden?
- [ ] Flower borders
- [ ] Vegetable garden
- [ ] Containers
- [ ] Privacy
- [ ] Patios
- [ ] Swimming pool
- [ ] Sitting areas
- [ ] Summer house
- [ ] Greenhouse

What kind of plants do you want to grow ?
- [ ] Annual flowers
- [ ] Year-round
- [ ] Foliage plants
- [ ] Perennials
- [ ] Shrubs
- [ ] Trees
- [ ] Fruit
- [ ] Vegetables
- [ ] Herbs
- [ ] Exotica
- [ ] Rock plants
- [ ] Water plants
- [ ] Organically grown
- [ ] Plants in containers

When do you want to be in the garden?
- [ ] Occasionally
- [ ] All the time
- [ ] Evenings
- [ ] Weekends
- [ ] During retirement

Who will be using the garden?
- [ ] Family
- [ ] Friends
- [ ] Children
- [ ] Pets
- [ ] Older people

What style of garden do you want?
- [ ] Formal
- [ ] Informal
- [ ] Romantic
- [ ] Cottage
- [ ] Exotic

What sort of features do you want?
- [ ] Lawns
- [ ] Paths
- [ ] Patio
- [ ] Arches
- [ ] Steps
- [ ] Pergolas
- [ ] Terraces
- [ ] Containers
- [ ] Rock gardens
- [ ] Trellising
- [ ] Secluded inner garden
- [ ] Raised beds
- [ ] Focal points
- [ ] Wildlife garden
- [ ] Stepping stones
- [ ] Tree-houses
- [ ] *Trompe-l'oeil*
- [ ] Shrubbery
- [ ] Water
- [ ] Greenhouse

What problem areas does my garden have?
- [ ] Slope
- [ ] Boundaries
- [ ] Entrances and exits
- [ ] Paths
- [ ] Drives
- [ ] Steps
- [ ] Surfaces
- [ ] Utility areas

What about the children?
- [ ] Safety
- [ ] Play areas
- [ ] Climbing frames
- [ ] Sand pits
- [ ] Tree house
- [ ] Swings
- [ ] Toy house
- [ ] Pet areas

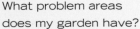

This compact climbing frame and swing in natural wood blend with the surrounding foliage.

Choosing the garden you want

Although every garden is as individual and personal as its owner, most gardens fall into four main categories, and when you are planning your own garden, it will be helpful if you think about your garden in terms of one of these styles.

Formal gardens

One of the keys to a formal design is simplicity. All fussiness is removed, and restraint is imposed. The lines and shapes are usually simple, consisting of straight lines and regular curves. The design is based on squares, rectangles, circles and ellipses, and the structure is provided by gravel or regularly paved areas. Within this framework lie various features and beds, all preferably with a regular outline.

Symmetry is another key to formality. Patterns should be regular, and plantings should be balanced from one side of the bed to another. The regular planting of trees or shrubs or the positioning of containers along a path or around a bed creates a pleasing rhythm. Not everything needs to be balanced. Often a single container as a focal point works extremely well.

Ponds are regularly shaped, often lined with concrete and with a fountain or spout. Containers with a single specimen, often a clipped tree or shrub, are a popular way of displaying plants. Plants are also often contained within a formal parterre or knot garden, consisting of low, clipped hedges of box. Instead of being filled with plants, the areas contained by these hedges can either be left empty or filled with coloured gravel.

Planting should be restrained and simple. Stand single plants, perhaps in pots, at strategic positions. Avoid mixing too many colours and anything that needs a great deal of maintenance. Many formal gardens rely almost entirely on foliage. Some people like to grow only trees and shrubs, partly because of their green foliage, but also because the foliage can be controlled by clipping.

Comfortable informality

Most gardeners feel more comfortable with an informal style – a garden where a football or watering can left lying around will not look out of place, a garden where a weed might just be acceptable. This style of garden has its origins in the cottage garden, where vegetables and flowers were often intermixed and plants were planted not by some great complex design, but simply because there was a gap to fill.

Not everyone feels comfortable with such anarchy, however, and many people prefer to take a more controlled approach, although still outside the straitjacket imposed by a formal garden. Colours in borders can be grouped so that there is some form of harmony. Planting can be precise rather than random, but the overall effect is one of relaxed control.

An informal garden makes it possible to blend various activities together. The garden is likely to have a lived-in feeling about it and to be something that is not so much for show as to be used and enjoyed. A barbecue or child's play area will, for example, sit happily alongside

decorative borders. Vegetable plots will mix with flowers and not need their own well-defined areas. Although such a layout may appear completely casual, it requires careful preliminary planning to make sure that the garden does not end up looking as if it thrown together.

An informal garden is a much more suitable environment for young children. A tangle of shrubs makes an ideal 'camp' and hiding place. Children will always leave playthings lying around and send balls crashing into the undergrowth, leaving temporary gaps. If the garden is likely to be used for ball games, beds with straight sides may prove to be more suitable than curved ones. A well-manicured lawn and active children do not suit each other. The practical solution is to select a tough grass, which will look far less formal but will stand up to running and cycling much better.

The shapes of the borders and patio and the lie of the paths can be anything you wish, but if a clumsily shaped patio fits the available space and feels comfortable, so be it. In general, curved beds look more appealing than those with straight edges, but it is best to avoid too extreme curves and awkward angles, which are difficult to plant successfully and hard to edge or mow up to.

The modern look

Some people are more conscious of trends and fashions than others, and just as the inside of the house reflects this, so the garden follows suit. There have always been gardens that followed the style of the day. In the past it was necessary to employ the fashionable designer of the time to lay out your garden, but now modern styles and trends, still often designer led, are illustrated in a wide range of magazines for anyone to copy. Glancing through gardening periodicals, weekend supplements and fashion magazines will provide a wealth of ideas, which can be adapted to meet your own tastes.

The materials, especially of containers, play an important role in such a garden. An earthy look, with terracotta playing a leading role, was once

BELOW Pools in formal gardens are usually rectangular or another geometric shape. The regular paving around the pool enhances the formality of the underlying structure, which contrasts with the lush planting.

ABOVE A town garden often has a favourable microclimate, with the surrounding walls and buildings keeping temperatures slightly higher than in the open country. Such gardens are the ideal place for massed planting of species that might be susceptible to the elements elsewhere.

considered the height of fashion. Then the pots were painted. Later still, other materials took over. Galvanized containers, buckets and watering cans have played their part, and now the latest trend is for stainless steel.

As with materials, so with plants: some are more fashionable than others. In recent years, for example, there has been a resurgence of interest in grasses, which are ideal for small gardens as they can be used in so many different ways. They can be grown as specimen plants or as a tangled mass. Bamboos are used in similar ways. Brightly coloured plants are becoming more fashionable, as are cheerful annuals.

Another trend in modern gardens is to treat the space as an outside room and reduce the amount of actual garden. The space is paved in stone or brick and any visual interest is generated by objects of one sort or another, rather than high-maintenance, time consuming plants. Climbers and vegetation on walls and fences are replaced by mosaics or *trompe-l'oeil*. Shrubs and trees are displaced by sculpture and *objets trouvés*, and no lawn maintenance is required because all the grass has been replaced by hard surfacing. As well as presenting a completely different environment, all these changes also represent a major change in garden maintenance: it no longer exists.

The garden is reduced to its bare essentials. It has become a minimal, low-maintenance space. It has become a garden for those who hate or have no time for gardening, but still want an attractive space in which to relax.

Japanese style

As in all aspects of our lives, travelling to other countries has influenced our gardens, but of all countries, Japan has probably had the greatest effect on garden design. The simplicity and tranquillity of the gardens there here been much copied in the West.

The essence of Japanese gardens is simplicity, which creates a sense of calm and peace. A Japanese garden is an area of total calm set around the house. One aspect of the simplicity is the limited use of materials and plants, and another is the way in which the available space is used. In the past every element in the garden was imbued with its own significance, and

to some extent this is still true, but now the symbolism tends to be retained for largely historical reasons rather than because it has any real meaning.

Nature plays a dominant role in Japanese garden design. Everything seems to flow from it, especially the natural landscape. Instead of making miniature copies of the landscape as we might do in the West, however, Japanese design is suggestive. Where we might build, say, a rock garden, a Japanese gardener would use rocks and boulders to represent mountains or islands, while raked gravel or sand is used to signify water. In nature there are rarely any straight lines, and so it is in the Japanese garden.

Streams and waterfalls are constantly used in Japanese gardens. They are usually imitations of natural streams, representing mountain torrents. Water is also present in the form of small pools, or water is introduced into the garden gently trickling through artificial courses, such as along split bamboo pipes. Sometimes the system is ingenious, with one pipe slowly filling before it tips and fills the next and so on. The water is calm or only just moving; there are no fountains to disturb the tranquillity. In addition to real water, there is much representational water in Japanese gardens. An area of raked gravel, for example, represents swirling water, while rounded rocks positioned on the gravel are islands set in the water. Often a ribbon of moss will pass through rocks and boulders, representing a stream.

A few ornaments are used within the garden, the best known of which is the Japanese lantern. These stone or metal lanterns, often like miniature buildings, are carefully positioned to illuminate key places along paths or water. They will often be placed next to water so that they produce reflections. Paths are of gravel or stone. Stepping stones are another popular feature, either made from slabs of stone or from sections of tree trunks. Bridges are often incorporated to cross either real or imaginary streams. In larger gardens there may be a pavilion or tea house, and a loggia may be built near the house from which the garden may be viewed.

BELOW Gravel and rocks are used in oriental gardens to represent water and mountains. Trees and shrubs are widely used, especially around the perimeter of the garden, to create a backdrop and to reinforce the idea of the 'borrowed landscape' beyond the confines of the garden itself.

Drawing up a plan

Once you know all about your site, exactly what you want from your garden, what inherited features are worth preserving and how much time you want to spend on maintenance, you can begin the design. But to generate any useful ideas, first stand in the garden – or on the patch of wasteland that is to become your garden – and think in terms of shapes and colours. As ideas begin to form, you can then explore practicalities and solve problems. At this planning stage, allow your imagination to wander and take plenty of time to consider all the options.

Marking out your garden

The practical business of designing – preparing drawings to scale, organizing plant lists and so on – appears to be far more daunting than it really is. Accuracy is important but is not that difficult to achieve; if you are methodical and careful, the site can be carefully measured and a true plan drawn.

If you find it difficult to visualize designs from lines on a piece of paper, there is really no reason why you should not use the garden itself as your drawing board. The site, if not already clean, will have to be cleared of any rubbish or unwanted objects before you begin. Then, using sticks and lengths of string (preferably strong and very visible baler twine) as markers, mark out where everything should go. Keep making adjustments to these markers until you have the layout you want. A length of hosepipe is very useful for marking out curves, especially of an informal border or pond.

Complicated details may need a more striking outline, which can be done with whitewash brushed over the ground. It is also worth visualizing height where this is a vital factor. A stepladder erected to the height of a mature hedge will give you a good idea of the ultimate effect. If this looks too tall, obscuring a fine view and casting too much shade, select a different hedging

plant. Put a chair in a proposed seating area and try it out. Is this the best place or will it be ruined by an unpleasant view?

When you have a clearer idea of the arrangement of your site it will be easier to transfer the details on to paper; this will be essential for reference once the heavy work has begun. Before you draw up the plan, however, leave the markers in place for a week or so to ensure that the idea really is going to be practical. Then, when you are finally happy with the main elements of the design, draw up the plan.

Drawing up your plan

When you have decided on your garden layout, you should draw up a scale plan that incorporates the main garden features. This may need to be reviewed several times as you dig, plant and build your garden. When

you have marked out your site, transfer your ideas on to the scale plan. Start by marking the areas of lawn, paving and border and, when the overall shaping is more or less complete, start to slot in the principal garden features.

It is likely that you will redraw your plan a few times because, even when you set out to dig and build, you may find that the design alters as you go along. A good garden is a blend of skilful advance planning and on-the-spot alterations. Although a plan is necessary, it should never be rigidly adhered to, otherwise the garden will be 'stiff' and out of harmony with its surroundings. Remember that a garden consists of living things that are constantly altering their size and shape; nothing is static and nothing grows in straight lines: compromise and adjustment are needed all the time.

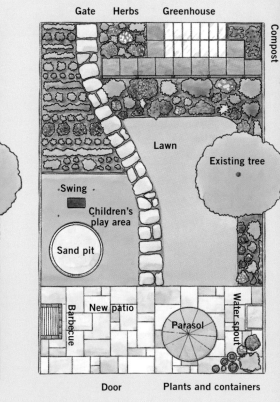

The basic garden plan

Plan 1 labels: Gate · Old shrubs and flowers · Old shed · Old shrubs · Old path · Existing tree · Lawn · Paved patio · Door

Plan 2 labels: Gate · Herbs · Greenhouse · Compost · Lawn · Existing tree · Swing · Children's play area · Sand pit · Barbecue · New patio · Parasol · Water spout · Door · Plants and containers

❶ Draw up a plan of your existing garden (above) and then incorporate your requirements into a new plan (above right).

❷ Sketch your ideas onto the plan and imagine how the different features might come together.

Drawing a plan

A scale plan drawn on squared paper will enable you to assess the space you have and see the relative space you have allowed for the different areas of your garden:

- Show the main wall of the house
- Mark boundary fences and walls
- Show the position of existing doors and gates
- Draw in the patio
- Indicate the size of existing features (ponds, established trees and so on) that you intend to keep
- Mark compass points
- Show where structures (shed, greenhouse, compost heap and so on) will be
- Indicate the lawn area
- Show areas for borders
- Mark areas for fruit and vegetables
- Draw in paths

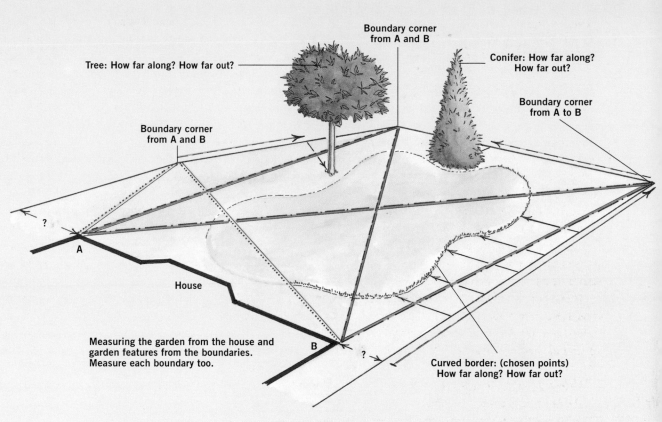

Tree: How far along? How far out?

Boundary corner from A and B

Conifer: How far along? How far out?

Boundary corner from A to B

Boundary corner from A and B

House

Measuring the garden from the house and garden features from the boundaries. Measure each boundary too.

Curved border: (chosen points) How far along? How far out?

This is an example of a simple garden plan showing how boundary corners can be plotted from A and B, the corners of the house. Note the attention paid to key features of the garden: the two trees and the curved border.

Measuring the garden

For an accurate, working scale drawing, you will have to measure your garden in detail. Include any contours and angled boundaries. Enter these measurements on to a couple of preliminary sketch plans first, before using them to produce the scale drawing.

Starting with the house, carefully measure and record the length of the walls and the position of doors and of downstairs windows. Next, measure and record the length of each different boundary. Very few plots are actually square, and it is quite possible that some of your boundaries are not straight and change direction more than once. Rather than trying to record all the corners in relation to each other, it is much easier to plot them in relation to two fixed points, such as the corners of the house. This places every change of direction and corner at the point of a triangle. Garden features, such as borders and existing trees, and plants can then be plotted off their nearest boundary.

Measure how far along and how far out at right angles the object is to the boundary and enter the measurement on to the sketch plan. For an object such as a shed or greenhouse, measure two adjacent corners to get the position and angle of the building and then the overall dimensions to complete it. To plot curves off a straight line, use a series of 'how-far-along', 'how-far-out' measurements. Finally, it is also a good idea to record the size of tree canopies and the diameter or width of shrubs.

Having marked the position of all the existing features, mark the orientation and record the amount and time of shade cast by buildings and plants, both in the garden and out.

Making a scale plan

The most useful scale to work to is 1 or 2cm to 1m (⅛ or ¼in to 12in), depending on how big your garden is and the size of the paper you are using. Work out the plan on squared or graph paper.

First draw the house. Next, plot the various boundary corners, using a pair of compasses for accuracy. Take the measurement between one house corner and one boundary corner, scale this down and set your compasses (that is to say, the length between the compass point and pencil point) to this length.

On paper, place the point of the compass on the house corner and, pointing roughly in the direction of the boundary corner, draw a broad arc. Repeat the process, this time using the measurement between the second house corner and the same boundary corner. Where the two arcs meet is the apex of your boundary. Repeat this exercise until you have reproduced every corner then join them to produce the boundary.

Check your drawing by measuring the distance from one boundary corner to the other and scaling it down – it should be the same as the equivalent distance on paper. With the basic framework on paper, you are now ready to add other objects and features.

Altering space

Inevitably, personal taste is bound to govern the final design you choose for your garden, but there are basic design principles that affect every scheme. These design guidelines will also help the less confident gardener to become more ambitious and to translate ideas successfully into real garden schemes.

First steps

To start with, since the garden will be viewed mostly from the house, go into the house and make all your major design decisions from the appropriate windows. Second, do not forget that the house is part of the garden; a garden design completely at odds with the style of your house will not look right.

It is a good idea to go out and look at examples of different types of garden for inspiration before you start to make your own plans. If you can, visit public gardens but also look at the way your friends and neighbours have treated their outdoor space.

Formality and informality

Gardens are sometimes classified as being either formal or informal. Formal gardens are mostly symmetrical, with a central path or lawn and identical features on each side, whereas informal gardens tend to be pictorial rather than patterned and scarcely ever repeat the same idea. They are more likely to consist of flowing curves than straight lines or geometric shapes.

One way of designing your garden is to make the area near the house formal and gradually make the layout less formal the further away from the house you go. This formula works very well since it ties the house into the garden in a gentle and subtle way. But there is nothing to stop you having a completely formal or informal garden, or a bit of both. You will end up with a garden full of variety and surprises, which will tempt any visitor to wander further to find out what is round the next corner.

Many gardens have an underlying formality that is often masked by a mass of informal planting. This can produce the most delightful results – a sort of controlled chaos.

Before deciding on a style, think about what suits you best. Formal gardens tend to rely on tidiness and precision for impact, which means constant weeding and trimming, while informal gardens can be left to grow and are easier to maintain. A formal scheme is not a good idea if you have small children.

Deciding on the basic layout

The starting point for any new design is deciding on a basic layout. Try to resist the temptation to line everything up in a series of parallel lines and instead explore more exciting shapes that make use of diagonals and curves.

Most gardens have a rectangular layout, a diagonal layout or a circular layout. A rectangular approach consists of symmetrical features and a lot of straight lines and predictable curves, a style perhaps more suited to a small town garden than a larger country one. The built-in angle of a diagonal layout will offset features to produce a less predictable, more relaxed and interesting effect. A curved layout is appropriate for large, rambling gardens.

ABOVE, LEFT The formal symmetry of the borders in this garden is softened by the planting. Note that the same plants are repeated in each of the borders, which emphasizes the formal theme.

LEFT Roses, French lavender (*Lavandula stoechas*) and peonies are among the array of plants in shades of pink and purple in this delightful informal garden.

Garden layouts

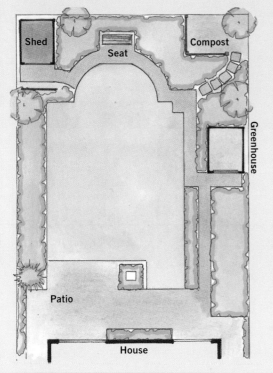

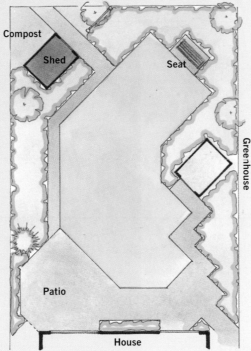

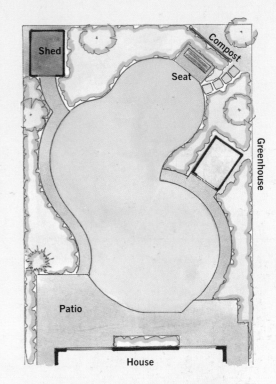

Rectangular layout
This formal, symmetrical design will work well for a town garden. Most of the lines will be straight and parallel or boldly curved rather than irregular.

Diagonal layout
A diagonal layout tends to have a semi-formal feel to it. Although it is mostly made up of straight lines, the offset angle makes it look more interesting.

Circular layout
For an informal look, use a curved layout. This creates irregular spaces, borders of different widths and hidden areas, using both straight lines and arcs.

Allocating space

If you have, or are planning, a patio in your new garden, consider what sort of focus you want it to have in the layout of the garden.

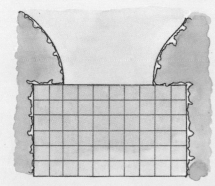

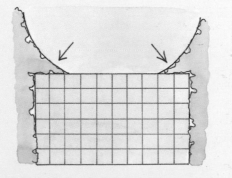

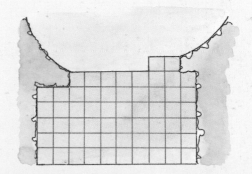

Curving the lawn towards the patio increases the border space. This tends to close in the patio, making it the centre of attention.

To open out the patio space, make the lawn circular. This creates more of a balance between paving and grass.

For a less formal approach, stagger the edge of the paving into the grass, which integrates grass and paving without dividing up the garden.

Shape and pattern

The use of different shapes and patterns is perhaps the single most important element in designing a garden. In a really good garden, the shape and pattern of every component, from the broad outline of a path or lawn to the contrasting shapes of miniature shrubs in a particular stone trough or terracotta pot, will have been thoroughly thought out.

Shapes introduce movement, balance and punctuation to a garden design. Movement can come from the repeated use of upright shapes, such as arches, which take the eye away into the distance. The effect will work both in a formal symmetrical

BELOW A cobble and brick path leads the eye to a circular area with an urn at its centre. The use of the strong circular shape for the paved area, together with the contrasting textures of brick and cobble, make a bold statement in this formal garden, which is underlined by the symmetrical planting.

context and in a more informal zigzag fashion. Balance will help the garden to look restful to the eye: a dramatic upright shape can be countered by an adjoining low mound, and the two can be held together by some horizontal shapes.

Some patterns, such as squares and circles within squares, are static and restful because they are self-contained shapes that do not lead anywhere, whereas diagonals and curves are active and full of movement as they lead from one place to another. A static design is appropriate for a formal, regularly shaped garden, while an active design is better for an informal garden. Make sure all the lines of your

ABOVE The steep contours of this garden have been turned into a positive feature by the use of an unusual timber retaining wall, which has been stained grey to match the slate steps. Pelargoniums add a bright touch and contrast perfectly with the grey shades of the hard landscaping.

pattern lead the eye towards some focal point, be it a specimen tree or a statue. This will create the pace of the garden and link it up into a coherent and satisfying whole.

Horizontal and vertical surfaces

Use vertical structures (walls, fences, screens, gateways, pergolas and garden buildings) and horizontal structures (drives, paths, patios and steps) sensitively, because some shapes and materials relate to one another while others do not. For a successful garden design you should use the vertical and horizontal together in a pleasing and harmonious way to create a unified whole. Try to achieve a balance between both planes. For example, an arch will complement a straight pathway, and so will a low wall built round a patio.

Contours

Not everyone is blessed with a level site for a garden, but those who are often long for a more varied terrain. Steep slopes can be used for streams or waterfalls, but to maximize on planting space you can terrace the slope using either retaining walls or grassy banks. Groups of Mediterranean type plants, such as lavender and santolina will thrive on sunny slopes, where drainage will be quick and efficient. These are also good conditions for a scree garden. Cold, shady slopes make good woodland gardens, but will

Assessing your garden with photography

One of the easiest ways to judge how new features will look in your garden is to take a series of photographs of your garden from different angles – black and white will do – and enlarge them. Draw new paths, patios, greenhouses, arbours or whatever feature you want to change or add on tracing paper and place them over the photograph. You can combine several overlays and alter the shape and size of the different elements until you are happy with the new arrangement.

Planning on paper

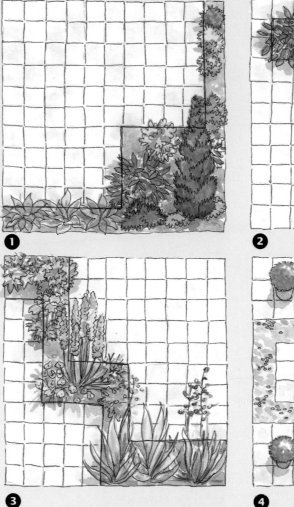

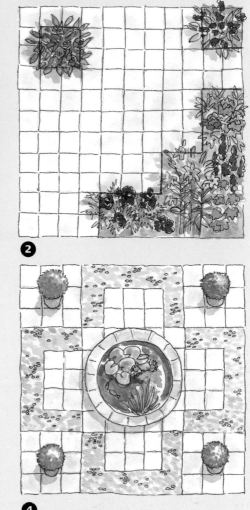

Before committing yourself to any one design, try out several schemes on paper first. Here, four simple designs create very different effects. The most basic design (1) shows how simple it is to break up the regularity of the square while retaining a feeling of space. A more complicated version of this (2) consists of the same paving stones but with slabs removed in a more random pattern. The most formal design (4) has gravel and paving arranged in a static, symmetrical pattern. This makes the space seem smaller, but detracts from the garden's squareness. The most active design (3) has a diagonal line across the square. This simple division helps to create two complementary areas.

equally make an ideal site for a terraced alpine garden because they are naturally well drained and fully exposed to light, but do not have the drying heat that is found on a sunny slope.

What you decide on also depends on the relationship of the slope to the house. A garden that slopes up from the house will always be far more dominant than one that slopes away.

Irregular changes of level within a garden can make it more interesting and offer the chance to create surprise views and features. The move from one level to another does not necessarily have to be negotiated in one go; a flight of steps can be split up and intermediate levels used. If the garden contains large mounds or hollows, consider enlarging them to create features, such as ponds or rockeries.

Eye-catching features

Below are some ideas for features to draw the eye. Restrict yourself to one feature if your garden is small or perhaps two, if you have a larger garden, so that features don't compete for attention.

- A spotlit specimen plant or mature tree
- Topiary
- A formal statue
- Sundial (see page 150)
- A large container, such as a terracotta urn, left unplanted.
- An elegant bench
- A pond or fountain (see page 158–159)
- One wall painted a dramatic colour
- A stylish gazebo (see page 130)
- A summerhouse (see page 138)
- A tall obelisk with a climbing plant growing up and around it
- *Objets trouvés*, such as rustic farm equipment
- Ornate bird bath
- Arbour or pergola (see pages 130 and 134)
- Large wall plaque or mosaic

Dark green foliage is the ideal background for an elegant statue.

Manipulating scale

If your garden is small or an awkward shape, you can disguise the fact by using various design devices. Most people want to increase the apparent size; others will want to make a broad site with little depth appear longer than it is or to make a long and narrow garden seem less tunnel-like. The aim may simply be to make a small garden seem less confined.

Making a small garden appear less cramped is often most successful when you avoid a single, unified design, which tends only to emphasize the size of the site. If you break the space down into even smaller portions, your eye will quickly move from one part to another and focus on the details of the planting and hard landscaping rather than on the larger picture. If you give these spaces different characters, you will increase a feeling of diversity within your small site. Try to create a garden where paths wind among the plants in such a way that the full extent of the site is not revealed.

Long, thin gardens can also be treated in this way. It also helps if you try to arrest the eye with some major feature in the foreground or middle distance, such as a circular lawn or a specimen tree, or place horizontal features, like low walls, wide steps, paving or hedges, across the axis. In a less symmetrical garden place features down the sides – perhaps a painted seat or the striking trunks of a multi-stemmed tree – so the eye will swerve and pause.

There are many ways of increasing the sense of depth in a garden. Vistas can be emphasized and 'lengthened' by stressing the distant perspective. Eye-catching features such as those listed opposite can be used to draw the eye away into the distance, but there is no need to rely solely on the contents of your garden to do this. Make use of the landscape outside: let the outside world become the focus of your garden vista. If you are fortunate enough to

LEFT The porthole in this brick wall frames the glazed pot and emphasizes the vista beyond.

RIGHT A mirror positioned behind a pond will enhance the reflection of the water and make a small garden look far bigger.

BELOW A circle of closely clipped box (*Buxus*) and a container of trailing plants with spiky *Phormium* at the centre draw attention towards them and away from the boundaries of this garden.

Using mirrors

Mirrors can be used simply to create the illusion of space or to reflect and amplify specific features, such as movement, foliage or a view. If they are cleverly placed, they can create the illusion that there is more garden beyond.

In a small garden with a tiny patch of sky, a carefully placed mirror can reflect the sky and so increase the impact of light on the garden. Placed behind a small pool, a mirror will likewise enhance the reflection and movement of the water.

Mirrors can be all kinds of shapes and can be mounted on walls, set in hedges or among shrubs. They must be safe, carefully and securely mounted and should be kept clean to create the proper effect.

Position mirrors high or low or use them to cover entire area behind a feature to reflect part or all of it. Remember to try to cover the edges of the mirror with foliage for a more realistic effect. An amazing illusion can be created by using one or more round mirrors recessed in a hedge to reflect the sky, giving the effect of portholes.

Mirrors are great accompaniments to garden lighting, and the two can be used together to great effect. Tiny mirrors behind spotlights create a mesmerizing effect and can be useful if space for other light-reflecting features is limited.

Mirrors can work wonders if they are used in flower beds behind areas of lush planting when they can create the sense of a dense, wide area, or reflect the colours of the flowers.

have a garden with an extensive view, make the most of it and use trees and shrubs in your own garden to frame a glimpse of the scene beyond.

Creating false perspective is another useful trick. If you place large plants in the foreground and small ones of the same shape in the distance, they all appear to be the same size although they recede into the distance. It is possible to do the same with foliage by planting thin, airy foliage close by and denser foliage further away. Lawn-mower stripes in a lawn can be used to give direction to a view or to pull your eye in a

particular direction, lengthening or shortening the perspective.

Arches, pergolas, trellis and fences all have a strong linear impact, which can be a tremendous help when you are trying to make sight-lines. Trellis can also be used for *trompe l'oeil* effects, giving the impression of three dimensions where only two exist. There are many ways of achieving these effects. Mirrors have been used in garden doorways to double the length of a vista (see above). Water will also reflect the garden, light and movement and so give the impression of space.

SURFACES

Surfaces

Surfaces in the garden have both a visual and a practical function. Visually, they provide places where the eye can rest between areas of planting, thereby defining spaces and emphasizing the layout of the garden. Practically, they provide the areas for walking, sitting, working and playing. The materials must, therefore, be chosen with care, so that they are appropriate both to the overall garden and to their specific function.

Types of surface

There are two types of surface – hard and soft. Soft surfaces are, of course, mainly lawns, although other materials, such as bark chippings, can be used for paths or in play areas to provide a surface that is easier to walk on or less dangerous for children to fall on. Soft surfaces are better for occasional use in dry weather, and they are usually easier on the eye than hard surfaces. However, they tend to require more maintenance, especially if they are subject to heavy use, and, in general, they cannot be used in wet weather.

Hard surfaces, on the other hand, although more expensive to install, are cheaper to maintain and can be used all year round, no matter what the weather. Problems such as unevenness, sinking or breaking up, which are sometimes experienced when a surface is in regular use, are nearly always the result of poorly laid foundations or bad drainage. Tree roots are another source of potential problems. Weed growth can be disfiguring but is not serious and can be avoided by thorough preparation before laying or by the use of spot weedkillers after laying.

If a garden is to look its best, all surfaces, whether hard or soft, should be properly laid and well maintained. Because they are such prominent features, carelessness or poor finishing will affect the appearance of the entire garden.

Design considerations

The type and nature of the proposed surfacing material should be assessed carefully for its functional and its aesthetic qualities. Your initial assessment of your garden during the planning process will have made you think about the style of garden you want, and your choice of surfacing material will be an important step in achieving your goal.

The functional aspects of the surfacing material are, perhaps, easier to identify than its aesthetic qualities. The material may be used for access – for people, wheelbarrows, bicycles and so on – for a child's play area or for sitting and sunbathing, and selecting a material that is fit for its purpose will be a relatively straightforward process.

The aesthetic qualities may be harder to define. Not only must the material fit the style of your house – modern, traditional, cottagey, formal – and the boundaries and other outbuildings, but it must also be appropriate for the mood of the garden. Do

Planning for success

Well-laid surfaces depend on the following factors:

- Plan for good drainage from the outset, making sure that the surface is laid on a well-drained, stable base to avoid problems with waterlogging and subsidence, including the introduction of underground drainage systems if necessary in areas with a high water table.
- Remove all topsoil because it contains organic matter that will decompose and may settle.
- Lay hard surfacing materials on well-compacted subsoil or, better still, on well-consolidated hardcore blinded with building sand.
- Build all hard surfaces with a fall (slope) of about 1 in 40 to allow rainwater to drain away safely.

BELOW Decking can be an attractive choice for patios and seating areas, especially in modern gardens. Always use tanalized wood and make sure that it is supported on well-built foundations.

LEFT A well-maintained lawn can make all the difference to a garden, providing a large, smooth expanse of a single colour and texture that can act as a fine foil both to hard landscaping and to planting.

LEFT Different coloured paving can be mixed successfully in a patio if planned carefully. Here the line of larger slabs divides the dining area from the rest of the patio while the coloured bricks form strong links with the terracotta urns and the dark table.

BELOW This line of dark slabs creates a striking, informal transition between the lawn, gravel and beds, as well as preventing the gravel spreading.

not use too many different materials, especially in a small garden, because this will confuse the eye and create a restless, unrelenting effect in an area that should be dedicated to relaxation and pleasure.

Using surfaces

The two main areas that will be surfaced and the two areas that can dictate the appearance of the whole garden are the patio and the paths.

Patios

The primary consideration in surfacing a patio is to create a clean, smooth surface that drains and dries quickly after rain. It should also be weed free and large enough to accommodate chairs and a table if you intend to use it for entertaining. Patios generally look better if they are laid in a formal style with uniform sized paving stones, pavers or bricks. The material should be in keeping with the colour and style of the house.

Decking, which blends well with most planting schemes, tends to create a more relaxed, informal effect. Wood is a material associated with informal outdoor living and leisure, and because it is relatively soft it may be an appropriate choice for a family with young children. Decking also lends itself to curves and changes in level.

Paths

The path in the garden that is going to take the hardest wear should be paved or concreted. This may be from the back door to the compost heap or greenhouse or from the patio to the shed. Before you finally decide on the position of the paths, note how people move about the garden. It is likely that they will avoid sharp corners and cut across lawns, so it is better to make a curved path in the first place to minimize wear and tear on the grass. Paths that are less often used can be made with gravel or bark chippings or even log stepping stones across the lawn.

Materials

There is a wide range of surfaces available now, each with its own advantages and disadvantages. You need to list your own particular requirements, such as durabilty, cost, texture and colour, in order of importance and then choose the material that suits you best. The materials for surfacing are likely to be the largest single expenditure you will make on your garden, so it is as well to make the right choice.

Natural stone

York stone, limestone, granite and other kinds of natural stone have one major advantage: once laid, they look instantly mellow, as if they have been in place for a long time – making them an ideal choice if your house is an old one. But they are extremely costly, even when bought second-hand, and are not always readily available. If you are buying second-hand stone from a demolition yard – the cheapest source – you may find that the slabs vary greatly not only in size but in thickness, too, which you will need to take into account when laying them.

ABOVE A bold approach to mixing materials and colours can be effective. Here, the large blue ceramic tiles mark the beginning of a meandering path.

Bricks and blocks

Bricks are not widely used as paving because of the cost involved and the time needed to lay them. However, if they are carefully laid, bricks of appropriate texture and pattern can give an extremely pleasing appearance indeed. Hard, dense, impermeable types should be used: they must be frost resistant and not prone to efflorescence. Engineering bricks are mostly suitable, but unless you are confident stick to mellow colours. The bricks can be laid either on their side or flat. The latter way is cheaper, but make sure that the top surfaces have a suitable finish: on many facing bricks only the sides and ends are suitable for exposure to the elements.

A good selection of paver bricks and concrete blocks is available, and some of them incorporate patterns in their surface. One of the attractions is that they can be laid in a wide variety of patterns to create visual interest and sometimes also an

ABOVE This formal courtyard garden is intimately connected to the house beyond through the use of similar-coloured reclaimed bricks. The inset of quarry tiles in the centre and the offset line from the french windows lighten what could be an overwhelmingly formal feel.

illusion of extra space, width or depth. Because there is some variation in the size of bricks, it is best not to try a very elaborate pattern, as the bricks might require trimming. Herringbone patterns, for example, would entail the cutting of bricks or blocks diagonally at the edges.

Tiles

Tiles are made of hard-fired clay and, depending on the composition of the clay and the temperature of the firing, they can be very durable. Quarry tiles are popular for paving; these are unglazed, geometric in shape (usually square or octagonal) and regular so they can be used to make formal, smooth surfaces. However, they are very difficult to cut and should be reserved for areas with long, straight edges rather than complicated curved perimeters.

For a more eye-catching effect, use glazed paving tiles, which come in different shapes and colours, often with painted motifs or designs. The more decorative tiles look best in the strong sunlight of hot climates. Glazed tiles are both fragile and relatively expensive, so they should be employed only in small quantities. Fragments of tiles can be used to make floor mosaics.

ABOVE The combination of precise geometric brick patterns and gravel has made what could be a very awkward corner into a very pretty formal area.

Prefabricated slabs

If you are laying a large area, it pays to use two colours, chequerboard fashion, to avoid monotony. For instance, although grey and honey-beige slabs are uninteresting if used by themselves over a large area, when combined they can look very attractive. However, be careful in your use of combined colours.

Slabs vary in shape from the 60cm (24in) common grey square slabs to polygonal and circular forms; most of them are 5cm (2in) thick or less. More expensive types are made of reconstituted stone, and you can even find them in a texture that has the appearance of water-worn stone. It is important to make sure that the surface finish is non-slip: a smooth finish encrusted with algae will be treacherous in wet weather.

Crazy paving

Although crazy paving is sneered at by many, it can be the ideal surface in some gardens, provided that the broken stone of which it is made is natural and that it is correctly laid. Random paving can look perfect in a country setting, although it would seem out of place in towns or combined with avant-garde architecture.

If you intend to use natural stone for crazy paving, bear in mind that the pieces are likely to vary considerably in thickness. Prepare the ground carefully if the paving is to present a flat, even surface.

Decking

Wooden decking is visually and physically softer than other surfacing materials. It looks good in rural or town surroundings and is warm to walk on. It makes a convenient alternative to paving if you are laying a patio over several different levels or on a very uneven surface. It can be laid in many different patterns and is easy to construct. Use hardwoods or softwoods that have been thoroughly treated with preservative and good quality fixings for durability.

ABOVE The contrasting colours and textures of wooden blocks and pea gravel set in a chequerboard make a stunning path.

ABOVE Here, small pebbles, flagstones and alpine plants are combined to create the feel of a mountain slope as an innovative finish to an informal patio.

BELOW Over a period of years, concrete will mellow and algae will grow on it. In small areas this can look picturesque, but will be slippery when wet.

Gravel

Gravel makes a relatively inexpensive and quickly laid surfacing material. Curves are much easier to form with gravel than with paving slabs, and slight changes in level are readily accommodated. Gravel offers the advantage, too, that it can easily be taken up and replaced later if underground piping and other services need to be installed at any time. Finally, if you become bored with it, the gravel can be used to form a good base for an alternative surface material.

The main disadvantage is that, unless it is carefully graded, the surface will be loose: pieces of gravel spilling on to an adjacent lawn could cause serious damage to a mower, and they are easy to bring into the house on the soles of shoes. Avoid gravel spilling over by creating a firm edge, such as a kerb of bricks on edge.

Gravel is available in two main forms: crushed stone from quarries and pea gravel from gravel pits. The former is of better quality, but will be very expensive unless the stone is quarried locally. Gravel occurs in a variety of attractive natural colours,

and your choice should, if possible, complement any stone employed in the garden for walling or rock gardens. The alternative, washed pea gravel, comes in a variety of shades, ranging from near white to almost black.

Whichever type is used, make sure that the stones are neither too large (which makes walking uncomfortable), nor too small (they will stick to your shoes). For most purposes the best size is in the range 10–18mm (⅜–¾in) in diameter.

Concrete

Used in mass form as a garden surfacing material, concrete is hard, durable and fairly easy to lay. Colouring agents can be added, and these will help to relieve the monotony if the concreted area is fairly small and the colours chosen with care, but a more interesting effect can be achieved by modifying the surface texture.

Concrete can be made to look much more acceptable and less harsh if its surface is brushed while still damp to reveal a pebble or gravel aggregate. This mellow, soft appearance is better suited to a garden setting.

Cobbles

These smooth, rounded stones look very attractive if you use them on a small scale, setting them around a tree, for instance, or infilling an odd corner, where it might be difficult to cut larger paving materials. They are not suitable for large areas, because they become slippery when wet, and are too unstable to support garden furniture. However, they can look very attractive when used to break up a large expanse of concrete – set in a circular swirl, for instance, or ranged into a square. Granite setts, too, can be used in the same way, to provide patterns on what might otherwise be a dull expanse of paving or concrete. Bed them in carefully to achieve a flat surface.

Bark

Chipped or shredded bark is a popular material for creating visually and physically soft surfaces. Its somewhat unruly appearance makes it unsuitable for formal areas and, because of its natural affinity with wood, it is generally used in wilder parts of the garden. Bark is particularly suitable for woodland areas, where its colour and texture blend in well with the trees. Chipped bark is a good choice in areas where children play because it is relatively soft. Heavier pieces of bark are better than composted bark, which is more like peat in consistency and can be more difficult to control.

RIGHT This broad bark path divides two parts of an informal border. The brick edging keeps the chippings off the beds and other paths.

Combining materials

Don't feel that you must restrict yourself to one sort of material in your garden. Instead of having a uniform patio area of, say, brick or paving, experiment with more than one type of paving material. You can create many imaginative yet subtle surfaces by mixing materials of different colours, shapes and textures. You could define and soften a patio of square slabs with borders of brickwork or make circular patterns with cobblestones and bricks for a less formal approach. Intersperse areas of gravel within areas of paving slabs and then grow a selection of rock plants in the gravel.

Mixing slabs

By mixing paving of different colours you can create random or formal patterns. Some ideas include highlighting diagonal lines across a patio with red slabs to contrast with the overall green or buff ones; picking out alternate rows of slabs in another colour; and working from the perimeter of the patio to form squares within squares, finishing with a solid block of slabs at the centre.

You do not have to stick to square, rectangular or hexagonal paving stones. Mix them for a more creative finish try combining hexagonal slabs with square or rectangular slabs of different colours.

If an area of your garden has a theme, choose materials to suit it. This dry river bed with stepping stones is, in fact, on a patio.

Four contrasting textures make this curving boundary between the matt brick path and crunchy gravel particularly pleasing.

The addition of the square terracotta-coloured tiles has transformed what could have been a dull corner into a stylish detail.

Drainage

There is nothing worse than having to splash your way through puddles of water every time it has rained. Good drainage is absolutely essential.

Draining hard surfaces

Patios and paths can be made unusable by every shower of rain if they are not constructed so that they shed water. When you are making a paved or concrete area, build in a slight slope so that water is shed and does not form pools. A fall of about 1 in 40 will move water quite quickly either on to border soil (where it can be used by plants) or into a shallow gully, which can lead to a soakaway or drain. This slope should always lead away from the house, walls or other garden structures. Construct the gully from half-round ceramic pipes bedded in cement or from cement that has been trowelled into a similar shape. If you wish to disguise the gully you could perhaps fill it with loosely packed small cobbles or a similar material that suits your garden and use a small grille so that the stones do not get washed into the soakaway or drain.

If a completely hidden gully is desirable on a patio or path, before you lay the slabs set half-round ceramic pipes down the centre of the area and slope the paving or concrete very gently towards the gully, overlapping the edges. A 12mm (½in) gap in the centre will allow the water to run into the channel.

Constructing a herringbone drainage system

Make sure the side drains meet the main drain at an angle of 60°. The drains must run towards a ditch or soakaway at a gradient of at least 1 in 40.

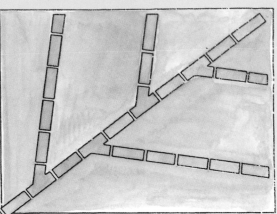

❶ Following the slope of the land, dig V-shaped trenches at the same level as the subsoil, up to 90cm (36in) deep and wide enough to take a 10cm (4in) diameter main pipe. At the same time dig side trenches for 7.5cm (3in) diameter drains.

❷ Cover the bottom with a 5cm (2in) layer of gravel. Lay the pipes on the gravel bed.

❸ The pipes are butted, not joined. Where the side drains lead into the main drain, break the pipes to fit them together and cover them with tiles. Any excess moisture will soak through the gaps between the lengths of piping.

❹ Cover all the pipes with coarse rubble or stones, then finer rubble, finishing with a layer of topsoil.

TOP RIGHT Plan for an ideal arrangement of side drains meeting the main drain at the correct 60° angle.

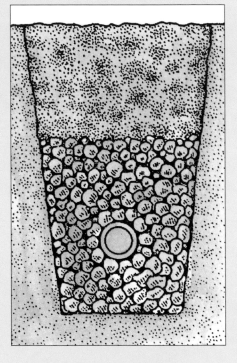

ABOVE A cross-section shows the pipe buried in coarse rubble, topped with finer rubble and a dressing of topsoil.

Building a soakaway

A soakaway is a pit filled with rubble or gravel. Water drains into it and then percolates away into the surrounding soil. If the soil in your garden is very compacted and poorly drained you will have to construct a soakaway if there is no suitable watercourse for a drainage system to run into. This is a fairly major excavation task. Dig a hole 0.9–1.8m (3–6ft) in diameter and at least 1.8m (6ft) deep. A drainage pipe from the herringbone drainage system should be laid so that it drains directly into the pit. The hole should be lined with loosely stacked bricks so that water can seep through the sides, and the pit is then filled with rubble, clinker or gravel. Cover the pit with topsoil and plant it up or lay turf over it to disguise it.

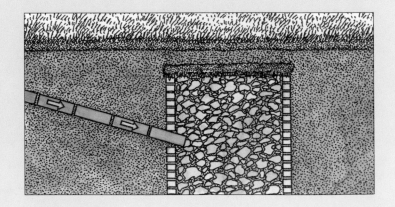

Mortar and concrete

Concrete paving slabs and mortar are a good choice for most patios and garden paths, although laying slabs can be quite a strenuous job, and you may need help.

Ready-mixed mortar

Some ready-mixed paving mortars have polymer additives, which are designed to allow heavy slabs to be slid into position and held in place while positioning adjustments take place (in way that ceramic wall tiles are fixed). Once the mortar has set, the slab will be held permanently.

Each 40kg (100lb) dry pack of ready-mixed mortar is sufficient to lay about 10 slabs that are 60cm (24in) square or about 14 slabs 45cm (18in) square. The material is used with a fairly dry texture and applied in four generous dabs at the corners of the slab and one in the centre: the slab is lowered on to the dabs and slid into position. Once you are satisfied with the alignment you can simply tap the slab down to the required level with the shaft of a club hammer, compressing the mix by about 2.5cm (1in).

Mortar ingredients

Mortar for slab-laying consists of cement and sharp sand mixed with water to form a self-hardening paste. Mortar mixed in the proportions 1 part cement to 5 parts sand is adequate for laying slabs. It is vital to mix the ingredients in the correct proportion. Use a bucket as a measure, tipping the ingredients on a hard, flat surface or mixing board.

Plasticizer

Often a plasticizer is added to the mortar to aid the workability and flexibility of the mix. Traditionally, lime was used but modern science has developed chemical plasticizers, which are easier to mix in and are now used instead. Chemical plasticizers usually come in liquid form with the amount that you need to add specified on the container.

ABOVE Mix mortar in small batches, so that it does not start to go off before you use it. Using a mixing board will help to keep your site clean.

Mixing mortar

1 Pile the sand into a heap, form a crater in the top and pour on a bucket of cement.

2 Turn over the sand and cement repeatedly with a shovel until a consistent colour shows that it is thoroughly mixed.

3 Add the plasticizer to the water in accordance with the manufacturer's instructions, then form a crater in the centre of the heap and pour in about half the water.

4 Collapse the sides of the crater inwards to mix the water with the dry mortar. Gradually add more water as the mortar absorbs it, continually turning over the mix until you achieve a really smooth but firm consistency.

5 Draw the spade across the mix in steps until the ridges remain. Adding too much water will weaken the mix, but you can stiffen it by sprinkling on handfuls of dry cement.

Concrete

Choosing a concrete mix

It is vital that you mix the concrete ingredients – sand, cement and aggregates – in the correct proportion to give the most suitable strength of mix for the job.

There are three basic mixes:
A: general purpose, for surface slabs and bases where you need a minimum thickness of 7.5–10cm (3–4in).
B: light duty, for garden paths and bases less than 7.5cm (3in) thick.
C: bedding, a weaker mix used for garden wall foundations and bedding in slabs.

What to order

When ordering the ingredients to make up 1 cubic metre (35½ cubic feet) of the three different concrete mixes described above, consult the chart below.

What to mix

Concrete mixes are made up by volume, and it is convenient to use a bucket as your measure. For the concrete mixes listed above, mix the following, remembering that each mix requires about half a bucket of water (although this does depend on how damp the sand is).

Mix	Cement: no. of 50kg (110lb) bags	Sharp sand + aggregate	OR	All-in aggregate
A	6	0.5 cu m (17⅔ cu ft) + 0.75 cu m (26½ cu ft)		1 cu m (35½ cu ft)
B	8	0.5 cu m (17⅔ cu ft) + 0.75 cu m (26½ cu ft)		1 cu m (35½ cu ft)
C	4	0.5 cu m (17⅔ cu ft) + 0.75 cu m (26½ cu ft)		1.25 cu m (45 cu ft)

Paving foundations

Paving slabs, block pavers and other paving materials must be laid on a firm, flat and stable surface. A base of well-compacted subsoil covered with a thick layer of sand is sufficient for a path, but for large, well-used areas or if the soil is soft you will need to add a layer of compacted hardcore to prevent the paving from sinking.

Hardcore

To make a firm foundation for a paved area or path, excavate to a depth of about 10cm (4in), deep enough for a layer of hardcore. On soft soil double this depth. Hardcore is a mixture of bricks and concrete that when compacted tends to have hollows over the surface. To give a firm, smooth base cover the hardcore with a 5cm (2in) layer of builder's sand. Roll or tamp down the sand and level it with a garden rake. Small pavers and paving slabs can be mortared directly on to the sand. Before you excavate the area to be paved, check the position of pipes and cables.

ABOVE Good, level foundations are vital for any paved area, but especially for one where crisp, straight lines play an important role in the overall look.

Laying paving foundations

❶ To prepare the foundations for a paved area or path, stretch two parallel strings between pegs about 1m (39in) apart and at least 5cm (2in) wider than the finished area. Remove the turfs (which can be used elsewhere in the garden or stacked in a corner to break down) and the topsoil. Dig down to a depth of about 20cm (8in), to allow a depth of hardcore to 10cm (4in), a layer of sand to 5cm (2in) and your chosen paving material.

❷ Compact the base of the trench with a stout timber post, a sledgehammer or a garden roller. If you use a post wear thick gloves to protect your hands.

❸ Add a layer of hardcore (which is available from builder's merchants) to the base. This should be at least 10cm (4in) deep. Compact it with a sledgehammer.

❹ Bind the surface with some builder's sand spread in a layer about 5cm (2in) deep. Use a garden rake to smooth over the surface and even out any indentations in the surface of the hardcore.

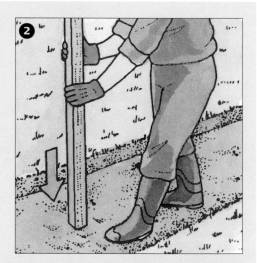

Laying paving

When the foundations have been thoroughly prepared you can lay the paving. The method is the same whether you are laying a path or a larger area, such as a patio. Establish a datum peg at the height you want the finished surface. This will be the point from which all measurements will be taken. Remember to allow a slope of about 1 in 40 to allow water to drain away.

ABOVE On this informal pathway, the gaps between the slabs could be left unmortared and filled with soil in order to allow plants to colonize.

Foundations

The foundations should be laid as described opposite. For a layer of sand about 5cm (2in) deep you will need to buy about 0.5 cu m sand for every 20 sq m of path or patio (1.7 cu ft for every 215 sq ft). Where traffic is likely to be very heavy and under patios, the paving should be laid on mortar. It is important to use string stretched between pegs so that you can check the height of each slab as you lay it.

Paving slabs

Concrete slabs are available in a variety of sizes and colours. The simplest designs are easiest to lay. They blend in with their setting more readily than complicated and difficult patterns. Detailed patterns can, however, be interesting to look at. Work out the pattern on squared paper before buying slabs so that you can calculate the exact requirements. Lay out all the slabs before securing them, then the whole pattern can be seen. Only cement them into place when you are happy with the effect.

Laying paving slabs

1 Put five dabs of mortar on the sand and put the paving slab in position. Check that it is level against the datum peg, laying your spirit level in both directions to check that it is perfectly level. Apply some mortar along one edge of the slab.

2 Place five dabs of mortar on the sand, one in each corner and one in the centre and carefully move the next paving stone into position, checking that it butts evenly against its neighbours.

3 Tap the paving stone into position with its neighbours with the shaft of a club hammer to tighten the mortar joint. Use a spirit level to check that it is level in both directions, tapping it gently until it is the correct height.

4 When the paving stones are laid, neaten all the joints and brush away any mortar that has oozed from between the paving stones before it hardens.

Paving blocks

Concrete paving blocks or 'flexible' block pavers can make an attractive patio or drive. They are extremely hard-wearing and can support considerable weight from vehicles; they can also be laid in such a manner as to provide an attractive, patterned surface. The blocks are known as 'flexible' pavers because they are laid dry on a sand bed without mortar, so they can be lifted and replaced if necessary, and they can be laid in a whole host of different patterns to create hard surfaces in a wide range of styles.

Block shapes and sizes

Paving blocks are usually roughly the same dimensions as house bricks, although square blocks are available. There are also small wedge shapes for creating circular patterns and wavy-edged blocks for more intricate designs.

Red and dark grey blocks are most common, but it is possible to get blocks in shades of browns and greys to imitate real stone. Others are made to appear old and weathered, which are perhaps more suitable for older properties. Choose a colour and style that complements your house. A mixture of similar colours laid

Preparing the base

Block pavers can be laid on a prepared foundation of compacted hardcore, topped with a layer of sand. They do not require concrete or cement. Start by digging out the area, then creating a retaining edge, if necessary. The depth that you need to dig out will depend on the thickness of the blocks you are laying. You will need to allow for a 10cm (4in)

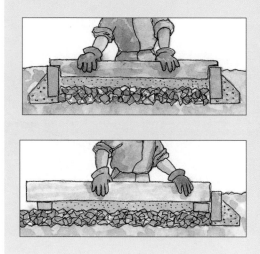

randomly will give a more natural appearance, or two or more contrasting colours can be used to make decorative patterns in the surface.

Some paving blocks have a smooth surface, while others are more textured. The surfaces of some are divided into small squares to give the appearance of mosaic. Before choosing blocks with a

layer of compacted hardcore, topped with a 5cm (2in) layer of sand. The blocks should be initially laid so that their top surfaces are about 1cm (½in) above the level of the edging to allow for subsequent compaction, so add the thickness of the block, minus 1cm (½in). When the area has been excavated, add the hardcore and level off the surface as much as possible.

❶ On paths and small areas of block paving, use a notched plank as a spreader to ensure the sand base is at a consistent level below the top of the edging planks or bricks. The plank should protrude below the top of the edging by the thickness of a block paver, minus 1cm (½in).

❷ For larger areas of paving, use a straight plank and levelling battens to lay the sand. The battens should be 5cm (2in) thick. Lay them on the hardcore base to create bays, then fill the space between them with sand. Draw the plank across the tops of the battens to level the sand.

ABOVE Square block pavers lend themselves to being used in a wide variety of interlocking decorative patterns, such as circles, quarter- and half-circles, fan-shapes and wavy lines.

Retaining edges

❶ To make a wooden retaining edge, nail wooden stakes along the wooden edging planks so that the tops of the stakes are 5cm (2in) below the top edge of the planks. Drive the stakes into the ground along the edge of the area to be paved until the tops of the planks are at ground level.

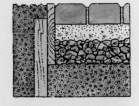

❷ To make a brick or kerbstone edging, dig a trench around the area to be paved deep and wide enough to accommodate the bricks or kerbstones, plus a 10cm (4in) concrete foundation. Position the bricks or stones while the concrete is still wet and hold them temporarily in place with a staked board while you pack more concrete behind them. When the concrete has set, remove the boards.

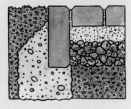

textured surface, consider the function of the area of paving. If you are planning a patio, you may be better off with smooth blocks so that your patio furniture will stand securely.

Before making your final selection, wet one of the pavers to see if it will change colour in wet weather and, if so, whether the colour still fits in with your scheme. You should also check its slip-resistance when wet.

The edges of block paving must be held within a permanent restraint, so unless the patio or drive is bordered by the house or wall, you will need to create one. Timber that has been treated with preservative can be used as edging boards. Position the boards so their top edges will be level with the surface of the paving, then hold them in place with wooden stakes. For a longer term edging, use concrete kerbstones or a line of bricks held in place with concrete.

Inspection covers

Never lay paving over an inspection cover. Metal 'trays' are available, and these can be filled with paving and lifted into position to disguise the cover. Alternatively, arrange some containers on top of the cover as a temporary, but moveable solution.

Laying block pavers

1 Check the position of downpipes, drain covers and other obstructions before working out the finished level of the pavers. The pavers should be laid initially so they are 1cm (½in) above the desired level; they will be lower once they have been bedded in.

2 Once the edge restraints are in place and the hardcore and sand base have been prepared, lay the blocks according to your pattern, starting at one corner and working diagonally across the area. Always work from a board to spread your weight.

3 When all the whole blocks are in place, start to fill the holes with cut blocks. Mark each one by holding it above its space and marking the cut line with a bolster chisel. Cut the blocks with a hired stone splitter for ease and accuracy.

4 If the pavers are laid over a small area, they can be compacted by hand. Work on a plank across the pavers so that your weight is evenly spread and use a length of wood and a mallet to tamp down each paver, working from one corner to the opposite corner.

5 For larger areas of paving, hire a motorized plate compactor to consolidate the surface and bed the blocks firmly in place. Choose one with a rubber base or place an offcut of carpet on the area you are working on.

6 Brush sand into the gaps between the blocks, then pass over the area again with the plate compactor to vibrate the sand into the joints. Repeat as necessary until you have a rigid and firm surface.

Laying cobbles and crazy paving

Used primarily for smaller areas, crazy paving and cobbles are somewhat more flexible to use than more conventional materials, such as paving slabs and bricks, but it is also quite easy to go wrong, especially with crazy paving. If you bear in mind the few basic rules about laying these materials they can provide an attractive, hard-wearing and individual surface for paths.

Cobbles

Cobbles can be laid loose like gravel, but they are more often set into concrete for a firmer surface.

1 To lay cobbles, first dig out the area to a depth of about 10cm (4in). Fill the area with a 5cm (2in) layer of wet bedding mortar, made from 1 part of cement to 5 parts of sharp sand.

2 Arrange the cobbles close together, with their bases set in the mortar and their top surfaces roughly level.

3 Allow the mortar to dry, then brush a dry mortar made of 1 part of cement to 3 parts of sand into the gaps between the cobbles, brushing off any surplus.

4 Spray the area using a watering can with a fine rose or a mister, to wet the mortar and clean the surface of the cobbles.

5 You can also set cobbles in 3.5cm (1¼in) of bedding mortar laid over a 7.5cm (3in) layer of compacted hard core.

LEFT The cobbled triangles in this formal path protrude slightly above the surrounding bricks, but not so much that they become a hazard.

Crazy paving

Crazy paving consists of pieces of broken paving slab laid to produce a complex, decoratively patterned surface. However, despite the apparently random effect of the paving, the pieces must be laid in a strict formula, both for a symmetrical appearance and for strength.

The sides of the paved area are formed by a row of fairly large slab pieces, which have at least one straight edge, which is placed outermost. Similar sized pieces with irregular edges are positioned in the centre of the area. Smaller irregular pieces are used to fill in any spaces remaining between the larger slabs.

Foundations

Prepare the base by digging out the topsoil. If the subsoil is not firm, dig this out, too, and replace with 7.5–10cm (3–4in) of compacted hardcore. Top with about 5cm (2in) of sand, raked and levelled.

LEFT The inset area of cobbles adds texture to the pale crazy paving path.

RIGHT Multicoloured crazy paving is unusual, but here it is combined with bits of coloured tile, pebbles and bricks to create a sunny Mexican atmosphere.

Laying crazy paving

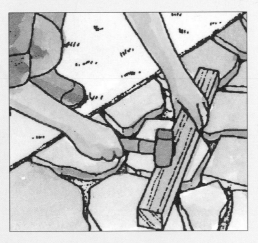

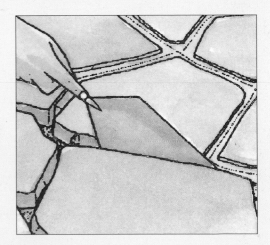

1 Dig out the base and fill with compacted hardcore topped with a layer of sand, raked and levelled. Starting at the sides of the paved area, bed each of the straight-edged slabs on five dabs of wet mortar.

2 Lay the larger central slabs and smaller infill pieces in the remaining gaps and tap level using a club hammer and a length of stout timber.

3 When the mortar is dry, point the joints between the crazy paving slabs with more wet mortar, making sure to bevel the mortar. This allows water to drain away efficiently.

Gravel

Gravel can be the ideal solution if you don't want a lawn or patio. It looks clean, easily repaired and replaced, and is almost maintenance free. It is halfway between a hard and soft surface and can be a good solution for gardens where lots of rubble has been left by builders. The rubble can help form the base for the gravel, which saves having to dig it out and dispose of it and bring in lots of new soil.

Gravel brings its own character to the garden too. It looks different in the wet and dry and can effectively reflect themes, such as Japanese or seaside gardens. The type of gravel you choose should provide the effect you want. Large, angular gravel is scrunchy to walk on and can be good if you want to hear who is approaching the house. It looks very different from small pea gravel. Gravel comes in several sizes as well as shapes and colours, so you will need to have a look around to see what is available and work out the costs to fit in with your budget.

Gravel looks good on its own but can look visually stunning when combined with other textures. Timber planks, large paving stones, decking, cobbles and sleepers all look good with gravel, either placed individually or as a large area next to gravel. However you use it, gravel can be used to create an attractive and low-maintenance garden. It creates a sense of movement and will withstand a lot of wear.

Gravel can also be used to create a flowing effect around features. It is one of the few materials that poses no problems going around corners and curves. The only maintenance it should need is an occasional raking over to keep it looking trim and to remove any bumps or indentations in the surface. If you don't lay a weed-suppressing membrane underneath it, though, you will need to weed regularly as seeds seem to germinate very well in gravel.

Laying gravel

First of all, draw the shape and design of your gravel garden on a piece of paper, then mark out the area on the ground and remove any large stones or bricks. Level the area as much as possible and tamp down the ground well using the end of a sturdy fence post or a garden roller if you have one.

If the area of gravel will get a lot of wear from cars or feet, it is best to lay a base of hardcore to make a firmer surface.

ABOVE Gravel provides a muted, low-maintenance background against which plant forms and colours can be seen to great advantage.

Laying gravel bed

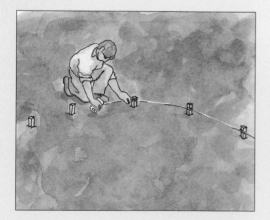

❶ Mark out your gravel area using wooden pegs and string. If the edges of the area are very curved, use a hosepipe to mark them out. This will give a smoother line.

❷ Dig out the area to a depth of about 15cm (6in) and remove any very large stones. Lay a 10cm (4in) layer of hardcore over the area and tamp it down with the end of a sturdy fence post or roll it over with a garden roller.

❸ Next, add a layer of sand over the top of the hardcore to a depth of about 2.5cm (1in) and rake it level. Compact it by treading it level or rolling with a garden roller.

Dig out the area to about 15cm (6in) deep. Lay a base of hardcore about 10cm (4in) thick. If you are planning to have areas of planting within the expanse of gravel, leave gaps in the hardcore where the plants will go then mark the planting areas with sticks. Cover the hardcore with a 2.5cm (1in) layer of sand, again avoiding the areas where the plants will go. Level again and tamp down.

Next, if you are using one, build the edging to contain the gravel. Log roll or concrete edging stones are secure and look good against gravel. You could also use bricks laid on their sides or at an angle or special edging tiles. If you are including large permanent features in the gravel garden, such as raised beds, build these now. This is far easier than trying to clear space and build after laying gravel.

If you don't want plants to seed themselves into the gravel or perennial weeds to grow up through it, it is a good idea to put down a weed-suppressing membrane before you lay the gravel. This is particularly important if you are laying gravel in a previously derelict piece of land, where perennial weeds are likely to be a major problem. Lay the membrane over any areas of bare ground you have left for plants.

Planting in gravel

Scrape away the gravel and cut an X-shaped hole through the membrane with a sharp knife. Loosen the soil underneath and add a little soil conditioner and fertilizer if necessary. Plant the plant, then replace the membrane and gravel. If you are planting a group of plants together, just clear a wider area and cut away the membrane altogether.

Plants such as lady's mantle (*Alchemilla mollis*) thrive in gravel gardens, as will phormiums and many grasses, which look stunning against a gravel background. Gravel gardens also offer perfect conditions for many of the Mediterranean plants that enjoy hot, dry conditions.

Plants in containers can look good on gravel as well, and you can chose the colours of your containers to make a strong impact against the gravel. Alpines and rock plants look stunning against cream or other plain coloured gravel as the neutral background enhances the intense colours of the small plants.

Next lay the gravel to a depth of about 5cm (2in). Compact it well and add another layer. Compact again.

Maintenance

To maintain a gravel garden, rake over when the gravel becomes displaced. If possible, roll over with a garden roller from time to time to keep it compacted and looking smart.

Remove any weeds by hand as soon as they appear. Although a weed-suppressing membrane should keep the area fairly clear, if some do get started it will certainly stop them becoming well rooted, and they should be easy to remove.

If you have not laid a weed-suppressing membrane under the gravel, use a granular weedkiller once a year.

4 If you are making an edging around the gravel area, do this now. Set bricks, edging stones or tiles into a shallow trench filled with mortar and leave overnight to harden.

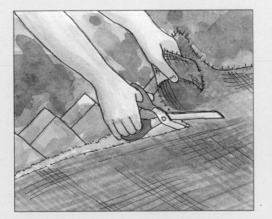

5 Cover the entire area with a weed-suppressing membrane or thick polythene, overlapping the sheets by about 2.5cm (1in) and trimming to fit around the edges.

6 Lay the gravel over the top, raking it to cover the entire area in a layer about 5cm (2in) deep. If possible, tread down well or use a garden roller to compact it, then add another layer the same depth on top.

Building a patio

Patios can be constructed from many different materials – practically all types of paving are suitable, as is wood – to complement the construction of your house and blend in with the overall theme of your garden. They can range in style from a simple paved square to a complex 'mini garden' on various levels, and can include features such as a built-in barbecue and seating, raised beds or even an ornamental pond. Many of the principles that apply to designing patios can also be extended to a small walled courtyard with great effect, turning it into an outdoor living room.

ABOVE The striking, formal square pattern on this small area of patio contrasts strongly with the loose planting surrounding it.

Planning your patio

Before you start building a patio you should give careful thought to where you will put it and how you want to use it. Normally, it will be adjacent to the house so that you can walk directly on to it. Sited close to the house, a patio provides a link between house and garden. However, that may not always provide the best exposure to the sun for most of the day, according to which way the back or side of your house faces. Depending on what you want to use the patio for, it may be better to build a separate patio away from the house and link the two with a pathway. A patio sited at the far end of the garden will have a different feel from one next to the house and may perhaps serve as more of a 'retreat' than an outdoor room.

Sun and shade

The first thing to do is to spend a few days in summer watching how the sun and shade strike various parts of the garden at different times of day so that you can select a suitable site. Although you may want the benefit of the sun for most of the day, some shade on your patio will also be desirable, particularly if you want to eat outside.

If your ideal site, from a functional point of view, is shaded by the house for most of the day, there's not much you will be able to do about it; however, if it is in the shadow of a tree or hedge, you may be able to solve the problem by judicious pruning or even by the complete removal of the offending shrubbery, bearing in mind any planning regulations and the neighbours. If a fence is the culprit – assuming that you do not need a tall solid barrier to provide seclusion – you could replace it with a lower one of open construction, such as a trellis.

If your ideal site is in full sun throughout the day, you can provide the patio with some shade by building a screen wall along one side, by erecting a pergola or trellis as a support for climbing plants or even by fixing a folding awning to the house wall. However, you could always rely on a large sunshade.

Size and shape

The size of the patio should be considered carefully – you do not want it to overwhelm the rest of your garden.

Decorative ideas

Regardless of the material you choose for your patio, there are a number of simple ideas to make it more visually appealing and stylish.
- Combine two or three materials to create different textures and interest. For example, crazy paving could be edged with brick, or paving slabs in two colours could be used.
- Lift random paving slabs or bricks and plant aromatic herbs in the soil. Good choices are creeping thyme and camomile, which will soften the hard lines of the patio and release a heady scent when you step on them.
- Edge the patio with raised beds to allow you to appreciate your favourite plants at eye level.
- Plant a low formal hedge of box or a fragrant informal lavender hedge along the garden side of the patio.
- A built-in barbecue is a good idea if you are a fan of outdoor cooking. Alternatively, a bench or table made of the same material as the patio – wooden decking or brick, for example – is practical and will create an integrated feel.
- A patio is a good place to position a small water feature, like a bubble or millstone fountain , so that you can enjoy the soothing sound of running water.

As a guide, a patio measuring 3.6m (12ft) square should be considered the absolute minimum. To be practical as an area for sitting and eating, there has to be sufficient space for a table and chairs and for people to be able to push their chairs away from the table. As a rule of thumb, allow an area of at least 1m (39in) all round the table for easy access and comfort.

A patio designed for seating should be made of material that is level and smooth, like decking or stone flags, so that garden furniture rests securely on it. The surface should also be sufficiently hard-wearing to take a fair amount of wear and tear. However, there is no reason why the patio should be the

Materials

Just about all types of materials are suitable for surfacing a patio – bricks, pavers, stone or concrete slabs, setts, cobbles, gravel and wood. However, take care in selecting a surfacing material, because you will be laying a wide area and some textures or colours may be too much to bear in large quantities.

You may want to use the same materials to pave a patio as those used for paths elsewhere in the garden, or you may want to match materials used in the construction of your house. This helps to give a unified appearance to your garden. To provide visual interest in the surface, consider adding sections of a limited number of other materials – areas of gravel or cobbles in a patio paved with slabs or bricks, perhaps, or a mixture of pavers and slabs.

Patio lighting

If you want to get the most from your patio in the evening, it is well worth considering installing some form of lighting. If lighting is too expensive an option, remember that simple candles and lanterns or garden torches will cast an atmospheric glow.

LEFT The basketweave pattern on the brick floor of this small courtyard garden introduces subtle variations in colour in what could be a rather dull area.

BELOW The floor of this summerhouse has been raised slightly to distinguish it from the surroundings.

traditional square: a circular patio or one that is irregular around the edge is far more interesting. Paving slabs are now widely available in a wide variety of shapes, so there is no need to confine yourself to a formal square or rectangular pattern.

Safety

Your plan should also take into account any changes in level between the house and patio and between the patio and the rest of the garden. Include steps or low ramps where necessary, and find interesting ways to block off potentially hazardous drops off the edge of the patio, for instance, raised beds, low walls or simple pots.

Building a patio

Patios that will receive a lot of heavy traffic should always be set on a compacted rubble and sand foundation (see pages 36–7). But before you start to dig the foundations, it is vital that you measure up and plan the base correctly to ensure the surface has a firm, level foundation that will not collapse.

Most patios adjoin the house and must be laid so that the surface is at least 15cm (6in) below the damp-proof course so that ground water is not drawn up the walls. To set the level of the finished patio use datum pegs, a series of wooden pegs made from offcuts of 2.5cm (1in) square timber. Starting at one corner, against the house wall if applicable, drive the first datum peg (the prime datum peg) into the ground so that its top is level with the proposed

Drainage

The hard surface of the patio will prevent rainwater soaking through into the ground beneath, so you need to plan where the excess water will end up. The entire patio should slope slightly to let the water drain away – about 2.5cm (1in) in 1.8m (6ft) is sufficient, but make sure the slope is towards the open garden and not towards the house wall or you will have a damp problem.

When levelling the datum pegs, use a 2.5cm (1in) thick piece of wood under the plank at the proposed lower end of the patio and adjust the heights of the pegs until the spirit level shows the plank is horizontal. This will build in the slope.

Setting out the base

1 Drive wooden pegs around the outline of the patio and stretch string lines between them. Mark the corners of the patio with datum pegs set at the proposed level of the top of the foundations.

2 For square or rectangular patios, check the corners of the patio using a simple builder's square to make sure the string lines are at right angles. Adjust them if necessary.

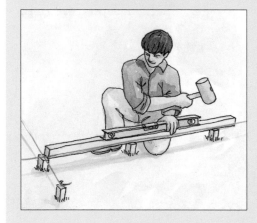

3 Level all the datum pegs by spanning a long plank across the tops and checking them with a spirit level. Raise or lower the pegs as necessary.

4 Add more pegs to level the whole base, spacing them at 60cm (24in) intervals across the entire site and levelling them to the perimeter pegs.

surface of the patio foundations, that is, at the level required for the bottom of the paving slabs.

Drive in another datum peg at the other side of proposed patio and set it at the same level as the prime datum peg by spanning the two pegs with a plank of wood and checking the height with a spirit level. If the area is very large or the plank you have is fairly short, set a datum peg about half way between each pair of pegs and use it as a 'stepping stone'.

Next tap nails gently into the top of the two main datum pegs, attach string lines to them and stretch these away from the house to the two bottom corners of the patio. Drive in two more datum pegs about 30cm (12in) beyond the patio so you have space to work, and attach the string lines to them. Bear in mind that you may need a slight slope for drainage (see left). Fix another string line between the two to mark the bottom edge of the patio, again setting the pegs outside the patio area. Indicate the corners of the patio

Laying hexagonal slabs

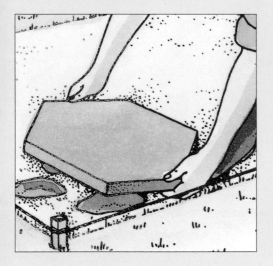

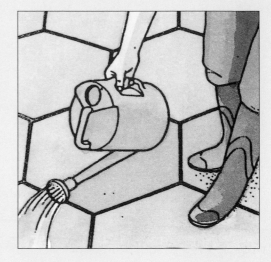

1 Lift the first slab and place its outer edge on the sand, then lower it gently on to five mortar dabs. Tap the slab down carefully, with the club hammer handle. Place a spirit level on top to check that it is perfectly level in both directions.

2 Position the second and subsequent slabs in the same way, using spacers to keep them evenly apart and checking across the tops with a spirit level. Pack more mortar under slabs that are too low, or tap down slabs that are too high, so that they are level.

3 Mix 3 parts dry sand to 1 part cement and brush between slabs. Water in the mixture using a watering can fitted with a fine rose. Once it has hardened, this filling will help to keep the slabs in place and discourage weeds.

by driving in more pegs set to the same level as the prime datum peg. Check that the corners are square with a builder's square.

Levelling the entire base

It is vital that the patio foundations are flat across the whole site. To achieve this, drive in more datum pegs around the edges of the patio, spacing them at about 60cm (24in) intervals and level them to the prime datum peg by working around the patio and levelling each to the height of the last. When the perimeter pegs are set and level, drive in more pegs at 60cm (24in) intervals over the entire surface of the patio and level them as before. The top of each peg will be at the desired level of the patio foundations.

The area is now ready for digging. See pages 36–7 for details of laying foundations. Leave the datum pegs in place, using them as a guide to levelling the layers of hardcore and sand. The final layer of sand should be flush with the tops of all the pegs so the surface can be laid on top. See the relevant sections for laying different surfaces: pages 38–41 for blocks, cobbles and crazy paving, and pages 48–53 for decking and duckboards.

ABOVE Decking patios are easy to lay and especially suitable for modern gardens with bold planting.

Decking

In many countries installing wooden decking is the most common way of creating a sitting area. It is a natural extension of the idea of having a veranda running along the back of a house, but remember that a deck can be built anywhere in the garden and need not be adjacent to the house.

The main advantage of decking over more traditional forms of hard surfacing lies in its versatility. Decks can be built on sites where it would be difficult to install a traditional patio, such as slopes, or out over water. For instance, a deck by a pond could be extended as a jetty, so that you could lie on the edge and watch the fish. In addition, wooden decks can be built to almost any height, from ground to roof level. Rather than simply build a low-level deck, you could take advantage of a high point in the garden to create a viewing platform. Because they are made of wood, decks are relatively soft and yielding, unlike concrete, brick and stone. Wood will deteriorate with time, of course, but provided it is maintained regularly, it should last for many years.

Roofing it in

If some shade is needed over your decking, one solution would be to build a slatted roof over it. This would let through a certain amount of light but filter out much of the direct sunlight. It could, perhaps, incorporate an awning that could be pulled over to provide additional shade when necessary. Another possibility would be to build a pergola over all or part of the deck and grow climbing plants over it to provide shade, colour and perhaps perfume, depending on which plants you choose: grape vines (*Vitis* spp.) produce a wonderfully dappled light, which is perfect for eating under during warm summer days.

Deck shapes

Shaded dining area

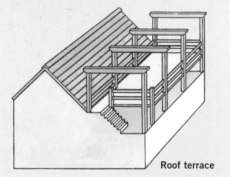

Roof terrace

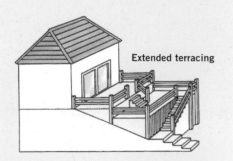

Extended terracing

Deck shapes

Many decks are just square or rectangular simply because these are the easiest shapes to construct. However, if a different shape, such as a triangle or hexagon, for instance, would suit the design of your garden, there is no reason not to build it that way.

Because wood comes in long planks and strips, one tends to think of things made of it as being composed of straight lines. Most decking does have straight edges, but there is no reason why it should not be cut to make curves. A series of circles, perhaps at different levels, for example, could be

extremely attractive, or the edge between the deck and a shrubbery or lawn could form a long sinuous line.

Rather than a simple expanse of wood, it is possible to create a space or spaces within a decking area for one or more small beds, perhaps with foliage plants or bushes growing in them. Likewise, established trees or shrubs that are growing in the area that is to be covered by decking need not be cut down: the deck can simply be fitted around them. This approach can be effective on steeply sloping ground, where a deck might jut out near the tops of the trees growing

Decking patterns

Attractive geometrical patterns can be formed by decking. The more complex, intricate patterns may require more elaborate supports underneath. Some of the options available include checkerboard, angled checkerboard, concentric rectangles and traditional herringbone. In some situations it is preferable to consider using a simple arrangement of parallel slats, perhaps laid on a diagonal in relation to the house wall, to give a dynamic effect.

RIGHT The timbers of this deck have been laid so that the pattern they form increases the apparent distance to the staircase and makes the garden feel larger.

LEFT Decking is an ideal material to use in conjunction with a water feature. The supports should be made of tanalized timber and will need to be checked regularly for any signs of deterioration.

Decking joists

The number and alignment of the supporting joists will depend on the pattern in which you are laying the decking. The main joists must run at right angles to the planks, with cross-pieces in between to strengthen the base.

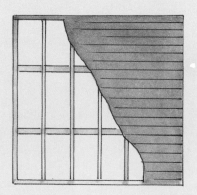
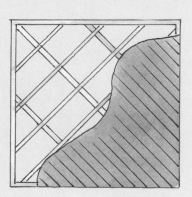
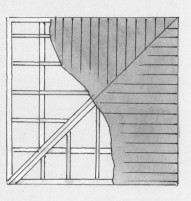

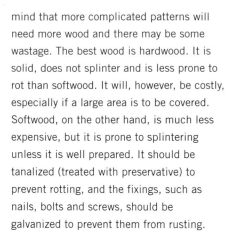

mind that more complicated patterns will need more wood and there may be some wastage. The best wood is hardwood. It is solid, does not splinter and is less prone to rot than softwood. It will, however, be costly, especially if a large area is to be covered. Softwood, on the other hand, is much less expensive, but it is prone to splintering unless it is well prepared. It should be tanalized (treated with preservative) to prevent rotting, and the fixings, such as nails, bolts and screws, should be galvanized to prevent them from rusting.

Ground-level decking

Ground-level decking is not only the most popular type of garden deck, it is also the easiest to install. If built correctly, a straightforward deck can be assembled in less time than it takes to lay a patio or gravel garden. However, speed should not be the key; it is far more important to ensure that you create a level platform and a stable deck. If built methodically and maintained regularly, a ground-level deck should last for many years.

Use pegs and string to mark the position of your planned deck, taking care to ensure that the corners, if you have any, are at exact right angles.

The simplest site on which to install a deck is an existing patio, which, as long as

ABOVE Low-level decking can be an attractive surface material for balconies and roof terraces. It is constructed in the same way as decking laid directly on to an existing patio surface.

through from below, or it could be equally effective at ground level, where the trees will provide natural shade.

Building a deck

Draw a scale plan of your garden on graph paper and mark the intended position and size of the deck, together with access arrangements and other features that might influence the design. If the ground slopes, draw an accurate side elevation of the site.

Think about what you are likely to use the deck for, as this will helps you to determine its overall size. If you intend to eat out of doors, it must be large enough for a table and chairs with space for people to pass behind when serving a meal. On the other hand, if the deck will be used as a sunbathing area there must be sufficient space to set out loungers.

Think about the size, shape and proportions of the deck in relation to nearby objects. For instance, a long, fairly narrow deck – perhaps 6m (20ft) by 3m (10ft) –

would look more in proportion running along the wall of the house rather than projecting out into the garden. A squarer deck, on the other hand, would be more in keeping with a corner location, set in the angle between two walls that meet at right angles.

From your plans you will be able to work out the amount of timber needed, bearing in

Laying supports

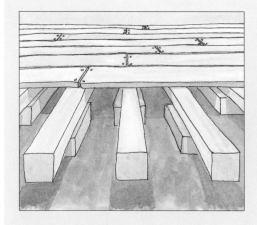

❶ Decking should be laid on wooden joists that are held above the soil level to prevent them from rotting.

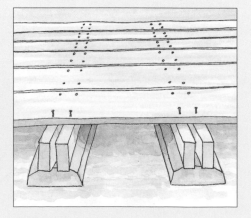

❷ Alternatively, wooden joists can be laid on concrete joists or even pillars if the ground is sloping.

it is flat and stable, should need no special preparation. If, however, you are installing your deck on an area previously covered with lawn you will need to clear all the weeds and remove the soil to a depth of around 10cm (4in), lay an appropriate waterproof membrane on the exposed earth and then level the area with gravel.

Standard paving slabs, tiles or bricks can be used as a simple but effective base for your deck. Position the slabs underneath

A note on safety

- It is wise to get any garden deck construction checked by a building professional before it is used. This is particularly the case with elevated decks.
- Avoid laying a deck with wide gaps between the planks. Chair legs will tip into the spaces, and small articles will constantly drop between the planks, perhaps into an area from which they cannot easily be retrieved.
- Children could easily get their feet trapped or twisted between deck planks if they are too widely spaced. It may seem to be a way of saving costs because it will obviously use less wood, but such a deck might well create more problems than it solves.

Elevated decks

There are several ways to build an elevated garden deck, but decks above 50cm (20in) high, should be left to a qualified builder. For low-level elevated decks, install specially manufactured posts, attached to a hard surface or concreted into the ground.

A stronger frame is required for an elevated deck than for a ground-level deck. First, double-thickness end beams should be used. Joists, spaced no more than 45cm (18in) apart, should be attached to these end beams with galvanized joist hangers. To attach a deck to a wall you should use a wallplate (below right), attached to the wall at close intervals with expansion bolts.

Raised decks can also be built on low brick walls or concrete piers about 30cm (12in) high and spaced at intervals about 1.2m (4ft) across the site. Make sure there is some form of damp-proof course (such as bituminous felt) beneath the supports to prevent damp rising up through the brickwork and attacking the wood. For neatness, it is a good idea to build a continuous peripheral wall too, so that the underside of the deck is not accessible to pets or children. Make sure that the tops of the walls are all level with each other as they provide

the supports for the deck's main supporting joists. It is important that the surface of the deck remains at least 15cm (6in) below the house damp-proof course to prevent damp penetrating the walls. Elevated decks and stairs should have boundary walls or railings.

Making duckboards

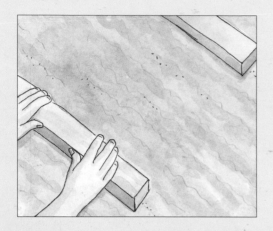

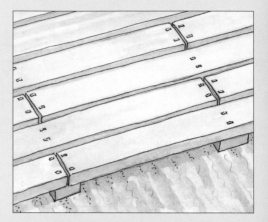

1 Use 7.5 x 2.5cm (3 x 1in) timber for both the bearers and the slats. Space the bearers about 75cm (30in) apart, running parallel to each other.

2 Space the slats about 1cm (½in), using an offcut of wood as a spacer to make sure the gaps are consistent. They should be at right angles to the bearers.

3 Arrange the slats so that the joins are staggered and the ends of the slats meet over a bearer. Fix the slats to the bearers using floorboard nails.

ABOVE Boxing in decking units both hides the underlying structure and gives a very finished look.

each timber bearer at 1.5m (5ft) intervals. The spacing of the bearers themselves is determined by the size of your deck. Make sure that the slabs or bricks are level by laying another bearer across them and checking it with a spirit level.

A standard decking frame should be constructed from 15 x 5cm (6 x 2in) treated timber bearers. The bearers run parallel to each other and are usually spaced at around 90cm (36in) intervals; they should be joined to the end beams using galvanized brackets. The bearers themselves are spaced by staggered nogs, or cross-pieces, made from lengths of the same timber and attached to the bearers with galvanized brackets. Once your frame is constructed and positioned on the base you can begin the enjoyable part of the job: laying the decking itself.

Laying decking

Decking can be laid in a variety of different patterns, ranging from herringbone patchworks to straight laid decks; whichever you choose, the technique is the same. You should allow a gap of about 1cm (½in) between boards to allow for expansion and drainage. The easiest way to ensure that this is consistent right across the deck is to use a plank of this thickness as a spacer. Lay the boards as straight as you can and secure them to each bearer with a pair of 6.5cm (2½in) screws. Trim the edges of the boards with a saw and add a fascia board or moulding across the cut ends to tidy the job.

Basic duckboards

A basic timber-slatted duckboard platform can be constructed entirely from sawn or planed lengths of hardwood or preservative-treated softwood measuring about 7.5 x 2.5cm (3 x 1in) on a concrete surface. Assemble the duckboards on site. Such platforms are extremely straightforward to build, consisting of lengths of timber, which form the bearers, spanned by timber slats. To form the bearers, space timber lengths about 75cm (30in) apart and parallel to each other running in the direction of the slope of the ground. Cut slats of the same timber to span the width of the platform and place them across the bearers at right angles. Lay full lengths of timber across platforms up to 3m (10ft) wide; for wider platforms butt-join the lengths so they meet over the middle of a bearer and can both be nailed to it.

Stagger the joins at each side of the platform in alternate rows so that there are no continuous break lines across the duckboards. Secure the slats to the bearers with 4cm (1½in) long floorboard nails, two per bearer, positioning them towards the outside of the slats to prevent warping.

ABOVE If it is to bear heavy objects like the planters and plinths, decking may need extra supports. An alternative is to cut holes in the decking and rest heavy objects directly on the surface below.

Laying duckboards

Small duckboards, which can also be bought in kit form, can be laid so that the boards lie in alternate directions to create an attractively varied surface pattern. They are held loosely together by the ends of the bearers, which protrude at each side. Trim off any protruding bearers to neaten the outer edge. Duckboards also make an ideal material for surfacing awkwardly shaped areas because they are very easy to cut and slot into place.

Paths

Although paths have a practical purpose in the garden, allowing you to move about without wearing bald patches on the lawn or turning flower beds into mud baths, they don't have to look purely functional. They can be made to enhance the overall design, becoming features in their own right.

The prime function of any path is, of course, to get a person from one place to another. This may seem an obvious statement, but it is a point that is often overlooked when gardens are laid out. Too often a major, much-used path meanders around a garden or has a dog-leg bend in it rather than going direct to its destination. The result is that people take short cuts, wearing patches in the lawn or jumping over borders so that they can get to their destination in the shortest possible time. When a path is going to be used a great deal – for example, if it leads to the front door – make it as direct as possible.

Planning a path

A scale plan drawn on graph paper will be of tremendous help in planning the position and width of your path. Draw in all the major features and then try different positions for the path. Another way to do this is to take a photograph of the garden from the house and then use tracing paper to add overlays showing possible path positions.

If you intend to use bricks or slabs as paving material, you can sketch in these details and gain a better idea of how the finished path will look. By drawing in the actual pattern, you will be able to work out how many bricks or slabs will be needed to pave a predetermined length of path. Then this figure can be multiplied by the overall length of the path to obtain the total number of bricks or slabs required.

The pattern in which you lay the paving may mean that some pieces have to be cut, in which case a carefully drawn scale plan of the path will show you just how many will need cutting and allow you to adjust this figure by moving the pattern here and there before actually doing the job.

Very straight or angular paths will tend to segment the garden and give it a formal appearance, whereas curves will produce a more natural effect and an informal feel. A path that curves will not only display what lies to either side of it, but will also create a sense of mystery when it turns out of sight. Paths that disappear around a bend tend to draw the viewer on to see what might be around the corner. In a small garden it is especially valuable to be able to give the impression that something lies beyond what is immediately visible and that the garden is much larger than it actually is.

When planning a path, you should take into account the profile of the ground itself, both for the appearance of the path and for practical considerations. For example, a path on ground that slopes towards the house or another outbuilding will create a direct route for heavy rainwater, leading it to flow to the house walls rather than soaking away into the ground as it would normally.

Choice of materials

A wide range of materials can be used for paths. If there are paved areas in other parts of the garden, using a similar material for the paths could help bring a feeling of unity. It might, on the other hand, be more interesting to use different materials to create a different atmosphere.

Paving slabs are relatively easy to lay. Brick is more expensive but good to look at, although brick paths can become slippery if they become covered with algae. Gravel paths are attractive as well as being cheap and easy to lay. Grass paths are also cheap and attractive, but they need

LEFT The contrasting textures of the bricks and gravel are emphasized by the semi-formal planting and lead the eye to the distant focal point.

mowing and cannot be used in wet weather or in winter without damaging the surface. Bark or wood chips make a soft path, but will quickly get scattered and begin to look untidy, even if they are confined within some form of edging; generally such paths are best confined to areas between trees and shrubs where grass will not grow and where this type of surface will look more natural.

There is no reason why a small number of different materials should not be mixed. Paving slabs surrounded by gravel, for example, always look good, and bricks and granite setts are good companions for slabs or gravel. It is not a good idea to mix large numbers of materials or colours as this may look messy.

Gravel paths

The use of gravel as a paving material can be very effective in many styles of garden. Furthermore, it is easy to lay and easy to maintain. However, you must take steps to keep the tiny stones on the pathway by

TOP Gravel makes an ideal surface for a path running between beds in an informal garden.

ABOVE The narrow crazy paving and gravel path is an ideal contrast to the tumbling grasses.

LEFT The formal lines of this brick and paving slab path set off the curving, modern lines of the series of rose arches.

ABOVE Slices of tree trunk act as stepping stones in these paths of coarse, pale gravel.

providing some form of edging, such as bricks laid on edge or concrete kerbstones bedded in sand or concrete, or even stout preservative-treated boards secured by stakes driven into the ground. This is particularly important if the path adjoins or is near to a lawn, as the small stones would seriously damage a lawn mower.

To lay a gravel path, replace the sand layer in your foundation with a 5cm (2in) layer of coarse gravel and roll it well to compact it. Then add a 5cm (2in) layer of fine gravel, raking it level and rolling it again to make a firm surface.

Stepping-stone paths

Paths don't have to be continuous – you may prefer to make one as a series of stepping stones or rounds of log across a lawn, which will create a less obvious division between one side of the lawn and

the other. If you do this, however, give great thought to their spacing. If you don't place the steps at the right intervals, you may find yourself walking on the grass between them.

The steps' surface should be lowered to about 18mm (¾in) below the surface of the lawn so that they are not hit by the lawnmower's blades.

Simply place the slab or log round on the ground and mark around it with a spade or lawn edger. Remove the turf or topsoil and dig a hole about 4.5cm (1¾in) deep plus the thickness of the slab or log.

Line the bottom of the hole with 2.5cm (1in) of builder's sand and check that it is level with a short spirit level. Place the stepping stone in the hole and tap with the handle of a club hammer to bed it in firmly. Check that it is level.

If you have a stepping stone path crossing a lawn and leading to a pond, continue the line of stones on the other side of the pool and into the garden beyond to give the whole area a sense of unity.

BELOW The line of stepping stones shows the way in this path leading through a gravel-surfaced garden.

Wood and gravel paths

An informal and attractive path can be made from log rounds and gravel. Make sure the wood is treated thoroughly with preservative so the path lasts a long time. Set the logs on a sand and gravel base.

❶ Arrange the logs along the length of the path, making sure they are all the same height to ensure that the surface is even. Lay them close together, almost touching, then firm them down.

❷ Fill the gaps in between the logs with shovelfuls of the gravel and sand mix and compact it by treading on it. Top up any new gaps that appear.

❸ Brush more gravel over the logs for an even surface, using a stiff outdoor broom.

ABOVE The dark bricks make a stylish, non-slip surface in this ornamental vegetable garden.

Materials and patterns

Any of the following materials can be used for paths, either on their own or mixed. You can make lots of attractive patterns to give interesting variations in texture and colour. In fact, no matter what style of path you choose, you will be able to find a paving material that will suit your needs. Choose from:

- bricks
- cobbles
- concrete pavers
- concrete slabs
- gravel
- sawn logs
- bark
- decking
- macadam
- concrete
- stone slabs

Laying a brick path

When laying bricks or pavers, set them out in your desired pattern, keeping the gaps between them uniform and no more than 12mm (½in) wide. After you have placed a few, lay a wooden straightedge across them and tap it down with a heavy hammer until the faces of the bricks or pavers are all level.

Ideally, if the path does not run downhill naturally, you should arrange a slight drainage fall to one side or the other of the path (away from the house) so that rainwater will run off. Check this with a spirit level laid on top of a second straightedge held across the path. A small wooden wedge underneath one end of the level will allow you to obtain a consistent fall by keeping the level's bubble in the middle of its tube. Tap the bricks or pavers down more on the side to which the rainwater must drain, but make sure the tops of all the bricks remain in line.

❶ Place the blocks on the sand bed in your chosen pattern, making sure that the gaps between them are uniform.

❷ Set up string lines across the paving as a guide to laying the blocks symmetrically, especially when creating a diagonal effect.

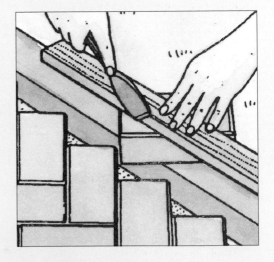

❸ Mark blocks for cutting by holding them over the space and scribing with a bolster chisel against a straightedge.

Edging

Just as gardens need a boundary and pictures need a frame, most patios and paths need edging, for without it they are likely to merge into their surroundings. Sometimes this is just what you want, of course, but a distinct edge is usually more satisfactory.

In some cases, edging is purely ornamental, but in others it is needed to keep surface materials such as gravel and bark in place, and to keep soil in the beds. Not all surfaces need to be edged but it often adds the finishing touch. Use bricks or tiles or, for a more informal, rustic effect, logs. Plants themselves can also be used as edging. Low clipped hedges of box go particularly well with brick or stone surfaces. Lavender is a more decorative choice that can also be clipped into neat shapes.

Use edging around flowerbeds to stop the soil overflowing on to surrounding areas, especially gravel or paths laid with chipped bark. Timber is particularly suited to this.

ABOVE Stained wood can be an attractive way of edging a flower bed, particularly if it tones in with the plants and flowers.

BELOW Brick rope coil edging makes a strong boundary between the gravel path and the densely planted bed.

Edging a path

Hard edges – concrete kerbing, for example – can be rather severe, or more relaxed looking, like bricks. Bricks can be run on the level, but they are often used on edge or emerging from the ground at an angle of 45°. There are also a number of decorative or plain edging tiles, made from terracotta or cement. All of these are best cemented into place so that they are firmly embedded and help to support the edge of the path.

Dig a narrow trench along the line of the edging, put a layer of cement in the bottom and position the edging in it. For a heavily used area, such as along a drive, a deeper layer of concrete will make the edge more secure.

Use wooden planks that have been treated with preservative as edging boards. Nail some stakes on to the timber and drive them in until the bottom edge of the timber lies flush with the ground. Alternatively, you might prefer to use bricks set on their edges to create a much more decorative and formal edge.

Soft edging

Softer-looking edges can be made from more natural or organic materials. These may range from running a strip of grass along either side of an area of paving, to using things like hoops bent from pliable sticks or lengths of metal, and hurdles or logs. Hoops and hurdles are ideal along the side of a border because they will prevent plants from flopping over the path or lawn. Log edging is ideal for a path of chipped bark, partly because the logs help retain the bark on the path and partly because the logs and the bark look like natural companions, especially in a shrubby or tree setting.

A positive edge to paths and borders can be created by using a low-growing hedge, and those formed of box (*Buxus sempervirens*) look especially attractive. They provide a barrier without totally separating the two areas, keeping the path from the border yet permitting the two areas to relate to each other. Keep such hedges clipped tightly so that they always look neat.

Edging lawns

Lawns normally just finish; there is no other edging material. There are times, however, when an edging is useful. Some gardeners like to lay a narrow row of paving slabs around a lawn, partly to obviate the need to cut the lawn edges and partly to allow plants to flop over from the border without ruining the grass. Such an edging should be just below the level of the lawn to allow you to run the mower right to the edge of the grass without blunting the blades.

ABOVE Plain timber is a timeless style of edging, and is particularly suited to raised vegetable beds in a kitchen garden.

Edging styles

Various forms of decorative edging can be used for paths and patios. Bricks, for example, can be laid in several different ways: they can be laid either in flat rows or angled for a serrated effect, or you can cement them together to make a low wall. Edging tiles can also be used. There are plain or decorative designs to choose from. Wire edging, which is available in a range of styles ranging from the very simple to the highly ornate, makes a cheap, versatile alternative and is simply pushed into the soil.

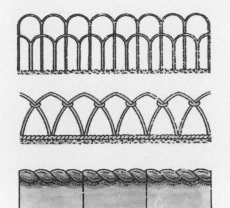

Edging a patio

The junction between a patio and the rest of the garden can be a difficult transitional area. So often the hard surface simply ends, and the garden starts in a rather unsatisfactory way. One way of make a positive termination of one and the beginning of the other is to edge the patio with a low wall. This can simply be a brick or block wall, or it can be a raised bed built at the edge of the patio so that plants can be grown in it. Leave drainage holes in the side of the brickwork so that excess water can drain from the bed into the garden.

Steps

Steps give pedestrian access to the various parts of a sloping or split-level garden, while also providing a visual link between the separate elements – vegetable patch, lawn, planting beds and so on.

Steps can be built of a variety of materials, including paving, bricks, timber and sections of tree trunk. The materials you choose should blend in with their context. There are many types of bricks, blocks, pavers, walling blocks and paving slabs that are all suitable. You can use bricks and blocks both for the risers and for the treads; face textures may be smooth, pitted or, in the case of decorative concrete blocks, resemble split stone. Slabs, although suitable only for the treads, may be smooth-faced, riven or even geometrically patterned for an ornate appearance.

If you have a collection of pieces of stone, all different sizes, you can use them to make crazy-paving steps. If you use logs, you can either cut them into discs or use them whole, with stakes in front to keep them firm. You can also use planks and lengths of square timber; if you can find them, railway sleepers make attractive steps. Wooden steps can be slippery when wet, however, so they could be wrapped in chicken wire to give more grip.

Casting a concrete footing

On a large flight – more than, say, about 10 steps – it is advisable to cast a concrete footing in a trench at the base to support the bottom riser and prevent the entire flight from sliding down the bank. Dig the trench under the position of the bottom riser, about twice the front-to-back measurement of the riser, and about 10cm (4in) deep. Ram hardcore into the base of the trench and top up to ground level with fresh concrete. Compact the concrete, level it and allow it to set overnight before building on the surface.

Step dimensions

The following dimensions are typical for comfortable, safe walking:
- Risers should usually be 10–12.5cm (4–5in) deep but may be up to 15–17.5cm (6–7in).
- Treads should not be less than 30cm (12in) from front to back (sufficient to take the ball of your foot when descending without the back of your leg scraping on the step above).
- Consider who will use the steps: treads 60cm (24in) wide will accommodate only one person; for two people walking side-by-side, make them 1.5m (5ft) wide.
- The front edge of the tread should project beyond the riser by about 2.5cm (1in), to define the shape of the step with an area of shadow.

Planning a flight of steps

Sketch the position and shape of the steps on squared paper to help you to determine how they will look and how they will fit in with your existing garden plan. Draw an accurate side elevation of the ground, which will show you exactly how steep the flight of stairs will need to be.

To work out how exactly many steps you will need, measure the height of the slope and divide this figure by the height of a single riser plus tread (see below). On a terraced site this is relatively simple as you can just measure the height of the retaining wall. On a sloping site the job is more complicated. Drive a peg into the ground at the top of the slope and a length of cane into the ground at the base of the slope. Tie a length of string around the base of the peg, then run it across to the cane. Check it is horizontal by using a spirit level. Measure the distance from the base of the cane to the string to get the height of the slope. Divide this by the measurement you have worked out for the depth of a riser and tread to give the number of steps that will fit into the slope.

ABOVE The contrast between the vine leaf terra cotta risers and plain stone treads helps to create a sense of recession on this tall, broad flight of steps.

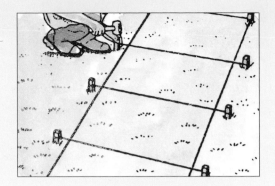

LEFT The contrasting textures and colours of the flat, darker stone and small, rounded cobbles make this flight of steps a dramatic statement.

Cut-in steps

These are used where you need to negotiate a slope or a bank. The shape of the steps is cut out in the earth itself and various materials can be used for the treads and risers. Cut-in steps may be formal, regular flights or meandering and informal.

1 First of all, measure the vertical height of the slope to determine how many steps you will need to construct. Mark out the shape and size of the flight of steps with nosing strings.

2 Working from the top of the flight, start to dig out the rough shape of the steps using a spade. Compact the earth at each tread position; take care not to collapse the steps while you are doing this.

3 Take precise measurements and go back over the surface, trimming each step accurately. Dig below and behind the nosing strings to allow for the thickness of the slab (or other) treads and brick or blockwork risers.

4 Construct the first riser, following the string lines. Start by troweling a 2.5cm (1in) layer of mortar along the length of the riser then position the bricks, following basic bricklaying techniques and staggering the bricks in a basic stretcher band.

5 Tip hardcore behind the riser and ram it down well – but take care not to dislodge the riser in doing so. Add more hardcore up to the base of the tread position and ram this down too.

6 Lift a slab into position on the prepared base. If it fits, remove the slab and trowel a layer of mortar around the perimeter of the riser. Alternatively, you can stick down the tread using five dabs of mortar (one on each corner and one in the middle) or a bed of mortar.

7 Place a spirit level on the slabs to check they are level with each other; check also that the slabs slope not more than 12mm (½in) towards the nosing for rainwater run-off. Construct the next riser directly onto the back of this tread and continue as from step 4.

ABOVE This curving stone staircase, which meanders up between dense mixed planting, invites you to see what is round the corner.

RIGHT This straight, narrow staircase, could appear very formal, but it is set off by the rounded forms of the lavender bushes.

FAR RIGHT These steps use an interesting mixture of shapes, with circles set into the strong straight lines of the paired terracotta tiles set between the bricks.

Types of steps

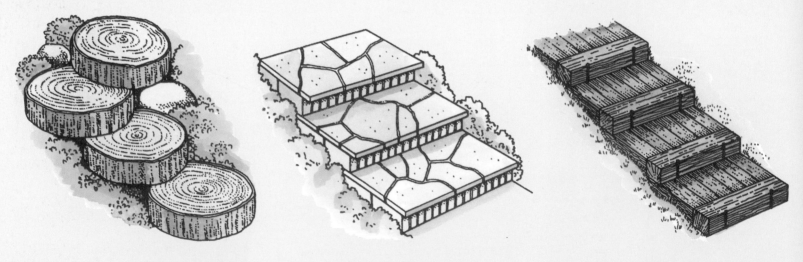

Large slices of log or tree trunk can be used to make substantial rustic steps in a woodland garden. They must be staked at the front to keep them stable.

Crazy paving steps can be combined with risers of various materials, including bricks laid on their sides. The stone may need to be cut to shape to avoid ragged edges.

Square-cut timber makes effective steps in a variety of informal settings, such as woodland or kitchen gardens. It would look particularly effective leading to a wooden bridge.

Making log steps

Masonry steps can appear incongruous in an informal garden, where timber steps are often more appropriate. Cut-in steps are more suitable for this type of garden, and using sawn logs as risers is a quick and easy way to form an attractive flight.

❶ To make each step, drive in two stout, rough-hewn stakes to align with the nosing position at each side.

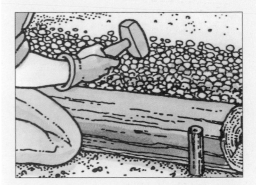

❷ Place a log behind the stakes so that they support it, then backfill with hardcore. Ram down the hardcore with a sledgehammer, then top with fine gravel or bark chippings.

You can also make up a single riser from two or more slimmer logs stacked on top of each other. Alternatively, you could use old railway sleepers. Fix them with stakes to create a more formal yet still rustic flight. Turning the flight is easily done by simply fanning out the logs or sleepers.

Be wary of the treads becoming slippery after rainfall. A good way of making a gripping surface is to staple chicken wire on top of the wood. Keeping the steps clear of moss and lichen will also reduce the risk of a slip.

Making curved steps

Garden steps need not always conform to a straight format. Where you have enough space, consider creating a flight composed of circular or segmental treads to scale a graceful shallow rise in the ground, perhaps leading to a formal terrace beyond.

Mark out the shape of the steps with an improvised pair of compasses made from a length of wood attached to a stake with string. Cut out the rough shape of the circular treads and cast concrete slab foundations beneath. There is no need to make the foundation slab round; just cover the corners with soil afterwards.

Use bricks or paving blocks laid on mortar to form the curving front edges of the treads, and fill the circles with gravel or cobblestones or concrete brushed

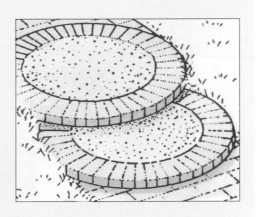

before it sets, to get an interesting texture. Alternatively, you could even lay turf in the circles for a grassy flight of steps, but it is important to bear in mind that these may be difficult to maintain and to mow satisfactorily.

Safety features

Steep flights of steps should include a handrail on each side at about hand height – 80cm (32in) – which extends about 30cm (12in) beyond the flight. It could be linked with existing fencing or railings for a unified scheme. Alternatively, you might prefer to build a wall (at handrail height) on each side of the flight.

Any flight consisting of more than 10 steps should be broken halfway up with a landing which provides a good resting place

and can also break a fall. Take this into account when designing the profile of your steps and the number of treads that you require to scale the slope.

The treads should slope slightly towards the front – a fall of about 12mm (½in) is adequate – so that rainwater will drain away rapidly. This is particularly important in winter, when ice could make the steps slippery and dangerous. For the same reason, choose only slab treads with non-slip, textured faces.

BOUNDARIES

Boundaries and vertical surfaces

Most gardens must have some form of physical barrier around them, partly to keep the world out and partly to keep the garden in. Boundaries and other vertical surfaces, including walls, fences, screens, trellis, archways and pergolas, define the limits of a garden or area of the garden and provide a backdrop for displaying plants and other features such as statues and ornamental garden furniture. Most forms of boundary – even a hedge – can be used to support climbing plants of one sort or another for a decorative effect.

Your choice of boundary material will greatly affect the overall appearance of your garden. Walls may create a more formal look than hedges, and give a greater sense of enclosure, whereas some types of hedging may encroach on the space.

ABOVE RIGHT A tall hedge provides an elegant living boundary and the dark green foliage is the ideal foil for red roses and grey green foliage.

ABOVE Trellis, painted crisp white to match the containers, screens a patio from the neighbouring garden.

Although it is often the case that fences, walls and hedges are used as screens to provide privacy in the garden, they need not turn the eye inwards and block off an attractive vista. If you have a very small garden but there is something inviting, like a meadow or even a neighbour's attractive tree beyond, leave gaps in your boundary, such as 'windows' in a hedge.

Walls

Walls are probably the most solid of vertical surfaces, the most long lasting but also the most expensive. They can be made from a host of materials, from traditional dry stone or smart brick to pierced cement blocks or even cobbles, to create a wide range of styles, from the old-fashioned to the starkly modern.

They can serve many purposes in the garden. High walls can provide an impenetrable barrier around the garden to stop prying eyes and deter trespassers, while low walls can outline other garden features, such as flower beds and patios. Walls can also be used to conceal one part of the garden from another or create a 'secret' walled garden.

Because of the cost and permanence of a wall, choose the materials and plan carefully. If you want your wall to take on a patina of age, choose a relatively porous material that will take on a mellow hue quite quickly.

Fences

Compared to walls, fences are quicker and simpler to construct, but are not as sturdy. Like walls they come in a wide range of styles. Simple picket fences add a cottage-garden feel, creating a low and not very solid barrier. Close-board, or panel fencing, on the other hand, creates a much more solid boundary and is probably the quickest and cheapest way to block out a view. With the addition of a coloured wood stain, panel fences can be made to look soft and sympathetic, or bright and cheerful, depending on the style of your garden.

Hedges

Hedges are living barriers and are visually sympathetic in a garden setting, but they may take some time to grow. They can be large, impenetrable garden boundaries or small hedges used to edge a border or patio. Choose your hedging plants carefully to match the effect you want to create. Yew (*Taxus baccata*) is a traditional plant used in formal hedging, whereas rhododendrons or hawthorn (*Crataegus monogyna*) make good informal barriers. Hedges do not have to be green: copper beech (*Fagus sylvatica* f. *purpurea*) or the purple forms of *Berberis thunbergii* will provide year-round colour. For year-round foliage, evergreen hollies are hard to beat. These also have cheerful berries in the winter, and you could introduce seasonal colour in spring or summer by planting a hedge of escallonia or potentilla.

Bear in mind the space available and how tall you want your hedge to grow, when choosing plants. All hedges will require some maintenance to keep them in shape and thick enough to work as a barrier, but buying something that will outgrow your needs in four or five years is wasteful.

Trellis

Trellis forms a less solid screen than a fence, but in many places this is desirable – for example there may be a pleasant view beyond that can be glimpsed through the gaps. Trellis can be made into more of a barrier by the addition of climbing plants, such as roses or clematis. Like fences, trellis can be stained or painted to complement or contrast with its surroundings.

Trellis can be used on its own to form a screen, but it can also be used with other materials. It makes a good top to a panel fence, extending the height of the fence without blocking out all the light, and can also be attached to a wall for decoration or as a support for climbing plants.

Pergolas

Traditionally used to support vines, pergolas consist of a series of arches,

ABOVE Trellis on top of a boundary wall adds height and allows you to grow climbers for extra privacy.

which can be covered in trailing plants to create a semi-solid barrier. Pergolas are perfect for setting off an area, drawing attention to a feature or simply providing a sheltered refuge to sit and enjoy the garden. They can be used to produce shade in sunny parts of the garden and offer relief from the sun in a hot spot.

Although usually made from wood, pergolas can be made from metal or plastic.

Arches

Like gates or doors, arches provide a definite delineation between one area and the next, but unlike doors and gates, they do not represent a solid barrier. They can also provide perfect illusions: a free-standing arch might be used to divide the garden without creating a solid barrier, because as you pass through it, you get a sense of transition from one area to another. Equally, placing an arch near a hedge, as if it were an entrance way, gives the impression that the garden stretches on beyond.

Building a brick wall

Walls provide shelter from prevailing winds for delicate plants and, depending on the site, will give beneficial shade or create sun-traps. They are among the most expensive of garden features but should last a lifetime.

Planning

Plan carefully before you start building your wall. How high will it be? What will it be built from? And, most important, why do you want a wall in the first place? It is best to start out by making a scale plan on graph paper. Draw in the outline of the garden and put in the major features, then draw in the wall. This will allow you to measure how long it will be and will show you if there are likely to be any problems with its run. Another way of doing this is in the garden itself, using pegs and string to mark the wall's position on the ground. Take into consideration any planning regulations that may apply.

Materials

When it comes to deciding what material to use to build your wall there are plenty of options, but whatever you choose, make sure it complements the materials from which your house is built and the overall style of your garden. You might want the formality of brick or reconstituted stone walling blocks, the rambling informality of natural stones, or the geometric precision of pierced screening blocks. If you have any concerns that the work is beyond your capabilities, you should always get a professional to do the job instead.

Single or double leaf?

Unless your wall is quite low, a single 'leaf' of bricks will not really be strong enough and will need to be reinforced with piers at regular intervals, or built so that the wall appears staggered or stepped when viewed from above. As well as these practical difficulties, single-leaf walls tend to look insubstantial.

A better way to create a solid-looking, substantial wall is to make each course from two rows of bricks laid next to each other and interconnected to produce a very strong self-supporting structure (see Bonds, opposite).

Brick shapes

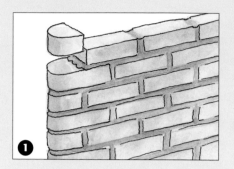

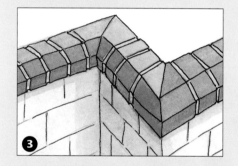

Bricks that are used for finishing off a wall come in a variety of shapes and sizes: bullnoses (1) are curved on one side and used at the end of walls, while coping stones, which prevent rain penetrating the wall, can be curved (2) and bevelled (3) or chamfered.

To achieve a strong bond, some bricks have a shallow depression, called a 'frog', which is laid uppermost and filled with mortar before the next course is laid on top. Cored bricks have holes pierced through them: mortar squeezes up through the holes as the bricks are positioned.

ABOVE This low curving brick wall is a decorative feature in its own right and acts as a demarcation between the lawn and the gravel path.

Bonds

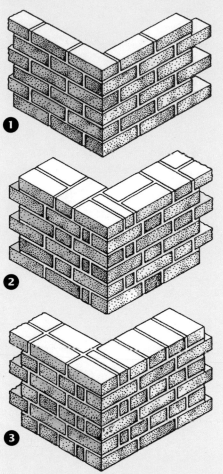

Brick walls can be constructed in several ways. The bonds are chosen partly for their decorative quality and partly for the strength they give a wall; for example, a retaining wall supporting a slope must be double leaf, while one supporting a shallow flower bed can be single leaf.

A wall consisting of more than one thickness must have ties through the wall to prevent the two layers pulling apart. The tie bricks, which show their ends, are known as headers. Those that are laid lengthways are known as stretchers.

The bonds illustrated are running bond (1), Flemish bond (2) and English bond (3), all combinations of headers and stretchers. Running bond is used for single-leaf walls.

Bricks may need to be cut: bricks cut lengthways are called queen closers, those cut across the width are called bats and one cut in half is a half-bat.

Bricklaying equipment

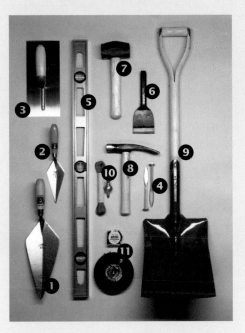

If you are going to do your own bricklaying you will need some tools and it is worth while having a look at the ones you might need before you start.

- **Laying trowel (1)** This is a large trowel with a blade 25-30cm (10–12in) long. It is used for spreading mortar when laying bricks and will help spread material evenly and cover a good sized area quickly.

- **Pointing trowel (2)** The companion to the laying trowel, this has a blade up to 20cm (8in) long and is used for shaping mortar joints.

- **A plasterer's trowel (3)** used as an alternative to a trowel for bricklaying.

- **Pointing tools (4)** These come in a range of sizes and are used for shaping joints. For concave joints you need a piece of bent copper tubing or hosepipe and for smooth joints a piece of sacking.

- A **spotboard** is a panel of chipboard, plywood or blockboard about 30–60cm (12–24in) square, used to hold the mortar. You can make your own from plywood and a broom handle.

- **A hawk** is a smaller board fitted with a handle, on which you can hold small quantities of mortar while laying the bricks.

- **A spirit level (5)** is used to check that individual bricks and complete courses are horizontal and vertical. This should have both vertical and horizontal vials and be around 1m (39in) long.

- **A bolster chisel (6)** has a sharp, straight edge and is used for cutting bricks.

- **A club hammer (7)** is mallet-shaped and is used with a bolster chisel for cutting bricks.

- **A masonry hammer (8)** is a quicker, but less accurate tool for cutting bricks

- **Shovels (9)** are needed for mixing the mortar on a hard, flat surface (such as a large square board).

- **A plumbline (10)** is useful for making sure walls are vertical. You can tie the line around a piece of board placed on the top course so it hangs down the wall as a guide.

- **A gauge rod** is a length of 75mm (3in) square timber marked in 50 or 75mm (2 or 3in) gauges and used for checking that each course of bricks is the correct depth. For screen blocks the gauges are every 20cm (8in).

- **Steel tape measure and 30m tape (11)** essential for accurate medium and long distance measuring.

- **Profile board** This is a board 45–60 cm (18–24in) long nailed across two batons 60cm (24in) long with pointed ends, are driven into the soil. It is used for marking the edges of strip foundations and walls. Two pairs are used for corners.

This starter range of tools should provide you with the basics necessary to carry out most bricklaying jobs in the garden.

Even with a single-leaf wall, the courses must be laid so that the bricks produce an overlapping pattern (known as the 'bond'). This locks them together, ensuring greater strength. However, you will have to cut some bricks to maintain the pattern, particularly at the ends of walls and possibly at corners.

Preparing the foundations

Normally a foundation consists of a strip of concrete that is about three times the width of the wall and that varies in depth, depending on the height of the wall. This strip is called the footing.

For walls up to 60cm (24in) high, a 10cm (4in) layer of concrete laid on top of a 10cm (4in) layer of well-rammed hardcore (broken brick and rubble) will do, but for a wall over that height, use 20cm (8in) of solid concrete.

On light, crumbly ground, these figures may need to be doubled, and in this situation you would be wise to seek professional advice from a local builder or surveyor. Always make sure that the concrete footing is laid below the frost line to prevent rising (heaving) during the winter.

Basic bricklaying techniques

Mix up the mortar either on a large board or in a cement mixer and tip it on to the spotboard. Only mix as much mortar as you can use in an hour – less in hot weather – and keep buckets and shovels for wet and dry ingredients separate. Scoop up two or three trowel-loads of mortar and transfer it to your hawk.

Practise slicing off some mortar and scooping it on to your trowel by sliding the blade underneath. Learn how to place the mortar properly: hold the trowel over the site and draw it backwards sharply, turning it

Laying bricks

❶ Set up profile boards and stringlines, then spread a 1cm (½in) thick screed of mortar over the concrete strip foundation. Furrow the surface with a trowel.

❷ Lay the first brick on the screed and remove the excess mortar. Butter the end of the next brick by drawing the loaded trowel across it, forming a wedge.

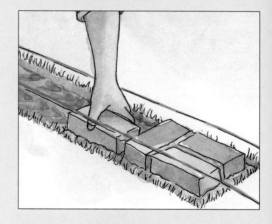

❸ Furrow the wedge and butt the mortared end of the brick up to the clean end of the previous brick, again scooping off the excess mortar with the trowel.

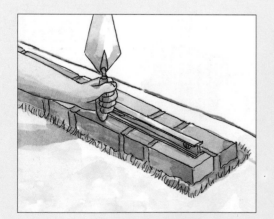

❹ After a few bricks, place a spirit level along the course and tap the bricks horizontal, using the shaft of your trowel.

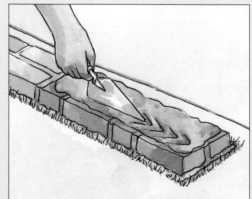

❺ Trowel a screed of mortar on top of the bricks of the first course, furrow the surface and position the second course on top.

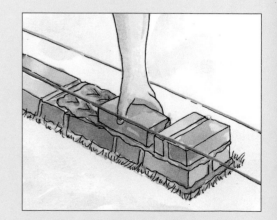

❻ Lay the second course as for the first, if necessary inserting a queen closer (a brick cut in half along its length) to maintain the bond.

ABOVE The way the bricks in the pier are laid forms an effect known as rustication, which emphasizes their strength and function.

over at the same time so that a sausage shape of mortar rolls off the blade. Spread a 1cm (½in) thick layer of mortar along the concrete strip foundation.

Furrow the surface by drawing your trowel blade back along it in ridges: the furrows will aid the adhesion of the brick to the mortar, and form a suction when the brick is pressed in place.

To mark the edges of the wall, transfer the positions of the string lines fixed to the profile board to the mortar by running a spirit level held vertically along each and scribing the mortar with a trowel blade.

Once the mortar is dry enough to hold its shape and is no longer sticky, you should neaten the mortar joints. A good basic joint can be achieved by pressing the blade of a pointing trowel against the vertical joints, bevelling the mortar to one side. Run the blade along the horizontal joints forming a bevel which will deflect rainwater from the wall. Once the joints have hardened a little you can clean any scraps of mortar from the bricks with a brush.

Corners and piers

Stability is all-important in a wall, and any straight sections of wall more than about 1m (39in) high, whether made from bricks or blocks, should be strengthened by piers along their length and at each end. These should be twice the width of the wall and built on wider footings than the rest of the wall. Hollow piers should be reinforced with steel reinforcing rods set into the footings (see Pierced cement blocks on page 72), Space the piers about 1.8m (6ft) apart. You can either continue the bonding pattern through them or link them in to the wall with metal bonding ties between every third course.

It is a good idea to build up each course of the end sections, piers and corners of a wall before filling in between them. This will allow you to check your levels and make sure the wall is straight along its length.

If your wall is going to turn a corner, you will need to maintain the bond arrangement, both to retain strength and keep a neat appearance.

An **intermediate pier** on a running bond wall is formed by alternating a half brick and two three-quarter bricks in one course, with two bricks sideways on in the next course.

An **end pier** is made by alternating two bricks side by side in the direction of the bond, with one and a half-bricks sideways on to maintain the bond in the next course.

To make a **corner** on a running bond wall, turn a brick at right angles in every other course. Use whole bricks, not half-bats at the corners to maintain the strength of the bond.

Intermediate pier

End pier

Corner

Decorative wall blocking

Decorative wall blocks come in a range of geometric patterns. They are particularly suitable for screening patios as they allow cooling breezes and light to filter through, but can also be used to build a low wall around a patio or to divide the garden.

The blocks are designed to make larger patterns when built into a wall, so they cannot be laid in an interlocking bond pattern. Instead, use a stack bond – that is, align the blocks directly one on top of another.

To ensure a strong structure, divide the wall with a vertical pier every 3m (10ft). These are constructed from hollow precast cement blocks that have slots in their sides to accept the ends of the blocks and are filled with mortar.

If the wall is going to be more than 1.8m (6ft) high, the piers should be reinforced by a steel rod embedded into the mortar in the holes in the middles of the blocks. Set the steel rods in the freshly cast concrete foundations; they should be bent at right angles at the bottom to hold them firmly in the concrete. Use a spirit level to check they are vertical and erect temporary props until the concrete has set. Build the piers first and wait for the mortar to set before you insert the main stretches of wall.

ABOVE Two designs of decorative wall blocks are used to effect in this modern garden. The red salvias form a strong contrast to the white blocks.

Decorative wall blocks

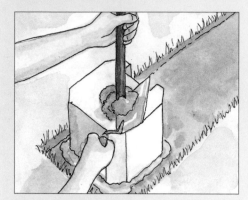

1 Slot the first pier block over the steel reinforcing rod and position it squarely on the foundations. Fill the hollow with mortar.

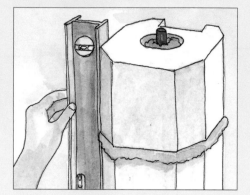

2 Continue to build the rest of the pier in the same way, stacking the blocks on top of each other and using a spirit level to check that the pier is vertical.

3 When the piers have been built, start on the wall. Lay the first pierced cement block on a bed of mortar, with one end inserted into the channel in the pier. Align using a string line as a guide.

4 Spread the outer edge of the first block with mortar and butt the next block up to it, using the string line to align it. Continue in this way.

5 Finish off the wall by setting coping stones on top, and capping pieces on the piers to deflect rainwater and give a smart appearance.

6 When the mortar has begun to stiffen, run a short offcut of hosepipe along all the joints to create a neat, rounded effect.

Dry stone walls

Dry stone walls are built without mortar so the stones must be laid to a strict formula to make the wall strong enough. They have a natural appearance that is best suited to country gardens. Soil can be packed in the crevices between the stones to accommodate plants, giving the wall a softer look.

Stones can be bought from stone merchants or garden centres. You will need approximately 1 tonne of stone per cubic metre of wall (1 ton per 1⅓ cubic feet). Choose the hardest stone you can, such as basalt or granite, as it will last longer.

A dry stone wall consists of the following elements:

- **Foundations** A row of large, flat foundation stones laid on top of well-compacted subsoil.
- **Edging blocks** Regularly shaped stones with at least one flat side used to form the front, back and end faces of the wall with a cavity between.
- **Infill stones** Small stones used to fill the cavity between the edging blocks.
- **Through stones** Large, flat rectangular stones laid across the wall at random intervals to join the two sides of edging stones.
- **Coverband stones** A row of large, flat stones laid in a row on top of the wall to cover the cavity.
- **Coping stones** A layer of flat stones laid on top of the coverband. They may all be laid on edge, or the stones can alternate, one on edge, one flat, and so on.

Creating the profile

A dry stone wall usually tapers towards the top for added rigidity. This profile is achieved by making two wooden frames, one for either end of the wall, which are used to align the stones. Use offcuts of timber, preferably 5 x 2.5cm (2 x 1in), to make the frames. They should be about 1m (36in) at the base and 30cm (12in) in width at the top.

Building a dry stone wall

1 Mark out the extent of the wall and erect a frame at either end to show the profile. Tie two lengths of string between the two frames, one on either side, at ground level. Remove the topsoil and compact the subsoil to create a firm footing. Position a layer of foundation stones with the flat edges outermost.

2 Next add a few rows of edging stones on either side and at the ends of the wall, flat faces outermost. This will leave a cavity in the middle of the wall. At regular intervals, lay a large through stone from side to the other to link the two rows of edging stones. Move the string lines up as you build.

3 Fill the cavity between the edging stones with small infill stones. Add a layer and ram it down, then continue adding layers until the cavity is filled.

4 Add more through stones along the wall to link the two sides, then build up more layers of edging stones, moving the string lines up as you build. Fill the cavity with infill stones.

5 Lay a row of coverband stones on top of the wall to cover the cavity and prevent rain washing into it. You can lay them at a slight angle to encourage rain to drain off.

6 Place a row of coping stones on top of the coverband, setting them all on edge, or alternating them one on edge, one flat, to give a crenellated appearance.

Decorative walls

Walls always seem to be desirable objects to have in a garden, but they often turn out to be rather boring and have few redeeming features, apart from their ability to keep out unwanted visitors.

Judicious use of paint will give them a new lease of life. There may well also be functional reasons for painting a wall: many small gardens, for example, tend to be shady and dark, and painting the walls white or a light colour will help to reflect light into the space.

Creating a background

In gardens where plants are the most important feature, walls tend to be either simply a background to, or a support for, plants. A well-built brick wall is perfect in its own right for this, but if it is constructed from ugly bricks or concrete blocks, it can detract from the plants. A way to deal with this is to paint it dark green, which will allow it to merge with the foliage and be far less conspicuous. If you want the colour to be more of a feature, try shades of blue-green: although they stand out a bit more than plain green, they can still be sympathetic tones to use with a wide range of plants.

Painting tips

- Although ordinary household paintbrushes can be used, a special masonry brush for applying paint to stone and brickwork will make it easier to get into all the pores and crevices.
- Paint on a dry day, preferably one on which there is no wind so that dust is not blown against the still-wet paint.
- Emulsion paints can be applied directly on to the surface, but oil-based gloss paints will require primers and undercoats to make sure that the best possible adhesion is achieved.

Brighter colours

In many situations plants may not be the dominant feature, either in the garden as a whole or in the vicinity of the wall. When this is the case, the wall can become a positive feature in its own right. Depending on the mood you want to create, you can use soft or bright colours to paint the wall. It can be painted all one colour or it can be several, possibly in bands or in some other pattern. Colour can be used to pick out certain areas – for example, in a predominantly red wall a green patch might be used behind planters containing red geraniums.

Maintenance

Exterior paintwork is exposed to the weather and therefore needs to be repainted regularly to keep it in good condition. Garden walls, however, are usually painted for decorative effect rather than to protect them, and so it does not matter if the paint becomes a little chipped or flaked. Indeed, this may be desirable, and the wall can be painted in such a manner that it looks as if it has not been painted for years. This distressed look can bring age and character to a setting.

Painting a wall

1 Brush a wall thoroughly with a wire brush to dislodge any loose material or flaky surfaces.

2 If the wall is dusty, flaky, or is already covered in peeling paint, apply an exterior – grade sealant.

3 Apply water-based emulsion direct to the wall, but use a primer first if you are using an oil-based paint.

Applying mosaic

Before you begin, brush down the wall to remove any loose pieces of material and dust. If the wall is uneven and you want a perfectly smooth finish to the mosaic, it may be necessary to render the area with cement. Seal the brickwork with an exterior-grade sealant. If you have worked out a design on paper, transfer the outline to the wall at the appropriate scale. Wearing protective goggles, use a tile cutter to cut the pieces of old pottery, tile, glass, mirror or shell to size and shape, then use cement to stick the pieces to the wall in the appropriate positions. Rub exterior grout or cement all over the mosaic, filling in all the gaps. Wipe off all the excess from the surface of the mosaic thoroughly before it sets.

❶ Brush the wall thoroughly to remove any loose material then wash it to remove any dust and dirt.

❷ Draw the pattern on to the wall, apply a small area of cement and stick on pieces of tile or other material.

❸ When all the tiles are in place and the cement is dry, apply waterproof grout, wiping off the excess before it sets.

ABOVE LEFT Painting walls in a shade of soft terracotta brings a Mediterranean feel to this garden, which is enhanced by the use of drought-loving plants.

BELOW Bold, colourful mosaic on the wall, steps and stepping stones makes a dramatic statement in the small, urban garden.

Painting a wall

The type of paint you use depends on the effect you want to achieve. For a long-lasting cover you should use an exterior wall paint that contains sand to make it hard-wearing and weatherproof. This is rather conventional, however, and exterior paints are usually available in only a fairly limited range of colours, so for more decorative effects ordinary household paints can be used. Emulsion paints will not wear well in the open, although they are perfect if you want a weathered look. Oil-based gloss paints will last much longer but will need to be repainted regularly if you want to keep the wall looking pristine.

The first task is to prepare the surface. Clean it down thoroughly. Brickwork can be brushed down with a wire brush. Unless you want a perfect finish it is unlikely that you will need to fill any gaps, although if you do you should make sure that you use an exterior filler that will withstand the weather rather than one normally used indoors. If the surface is dusty or flaky you will have to seal it with an exterior sealant before painting. This will also help to prevent the wall from absorbing the paint like a sponge and will thus make the paint go further.

Mosaic walls

Mosaics can be used to brighten up a wall as well as to give it intrinsic interest. A mosaic needs plenty of imagination and a bold hand as well as careful planning.

Mosaics were originally used for floor decoration and were made up of thousands of small coloured tiles. These are available from craft and specialist suppliers. However, a much wider range of materials can be used and one of the best is broken pottery. Fragments of white or brightly coloured ceramics are ideal for creating a modern mosaic. Pieces of old tiles can also be used, as can coloured glass. The mosaic could also contain three-dimensional objects, such as shells and pebbles.

The wall on which the mosaic is to be created should be sound and preferably flat. Because the mosaic will be out in all weathers it must be weatherproof, so use cement rather than an indoor adhesive for attaching the pieces to the wall. The grouting between the pieces should also be waterproof and should fill all the gaps and crevices so that no water can get into the design. If water does work its way in it may freeze in winter, expand and force the piece away from the wall.

Fencing

Like walls, fences can have several uses in a garden, in particular as a barrier around the edge of the property and to divide one part of the garden from another. A tall, solid fence will provide privacy, shade and shelter from the wind, while one of more open construction will allow light and breezes through.

Although not as sturdy and long-lasting as a wall, a fence is much cheaper and quicker to erect and makes an ideal temporary barrier while a natural one of shrubs or trees grows to maturity. Even so, a well-built fence can be expected to last for many years, particularly if its wooden structure is treated regularly with preservative.

There are many different styles of fence to choose from, but it is important to select a style that will match the property. Some, such as picket fences, will look more at home with older properties, whereas panel fencing, for example, will be more suited for use with modern buildings.

Home-made or ready-made?
Most types of fence need to be constructed piece by piece on site and can easily be tailored exactly to your needs. However, it is possible to buy ready-made solid fence panels in a range of standard sizes and styles. These speed up construction considerably, but will not be as sturdy as a custom-built fence. In addition, the length of your fence will rarely equal a whole number of ready-made panels, in which case you will have to cut one.

Another type of fence you may find in ready-made form – as a kit of prefabricated parts ready for nailing together – is picket fencing. This, too, will be made to a standard size and may require some trimming to match the length of fencing that you require.

Bringing in the countryside
A touch of countryside can be introduced using traditional hurdles, of the kind originally made for enclosing stock. These panels, which are made up of woven hazel or willow, are usually rather decorative. The craft of hurdle-making is increasingly being revived for the garden market, and more and more individual designs are becoming available. Some of the open-weave panels are attractive and suitable for internal screens, although they are not practical for external boundaries. Willow, in

BELOW Although not as sturdy and long-lasting as a wall, a fence should last for many years, particularly if it is treated regularly with preservative.

Fence styles

There are many types of wooden fence to choose from, both solid and open. The solid ones are good for privacy, while the open ones provide a boundary without interrupting the view of what lies beyond.

waney-edged

larchlap

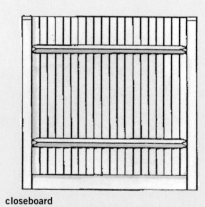

closeboard

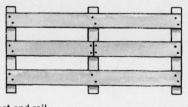

post and rail

Fence posts and spikes

The posts need to be strong and thick enough to support the fence, given the fact that a solid fence will take the brunt of any wind. How much post goes into the ground depends on the height of the fence. For fences over 1.2m (4ft) the post should be at least 60cm (24in) in the ground. For fences over 1.2m tall, especially if they are in a windy site, the fence will need extra support every third post using timber stays. For lower fences in windy sites, strengthen every fourth post.

Precast concrete posts are available and should be set into the ground by at least 60cm (24in). Otherwise, use fence spikes (also known as met posts or ground spikes).

Installing a fence spike

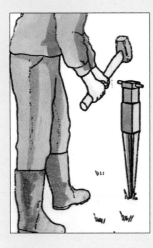  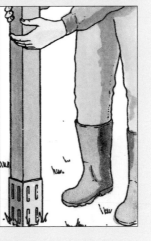

❶ Drive the spike into the ground at the post position with a sledgehammer and offcut of post (or a fixing accessory).

❷ Check at frequent intervals that the spike is vertical. Do this by holding a spirit level against each side of the spike in turn.

❸ Push the post into the collar of the fence spike. You may have to tighten integral bolts in order to secure it firmly.

particular, is becoming more generally available, and there is no reason why you should not make hurdles to your own design.

Fencing material

You can buy ready-made fencing panels and kits from garden suppliers and timber yards. The latter will also supply the necessary wood for making your own fencing. In both cases, the wood should have been pressure-treated with preservative – check that the preservative is harmless to plants, as some types are not. For safety's sake never burn scraps of pressure-treated wood or breathe in the dust when cutting it, as it can be toxic. If you are using untreated wood, make sure that the posts are allowed to stand in preservative for a few days before putting them in the ground. This will ensure that their feet are well protected. The rest of the fence can be treated by brush or spray once it has been erected.

When buying nails for fencing work, make sure they are galvanized. This treatment will protect them against rust.

Putting up fences

Ready-made panels are simply nailed between posts. Prop each panel on bricks or offcuts of wood so that it is level before driving the nails home. You can prevent the panel edging from splitting by drilling pilot holes for the nails first.

Concreting in a fence post

❶ Dig a hole and prop the post in it on a brick, with temporarily pinned-on braces.

❷ Set the post perfectly vertical, checking each side in turn with a spirit level.

❸ Ram hardcore into the hole around the post to support it firmly. Stop the hardcore about 15cm (6in) short of ground level.

❹ Trowel in concrete around the post and compact it to dispel bubbles. Shape the top of the concrete into a mound.

Fence panel fixings

1 Two-piece brackets consist of a pair of L-shaped brackets that are fitted one either side of the panel to hold it in place. The panel is slotted in the channel between them.

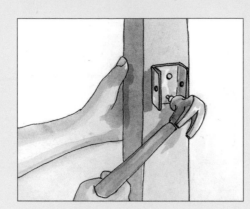

2 U-shaped brackets are simpler to work with but are not as strong as two-piece brackets on windy sites as they support a shorter length of panel.

You can also buy two-piece or U-shaped brackets for nailing to the posts. These allow the panels to be dropped into place and then secured with nails driven through the brackets. Where concrete fence posts are used, the panels are simply slotted in from the top.

Most types of ready-made fence panel are held together by short, thin nails or even staples, so if one needs shortening it is a relatively easy job to prise off the edging, cut the panel to length with a hand or power saw and nail the edging back on.

With tailor-made vertical closeboard fencing, horizontal supporting rails are usually added as the posts are erected. These are known as arris or split rails. They are triangular in section so that water will run off, and their ends fit into slots cut in the posts. The upright palings or boards of the fence are then nailed to the faces of the arris rails.

With vertical closeboard fences, it is usual to fit a gravel board between each pair of posts at ground level. This should be nailed to two short pieces of wooden batten nailed to the posts. Its purpose is to protect the bottoms of the boards from rotting through contact with the ground.

When horizontal closeboard fencing, or some form of post-and-rail arrangement, is being erected, you can nail the board or rails directly to the posts.

Erecting a panel fence

There are many different kinds of fencing to choose from but the most popular remains the simple panel fence.

If you are replacing one panel fence with another, have a look at the existing fence posts. If taking them out would mean spending a lot of time and energy digging out the old ends, it might be sensible to cut them off to just below ground level and make the first panel a half panel instead of a whole one so you can put the new posts halfway between the old ones.

Mark the line of the fence just inside the boundary using string and pegs. Measure the distance and decide how many posts and panels you will need, as well as gravel boards if wanted, and post supports if

Erecting a panel fence

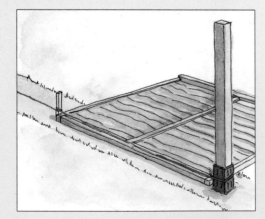

1 Fix the first fence post into position, then use a stringline to mark the run of the fence. Use a panel as a guide to the position of the second post and erect it securely, using a spirit level to check it is vertical.

2 Make a T-shaped gauge from offcuts of timber to position the brackets on the posts at the correct distance from the edge. Use two-piece brackets or U-shaped metal brackets.

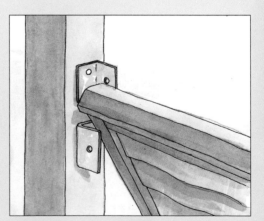

3 If using two-piece brackets, slot the panel between the top brackets, lift it up then bring it down in a straight line between the bottom pair of brackets.

Arris rail fixings

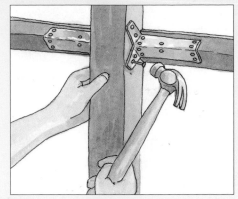

1 Galvanized rail brackets fit over the triangular shape of the rail and the pre-drilled flanges are held to the posts with nails. The ends of the rails have to be cut perpendicular to use brackets.

2 Morticed posts have holes cut in them, into which are inserted the ends of the arris rails. These are then held in place with nails. The ends of the rails are tapered to fit the holes snugly.

needed. Shop around for the best materials at the best cost and ensure the wood is all pressure treated with preservative.

Because the distance between the fence posts is vital for panel fences, put the posts up in pairs and fix each panel as you go along. Wooden posts can be concreted in place or fixed with fence spikes (see box, page 77). Concrete posts should always be concreted in.

If the end post is not secured to a wall, it will need supporting. For extra strength support stays can be fitted against any of the posts in line with the fence. Use pieces

ABOVE This blue-painted panel fence not only shelters the plants in front of it, but provides a soft background to enhance their sharper colours.

of timber about half the length of the post and cut the ends to an angle of 40°. Lean the cut ends of the support stays against the post and bury the square ends in the soil. Place a heavy stone under the buried end of the stay for support. Secure the top to the post using large galvanized nails.

The panels can be fitted to the posts using either two-piece metal brackets or U-shaped brackets. Prop the panel on the

gravel board, if you have fitted one, or on a brick while you nail it to the posts. Drilling pilot holes will make putting the nails in easier and you will be less likely to split the edge of the panel. Hold the panel in position and nail the panel to the first post, driving in the nails at a slight angle so they do not pull straight out in the wind. Position the other end of the panel against the second post, check that the panel and post are level using a spirit level and nail in place (see box left). Once the fence is securely erected, you can paint it any colour you want and start planting.

4 Stand the panel on the gravel board (if you have fitted one) or on a brick while you nail the panel into place, to make sure it is raised off the ground and therefore will not get damp.

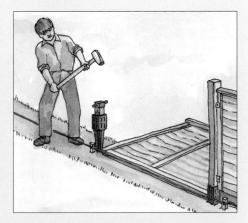

5 Lay the next panel on the ground with one end butted up against the second fence post and fix the third post into position using the stringline and panel as a guide. Continue as before until the fence is finished.

Erecting a closeboard fence

❶ Erect all the fence posts by either concreting them in place or using fence spikes, checking they are vertical using a spirit level. Fix the arris rails to the posts using galvanized brackets (see box, page 79).

❷ Next fit the gravel boards, made from 15 x 2.5cm (6 x 1in) timber. Cut them to length and attach them to the fence posts using short supporting battens fixed to the inner edges of the posts.

❸ Stand the first feather-edged board on the gravel board with its thick edge against the fence post. Tie a string line close to the tops of the fence posts against which to level the tops of the boards.

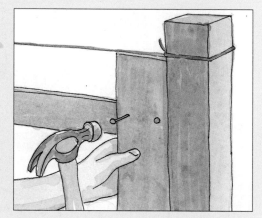

❹ Nail the first board to the top arris rail using two galvanized nails. Use a spirit level to check it is vertical, then nail the board to the bottom rail in the same way.

❺ Continue along the fence, adding boards and overlapping them by about 1cm (½in) as you go. Check they are vertical and attach to the arris rails using just one nail for each rail.

❻ A spacing gauge, made from an offcut of timber, can be used to space the boards quickly and accurately. Use the gauge to space each board at the top, nail the board in place, then slide the gauge down and repeat at the bottom.

Closeboard fences

Although it is possible to buy closeboard fence panels, it is better to erect this type of fence *in situ* as the result will be stronger and better tailored to the site.

A closeboard fence consists of a series of upright fence posts joined together with two rows of arris rails. Arris rails are usually triangular in section to allow rain to run off. Feather-edged boards are nailed to the arris rails overlapping one another for a solid boundary. As with any type of fencing, make sure the timber you use has been pressure treated with preservative.

There are two ways of joining the arris rails to the fence posts. The first is by mortise joints: holes are made in the fence posts into which are inserted the ends of the rails. Some posts can be bought with the holes already in place, or you can cut your own. Perhaps a better way of fixing the rails to the posts, however, is by using special galvanized brackets (see page 79). These will allow you to erect all the posts at the same time, then fit the rails later. If you are using mortise joints, however, you will need to erect one post, fix the rails, erect the next post and so on.

Picket fencing

Although ready-assembled picket panels are available, you may prefer to make up this attractive boundary fencing from scratch so that you can vary the design. Pales are normally spaced about 3.5–5cm (1½–2in) apart, but you may want to fit an arrangement of alternating long and short

Protecting a closeboard fence

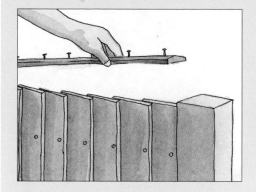

1 Fit coping strips along the top of the boards to repel rainwater from the end grain of the wood where it could soak in. Cut lengths of the bevel-edged strip to fit between fence posts and nail into position on top of the boards.

2 Fit post caps to the fence posts to repel rain in the same way and prevent the post rotting. Post caps can be bought in a number of different sizes and usually have chamfered edges. They should overhang the post all round.

ABOVE The screen of thin bamboo cane is relatively lightweight, delicate in appearance and very easy to construct. It is particularly suitable in small gardens.

pales to give a curving or zigzagging top to the finished fence.

It is best to erect the posts (see page 77), make up panels of picket fencing to fit between them, then fit the panels to the posts. It will be easier to make the panels on the ground where you have a firm surface against which to drive in the nails.

The posts should be 7.5 x 5cm (3 x 2in) in profile, set 1.8–2.7m (6–9ft) apart. Use

5 x 2.5cm (2 x 1in) softwood for the rails and the pales. For durability always choose pressure-treated timber.

Bamboo

One way of getting something more individual is to make your own fence. Bamboo fences provide a sympathetic backdrop in a small garden, and the simplest way to create a screen is to nail a roll of bamboo matting over

an existing fence. It does work best if only the framework of the fence is used so light filters between the individual canes, but it can be used over a solid fence to disguise it as long as none of the original fence is visible. Larger canes can be individually nailed to wooden rails held between posts. Canes can vary in height and thickness to provide interest, being placed either in a regular pattern or at random.

Making a picket fence

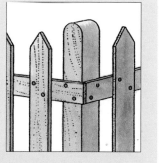

1 Assemble the picket fence on a flat surface by laying out the arris rails and securing the pales over them. Use a spacer to determine the positions of the pales, usually spaced 3.5–5cm (1½–2in) apart.

2 Nail the picket panels to the fence posts, driving in two nails per arris rail. Ensure that the rails are horizontal and the pales are vertical by checking with a spirit level.

3 When turning a corner, use a corner post and nail the cross rails of the two lengths of fencing to the post at right angles. Picket fencing is perfect for smaller gardens.

Decorative paling

For a more decorative finish, shape the ends of wooden fence palings. The simplest designs are rounded (1), square (2) and pointed (3), but more complex ones that might complement a garden scheme include intricately carved pointed Gothic (4 and 5) and ornate classical or Queen Anne styles with mock finials (6).

Gates

A gate is an essential part of a wall, hedge or fence if you want a continuous barrier with access through it. They are commonly made of wood or wrought iron. It is important to choose one that fits in with its surroundings: a very ornate wrought-iron gate would look out of place in a simple country garden, just as a simple picket gate would be highly inappropriate in a modern patio garden. Both wooden and metal gates can be painted in just about any colour, or you could simply apply a preservative to protect the gate in its natural state. Coloured and natural wood stains can also be used to colour wooden gates.

Internal gateways can be more frivolous than those on the garden boundary. They need not even be designed to shut but can be used to draw the eye to another part of the garden or become a focal point in their own right. Constructing a gate from scratch is not easy, so if possible buy a ready-made kit consisting of all the parts that can be glued or screwed together. In general, metal gates should be hung either from metal posts or

Security

Security is a tedious but, unfortunately, necessary consideration. You can adopt a cavalier attitude towards keeping intruders out, but if you have children or pets it is essential that there are adequate, safe gates with bars close enough together to stop them slipping through. Secure, out-of-reach catches are essential. Self-closing devices are useful to make sure that gates shut after visitors, such as the postman. Unfortunately, they can compound the problem, because if a child does manage to slip out they can't slip in again.

brick piers, while wooden gates should be used in wooden fences, wherever possible matching the style of the fence. Whatever type of gate you have chosen, make sure that the uprights are well concreted in or they will soon move and the gate will stick or constantly swing open.

There are many styles of gate to choose from, including functional ones and those that are more delicate and rustic. The choice of

ABOVE This simple gate, painted in a cheerful blue, is perfect for a small cottage garden.

gate depends on its proposed function and position: heavier gates should be used in walls, fences and hedges marking the outside property boundaries of a garden, while gates of lighter construction are suitable within the garden, used just as much for decoration as for practicality.

Hanging a gate on strap hinges

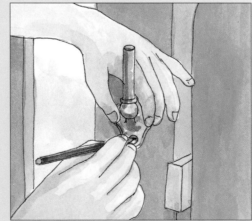

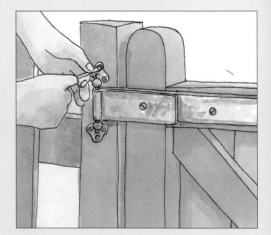

❶ Place the gate in the gap on two blocks leaving a gap of 6mm (¼in) at either side and 50mm (2in) at the bottom. It may be necessary to leave a bigger gap at the bottom if there is not sufficient clearance.

❷ Attach the strap part of the hinge to the gate, then, screw the lower hinge cups on to the end of the hinge pins, mark the position on the gate post and attach them.

❸ Slot the end of the strap hinges onto the hinge pins and secure by screwing in the top hinge cups to the posts.

Constructing a gate

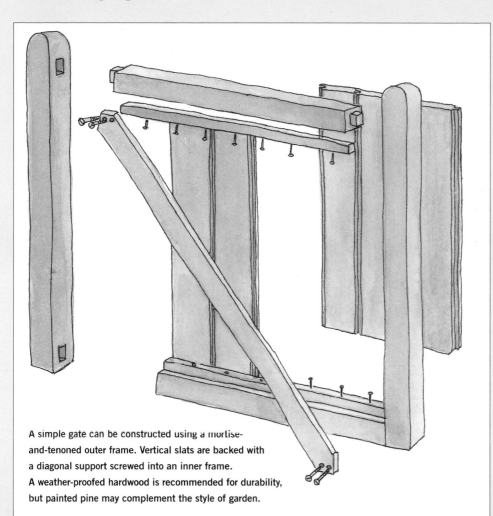

A simple gate can be constructed using a mortise-and-tenoned outer frame. Vertical slats are backed with a diagonal support screwed into an inner frame. A weather-proofed hardwood is recommended for durability, but painted pine may complement the style of garden.

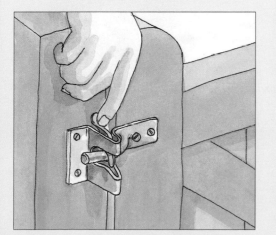

4 Latches come in all styles, shapes and sizes, but by far the most common is this simple automatic latch. Screw the locking bar in first (preferably in line with the strap hinge) and mark with a pencil where to attach the catch.

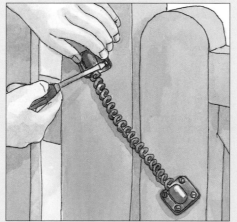

5 A spring closer is a good safety device if you have small children or pets, especially when used in conjuction with an automatic latch. Simply screw one end to the gate and the other to the gate post on the hinge side.

Gate styles

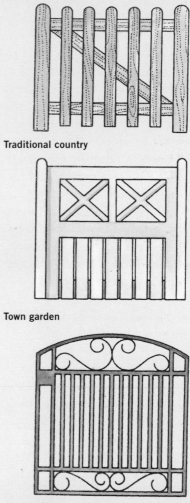

Traditional country

Town garden

Wrought iron

Rustic trellis

There are many styles of gate to choose from, including functional ones and more delicate and rustic types. The choice of gate depends on its proposed function and position: heavier gates should be used in walls, fences and hedges that mark the outside property boundaries of a garden, while gates of lighter construction are suitable within the garden, used just as much for decoration as for practicality.

Screens and trellis

Normally, screens are erected as part of a pergola or similar structure bordering a patio, being fixed between the supporting uprights. However, there is no reason why they should not be constructed as a form of fence between normal fence posts.

They tend to form a less solid boundary than a fence and so can be used where you want to create a divide but don't need to ensure privacy. They are also ideal where you want to preserve the view beyond the garden. Trellis and screens can be left bare or clothed with climbing plants for a more attractive finish.

Dappled shade

Trellis and screens are also perfect for creating shady areas for both humans and plants. Although sitting in the sun can be very pleasant, there are times when a shady spot is called for. Some plants do not

Attaching trellis to a wall

Some ready-made trellis panels will come with predrilled holes for attaching them to a wall. If not, drill your own. Hold the panel against the wall, checking it is level using a spirit level, then make marks through the screw holes onto the wall. Remove the trellis and use the marks as a guide to drilling holes in the wall. Fit wall plugs, then screw the trellis into place.

1 If you are planning to train twining plants on the trellis, you will need to create a gap between the trellis and the wall. Either mount the panel on wooden battens attached to the wall, or use cotton reels as spacers.

2 If the trellis is being fixed to a painted wall, attach the panel with hinges so that it can be pulled back when the wall is repainted. Mount the panel on two horizontal battens attached to the wall, fixing it with hinges at the bottom and hooks at the top.

appreciate being in the sun all day either – in fact, some plants don't like the sun at all. So if your garden does not have any naturally shady areas, it is a good idea to create some by erecting a trellis screen that will allow sunlight to filter through but create enough shade to provide comfortable conditions for both people and plants.

Supporting plants

Trellis and other types of screen have many uses around the garden as plant supports. They can be added to the tops of fences to extend the height and provide a framework for training clematis, for example, they can be fixed to walls to which plants could otherwise not cling, or they can be used to build pillars for ornamental arches.

FAR LEFT Trellis might have been designed for roses, in this case a beautiful light pink climber, *Rosa* 'Blairii Number Two'.

LEFT Trellis can be used to great decorative effect in its own right, not just as a support for plants.

ABOVE Trellis need not simply be attached to a wall or fence, if properly supported it makes a stylish barrier that supports plants, yet still lets light through.

Trellis styles

A trellis is usually a latticework of narrow wooden or plastic slats – about 2.5 x 1.5cm (1 x ½in) in profile – forming open squares about 15cm (6in) in size. Trellis panels can be bought ready-made, but it is not difficult to make them. The slats are simply nailed together and can be attached to a supporting framework of larger section battens at the edges.

Ready-made panels come in a range of sizes and styles, including square and rectangular panels, expanding panels and fan shapes. They can be made from hardwood or softwood (the former lasting longer than the latter). As with any exterior timber, make sure they have been pressure-treated with preservative.

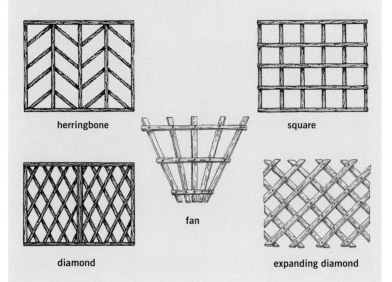

herringbone

square

fan

diamond

expanding diamond

Climbing plants

Following is a small selection of climbing plants suitable for screens and trellises.

Plant	Height	Description
Actinidia kolomikta	3–5m (10–15ft)	Striking pink, white and green foliage in summer. Flowers are white. Female plants bear sausage-shaped fruits.
Aristolochia	5m (15ft)	Vigorous climber. Dark green, heart-shaped leaves. Needs pruning back. Small, yellow, tubular flowers in summer.
Clematis alpina	2.5m (8ft)	Low-growing climber with lantern-shaped, blue flowers in spring.
Clematis armandii	5m (15ft)	Scented white flowers in spring and autumn. Handsome evergreen foliage. Easily trained.
Clematis montana	5–10m (15–30ft)	Masses of pink spring flowers. There are many cultivars of this vigorous, deciduous climber.
Hedera	varies	Ivies are grown for their superb evergreen foliage cover. *Hedera helix* 'Tricolor' has pretty green and yellow leaves. Flowers are usually small.
Jasminum officinale	10m (30ft)	White scented flowers in summer. Climbs well. Needs regular watering and rich, light soil.
Lonicera periclymenum	2–10m (6–30ft)	Many honeysuckles are scented. Creamy flowers in summer.
Passiflora umbilicata	5–10m (15–30ft)	Delicate leaves and pretty mauve passionflowers in summer and autumn. Requires a sheltered position.
Rosa filipes 'Kiftsgate'	5–10m (15–30ft)	One of many climbing roses, it bears many scented flowers and can be tied to climb over most structures.
Solanum jasminoides	2–3m (6–10ft)	Pretty foliage, with white flowers in summer and autumn. Does well in a sheltered position.
Vitis vinifera	varies	Large-leaved plant bearing grapes in favourable years. Rust-coloured leaves in autumn. Tendrils mean it can attach itself to many supports. Good for covering large areas.

PLANTING

Planting styles

Plants are an essential part of almost any garden. There are many ways to create different planting styles in beds and borders, rock gardens, raised beds, pots and other containers. The plants that you choose, and how you lay them out and group them, can be used to create an individual style that may be formal or informal, soft or architectural. Plants can be used to enhance attractive areas of the garden, to disguise parts you do not like or even alter the apparent shape of the garden.

ABOVE This mixed border is an eye-catching blend of purple and yellow, sharpened by the lime green of the tall euphorbias on the right and the golden hop (*Humulus lupulus* 'Aureus') at the back of the border. The distinctive rounded heads of dark purple alliums contrast with the softer plants at the front of the border.

Borders

Borders may be simple, narrow strips or they can be deep, curved, lush areas filled with all kinds of plants. What you want them to do will dictate their shape: if you want simply to define the boundary, keep the borders more or less to the shape of the garden, but if you wish to disguise the garden's shape, make the borders curved and irregular.

What will make your borders individual is what you put in them. For example, large, green plants (such as hostas and euphorbias) will create a lush backdrop, while tall, pale flowers like delphiniums will help the garden to appear larger. Lots of different sized flowers in hot colours, like yellow, orange and red, including red-hot pokers (*Kniphofia*) and Peruvian lilies (*Alstroemeria*) will make the border

appear closer and are a useful way to reduce the impact of space in a large area.

The shape and size of your borders, too, can affect the feel of your garden. Deep borders can be used to soften the edges of a very angular plot or simply to hide areas that are difficult to use.

Small narrow borders planted with lots of climbing plants will effectively create a green backcloth for a small garden and also increase the range of plants that can be grown in a limited area.

To make a border more individual, punctuate the planting with specimen plants or individual ornaments.

Beds

Beds are separate areas of planting within the garden itself. They can be of any size or shape that fits into your schemes.

As well as simply containing plants, beds can be used as part of the garden's structure: for instance, a sweeping bed planted with woodland species can be used to link the main garden thematically with a woodland area beyond. Small beds can be planted to take advantage of an otherwise unusable area, too. A tree may cast heavy shade, making the area beneath it unsuitable for lawn, but turn it into a bed for shade-lovers, such as ferns, and you instantly create an exciting, interesting area.

Beds do not have to be traditionally laid out. You do not have to stick with the 'taller at the back, smaller at the front' system. Try mixing different sizes and shapes of plants for added interest. You do not even have to stick to plants alone in your beds. Some beds can be mini-designs in themselves with perhaps stepping stones or a path leading through the plants, a statue here and there or a pond.

Rock gardens

Rock gardens are very attractive features and if well positioned can bring year-round interest and life to the garden. Make sure you choose the right size and shape for your garden and try to position them in a sunward-facing area. Rockeries can be built using large rocks and soil or can be made in troughs, dry stone walls or low raised beds. The growing medium depends on the plants you want to grow, and you should do some careful research before you make your final decision. Acid-loving plants require peat, or preferably peat substitute, some plants thrive best in scree, and others prefer ordinary soil. Pockets of scree can be incorporated into most rock gardens. If you build the rock garden in a raised bed, you can have different composts suited to different groups of plants in each compartment.

A rock garden benefits not only from the choice of planting but from the materials used to shape it. Many attractive stones are available in a whole host of different colours. If carefully thought out and sited, a rockery can provide year-round interest and can be especially effective if combined with a water feature, such as a pond or stream.

Raised beds

Raised beds are simply beds that are raised above the ground, and they can be built from many different materials, including bricks, dry stones, railway sleepers, logs or timber, each of which will create a very definite style. Raised beds add height to an otherwise flat site and can be useful for adding three-dimensional interest in a small garden.

They can be constructed on a hard surface to avoid the need for digging the soil underneath, and are also useful for providing a different environment than that in the surrounding garden. For example, a raised bed built in an area of alkaline soil can be filled with acid soil for growing azaleas, or a free-draining, raised alpine bed can be built in an area with moist soil.

Containers

Growing plants in containers adds a new dimension to your garden, bringing life to dull areas and introducing instant colour and interest. There is a vast range of containers to choose from: pots, urns, planters, troughs, tubs and windowboxes, made of terracotta, plastic, wood and stone, so you will always be able to find something suitable to include in your garden.

RIGHT The shapes and colours of various alpine plants – including houseleeks (*Sempervivum*) and saxifrage – blend with the rough weathered stone in a raised bed to create a natural-looking effect.

BELOW Repetition of tall plants like lupins and foxgloves draws the eye along the borders and provides continuity.

Plants in containers can be especially useful at creating a link between the house and garden. Placed on a bare expanse of hard paving or patio they instantly create a green bridge, linking the living area to the garden, inviting you to come out and explore. When secured to walls or window sills, they introduce a vertical element. Free-standing containers, such as urns and tubs, can be used to flank flights of steps with colour, to make focal points in lawns or to add height.

The greatest advantage of container gardening is that the containers can be moved around the garden at will, to create a series of different effects. They are ideal for bedding plants, which you can plant in succession as needed, so you have a continuous display of colour.

Groups of containers can themselves become a feature. Well thought-out arrangements of attractive containers can create the right atmosphere and enhance the theme of the rest of the garden.

Beds and borders

Beds and borders are like the clothes in a garden; they overlay the hard landscaping forms of walls, fences and paths and soften the overall effect. The plants in beds will probably provide the majority of the colour in a garden.

You can create whole borders of shrub or use them for punctuation and interest throughout the garden. Stunning beds using annuals and biennials can also be designed, while roses can be used in spectacular groups or as individual standards. However, the most interesting sight of all has to be the well-planned mixed border that provides something for everybody – annuals, bulbs, herbaceous perennials, shrubs and architectural feature plants. One of the great advantages of a mixed border is that you can change it from year to year. And as you become more adventurous and knowledgeable, it will be possible for you to create ever bolder and ever more spectacular border displays.

The types of beds and borders you can create are virtually limitless. Island beds can be made in areas of grass or paving and are viewed from all sides, while the traditional bed backing on to a fence or wall, planted with taller plants at the back and smaller ones at the front, offers different opportunities altogether. In a raised bed emphasis is on the plants at eye level, while some beds are designed so that you can walk through them and see the plants from several viewpoints.

Size and shape

A border needs a certain amount of space to be effective. The minimum requirements are roughly 1.2 x 3.7m (4 x 12ft). If the border is any smaller than this you should restrict the number of plants used to six or seven different types, ensuring that they provide a good mix of flowers and foliage over a long period of the year.

If you have more space you can create a host of different shapes and styles, incorporating varying widths and curves, which will be more interesting than a straight border.

ABOVE This lush border has a curved outline which is further softened by the tumble of pastel plants that edge the lawn.

Marking-out and preparing the bed

If you are creating the bed in an area of lawn, remove the turf first with a sharp spade or turf cutter.

If the ground has not been cultivated before and is therefore quite compacted, double dig the bed (see opposite) and incorporate organic matter into it before preparing it for planting. If you are going to make an edge, do this now before any plants are present. Wooden edging, large stones, logs or small walls will all stop soil migrating on to the rest of the garden.

❶ Before you dig out your flower bed, roughly mark out the area using a small mallet to drive stakes into the ground. Tie string around the tops of the stakes to define the edge clearly.

❷ If the border is very curvy, use a hosepipe to create smooth curves.

❸ Following the string or hosepipe, pour sand from a small drinks bottle with a hole in the top. Stand back and check the shape. Readjust where necessary.

Double digging

1 Take out a trench 60cm (24in) wide and one spit (spade's depth) deep at one end of the plot. Dump this soil alongside the spot to be occupied by the last trench in the plot. Divide the plot into two rows if it is very large.

2 When the soil has been removed from the first trench, break up the soil in the base of the trench to the full depth of the fork's tines. Fork compost or manure into the lower layer of soil.

3 Next, start to dig and throw forward the soil adjacent into the first trench. Make sure that the soil is turned over and remove perennial weeds as you go.

4 When the first trench is full, fork over the base of the second trench as before. Continue until the entire plot of soil has been dug to a depth of about 50cm (20in).

Practicalities

Some of the rules for creating a mixed border are:

- Most borders, whether shrub or mixed, need some sun, so try to site them in the sunniest part of the garden.
- Careful soil preparation is vital.
- If planting against a wall, hedge or fence, leave at least 45cm (18in) between the back of the border and the boundary. If you can, lay some sort of path. This will make it easy for you to tend to the back of the border and to repair the wall or fence or trim the hedge.
- Soggy land or a sunless position are the two great handicaps. Try for good drainage and full sun.
- Make sure you choose healthy plants suited to the soil and position to get healthy growth.

Digging sensibly

- Remember to keep the spade vertical; a slanting cut achieves less depth.
- Drive the spade in at right angles to free the clod of earth and allow it to be lifted cleanly.
- Lift up small spadefuls of soil that are light and easy to handle.
- Dig a little ground at a time on a regular basis. Cultivate a 1m (39in) strip every day rather than attempting to dig the entire plot at once.

LEFT Plants in dramatic colours combine with the formality of a circular island bed to provide a focal point.

Rock gardens

A rock garden, with its layers of large rocks and colourful alpine plants, can make a very striking feature if put together properly. Resembling a rocky outcrop on a mountain or a cliff face, it is an ideal way to link different garden levels. One of the most important features of a rockery is that it should look like a natural rocky outcrop rather than a heap of large stones with plants growing on it. This requires considerable skill in selecting the site and the stones, and in laying the stones so that they look as though they belong together.

Very little soil should be visible in a rockery – it should be packed into crevices between the rocks and perhaps covered with a layer of gravel or grit. This will not only disguise its presence but also help to retain moisture in summer.

Choosing stone

- Wherever possible try to use local stone for your rockery as this will be most in keeping with the rest of the garden and look natural.
- If stone is not available locally, choose sandstone or limestone, which weather well into attractive shapes.
- Ask your local stone merchant or mason's supplier, garden supplier or quarry for a selection of sizes, telling them that you want the material for a rockery. They may sell it by weight or size, and you will want a lot – several tons for a decent-size rockery.
- If you have wide enough access from the front to the back of the house, you could rent a mechanical digger and driver to shift the rock from your driveway (where it will be dumped on delivery) to the rockery site.

Choosing the site

As with so many features in the garden, it is vitally important to choose the correct site for a rockery. Although you can build a rockery on flat ground, it is difficult to ensure a natural look, and it is much better if you can build the feature into the face of an existing slope in your garden. This should be a sunny position, although not in full sun all day long. It should definitely not be in full shade, nor should it be under trees, which will drip rainwater on to the alpine plants.

The site and the rockery itself should be well drained and the foundations firm.

Safety when moving stones

One of the important things to watch is that you do not strain your back in attempting to move the rocks. Even apparently small pieces will be very heavy; if you are able to lift them, do so by bending your knees and keeping your back straight.

There are various ways in which you can move the rocks over the ground. Smaller pieces can be moved by wheelbarrow, but larger rocks will need to be rolled along, using stout wooden levers or crowbars.

You may also be able to move them using wooden rollers on a track made of wooden planks laid on the ground. Rope slings can also be fashioned and fitted around rocks so that they can be lifted between two people.

ABOVE LEFT Site your rock garden in a sunny position with well-drained soil.

ABOVE Houseleeks (*Sempervivum*) thrive in the crevices between rocks.

Building a rock garden

1 Mark out the shape of the garden on the ground using strings stretched between pegs or a garden hose curved to the right shape. Then dig around the perimeter with a spade.

2 Dig out the topsoil within the area of the rock garden and retain the fertile soil for mixing with grit as the growing medium. Compact the base by treading lightly; trampling may impede drainage.

3 Next, position the largest rock (the keystone) and build V-shaped arms away from it using smaller rocks. Try to arrange them so that they all have a flat side pointing forwards, if possible.

4 Fill in behind the lower outcrop of rocks with a mixture of topsoil and grit. Rake the mixture level and compact it by light treading, but do not dislodge the stones.

5 Build the second outcrop of rocks on top of the first tier, but set back from its edge, leaving adequate space for planting in between the two layers.

6 Remove the plants from their pots and place them in holes between rocks, crevices and stones. When planting is done, cover the bare soil with a layer of fine grit or gravel.

Growing alpines

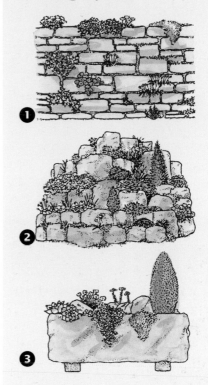

There is a variety of attractive ways to grow alpines and rock plants in the free-draining conditions they require to thrive. Old walls (1) make an ideal site, and seeds can be sown straight into soil pushed into the crevices. In a well-built rock garden (2), plants with different requirements can be grown in separate areas in a way that looks more natural. Troughs and old sinks (3) also offer the conditions required and look good on patios. They can have a few small rocks set into the soil for a rocky look.

Scree beds

Alpine plants that require extremely sharp drainage are best cultivated in scree beds, designed to simulate the conditions that occur naturally at the foot of mountain slopes where there is a deep layer of finely broken rock and a certain amount of humus.

A scree bed (pictured right) is essentially a raised bed with much of the soil replaced by stone chippings. Retaining walls of sandstone, brick or broken paving slabs may be used to support the sides of the bed, and these should be given an inward slant to make them stable. Lay the lowest stones on a concrete foundation; the upper courses may be laid dry or filled with soil between them to accommodate plants that enjoy growing in crevices (these should be inserted as building progresses). Leave drainage holes in the base of the wall at frequent intervals. The bed should be at least 60cm (24in) high if built over clay soil to provide good drainage, and at least 30cm (12in) high over sandy soil. Place a 10–15cm (4–6in) layer of broken bricks and rubble in the bottom of the bed and use the following compost to fill the rest of the space: 10 parts stone chippings, 1 part loam, 1 part substitute or leaf mould and 1 part sharp sand.

Raised beds

Raised beds are very useful and attractive features. They raise plants to eye level for more interest, and can follow the rise of steps or ramps and help reduce the impact of changes of level. They can also make gardening easier for people with a disability by reducing the need for reaching and bending, and they can be filled with different soils to create the right environment for plants that cannot be grown elsewhere in the garden. In garden design their most useful role is to introduce dramatic changes of level in even the smallest area and to extend the range of planting possibilities.

Another use for raised beds is to create a permanent area for plants in otherwise bare places such as patios. You can fit other features, like a seats, into their walls or link them to a raised pond of the same material.

Choosing a style

Materials for constructing raised beds vary and will greatly influence the style of the finished bed. Raised beds can be built from timber, logs, railway sleepers, bricks or stone, or you can buy pre-formed or self-assembly beds in a range of finishes. Your choice of material is limited only by your imagination, as long as the material you choose will hold the weight of soil and plants and is safe and secure.

Make sure the size, material and colour of the bed fit the overall theme of your

ABOVE The weathered stone of a dry stone wall is a perfect foil for the informal planting in this raised bed.

RIGHT The timber frame of the raised beds and the arrangement of pretty pebbles enhance the nautical feel of this coastal balcony.

Laying a strip foundation

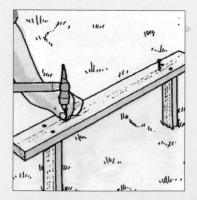

❶ Fix profile boards at each end of the proposed trench, with nails attached to the cross-pieces to mark the trench width.

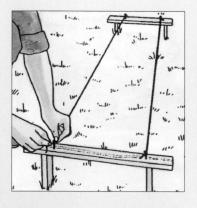

❷ Attach string lines to the width markers, linking both sets of profile boards at each end of the proposed trench, and secure.

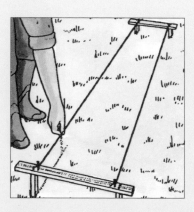

❸ Sprinkle a little sand along the strings in order to transfer the width marks to the ground, and then remove the strings.

❹ Dig out the trench to the required depth, making sure that you keep the base flat and the sides upright.

garden. Beds made from the same material as the boundaries can unite the garden, so you could choose brick to match the boundary walls or timber stained the same colour as your fence. Alternatively, contrast bed and boundary to add texture and interest. For example, you could try a bed built from old red bricks against a dark blue fence. Narrow or wide, large or small, raised beds are a useful addition to the garden and can even be used as a dividing wall themselves.

Siting a raised bed

Where you site a raised bed will depend on a number of factors. First, what are your reasons for having raised beds? If they are for easier access, then obviously the area around them must be easy to get to. If they are being introduced to define areas within the garden then you need to plan where they are going and their dimensions, any gaps between them and so on.

Planting

Next and very important is what you want to grow in them. Alpines and rock plants like a sunny site with some shade, cacti like full sun and most ferns require dappled shade. Whatever you want to grow in them, raised beds will need good drainage, so siting them directly on to

concrete or clay is not going to be the best idea unless you provide adequate drainage. By considering all these things you can create and site raised beds to enhance your garden and make them part of the overall design.

Strip foundations

If you are building a raised bed from bricks or stone, you will need to provide adequate foundations to support the walls. Strip foundations are suitable for small-scale features like raised beds. These consist of a trench filled with a layer of compacted hardcore (broken stones or bricks) topped with fresh concrete.

The foundation is built wider than the wall, so that the weight of the wall is spread out at an angle from its base into the foundation and on into the subsoil. To gauge the correct width of foundation for a given wall width, you should, as a rule of thumb, allow twice the width of the masonry.

The depth of the foundation depends on the height and thickness of the wall and on the condition of the soil, but in general it should be half as deep as it is wide and project beyond the ends of the wall by half the width of the masonry. For example, a wall that is six courses of bricks high would require a trench about 40cm (16in) deep.

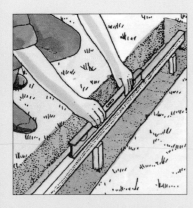

5 Drive in pegs so that they protrude to the final level of the top of the concrete foundations. Check that the pegs are level.

6 Soak the trench with water, then add hardcore and ram it down well into the soft ground with a sledgehammer.

7 Pour in the concrete and work in by slicing into it with a spade. This dispels bubbles that might weaken the foundations.

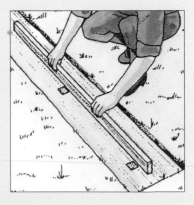

8 Compact the concrete by tamping with a straight-edged length of timber and level it to the tops of the guide pegs.

Containers

Containers planted with flowers or shrubs can be used for an instant effect in a new garden or to rejuvenate a neglected area. Terracotta chimney pots in different sizes, oak whisky barrels sliced in half, old metal fire buckets and tin tubs, watering cans, milk churns and stone, earthenware and porcelain sinks have all at some time been recycled for use in container gardening.

Look around you and see what might be transformed into a useful container for growing plants. You may choose to make a display of cacti or a table centrepiece for outdoor entertaining, or find a new lease of life for a redundant vessel by filling it to overflowing with flowers and ferns. You can transform an orange box into a container for herbs or as an attractive table decoration, convert a polystyrene fish box into a 'stone' planter and make and decorate a number of more traditional wooden garden planters.

Creative containers

Many items can be adapted into unusual containers. Whatever you choose, make sure that it has adequate drainage holes and that you use good quality compost. Let your imagination go and think about the possibilities of things like:

- galvanized florist's buckets
- plastic buckets in cheerful colours or old zinc mop buckets
- steel dustbins
- old baths and sinks
- terrracotta pots decorated with mosaic or painted in eye-catching patterns and colours
- old teapots and kettles
- chimney pots
- wicker baskets lined with heavy-duty plastic
- old car tyres stacked up

Which container?

Containers can be used in all sizes of garden, from the largest area to the very smallest rooftop retreat. Portable planters are particularly useful for creating areas of interest, which can be changed around with the passing of the seasons and as different plants reach their peak. Create small focal areas in the garden by using gravel, pebbles and different coloured stones (paint stones, if you wish, for a striking effect) to set off displays of large-leafed plants in grouped containers. Secrete a hanging pot high among the leaves of a climbing creeper or create small displays of pots in areas to be discovered and rediscovered as you walk around the hidden areas of your garden.

Terracotta

Giant antique terracotta pots from the Mediterranean or Mexico, once used for storing olives, wine or water, make interesting focal points; large objects in small gardens can in fact provide an illusion of space. These hand-made vessels, some as large as two or three metres in height, have developed a unique character of shape, size and colour through generations of use. However, they are not always easy to find, and are becoming increasingly expensive.

Garden centres sell a wide range of modern terracotta both in modern styles and in imitation of antiques but, although reasonably priced, such containers tend to be mass produced and lack the charm of older pots. Certainly, do not dismiss all modern terracotta as there are some exquisite examples of plain and decorated pots and planters made by local craftsmen. Search out these potters and you will be fascinated by some of their contemporary wares and the designs still being made in traditional style. Your acquisitions will give you years of pleasure, as well as supporting local craftspeople.

LEFT Plants in shades of pink are displayed to great effect in wall planters, terracotta containers and an unusual old wooden wheelbarrow.

Urban garden

Within a garden, a good view can be emphasized or attention can be diverted from a plain wall with the careful positioning of terracotta, reconstituted stone or even concrete urns and pots, which eventually become so encrusted with lichen that they appear to be antique (paint them with milk or dilute yogurt to encourage this).

For the urban gardener with only a windowbox, a postage stamp-sized patch or roof-top garden, pottering about arranging and rearranging or replanting the various containers can give hours of pleasure and respite from the pace of a busy city life. When it comes to the choice of plants, it is preferable to restrict the range and colour scheme, as this will make a far greater impact in a small space than attempting to include a bit of everything.

The following pages show several planter projects for enlivening a patios or adapting existing pots.

LEFT Ordinary terracotta pots have been transformed into elegant striped containers with a lick of paint.

BELOW RIGHT Group small containers together for a simple, bold statement.

BELOW LEFT Containers of colourful flowers add instant impact to this sunny patio.

Terracotta wall planter

Wall planters overflowing with trailing geraniums or other drought-resistant plants are a feature of Mediterranean houses and gardens – the bright colours provide a striking contrast with the stark white of sun-drenched buildings. The simple hand-made clay tiles and pots found throughout much of southern Europe make particularly appropriate planters, but this project can be easily adapted to more easily available materials.

Take inspiration from a search around a building reclamation yard; you will find hundreds of different tiles that can be adapted to make a variety of unusual wall planters. If possible, choose a pot that already has a hole in its base. If it does not, you will need to drill either one large hole or a number of small holes in the base before you begin the project as it is vital that the plant has adequate drainage.

Materials and equipment

- Old 10cm (4in) terracotta flowerpot
- Old terracotta ridge tile
- Zinc-plated or galvanized 4cm (1½in) M5 bolt, nut and 2 washers
- Waste timber or board
- Tape measure
- Pencil
- Electric drill
- 5mm (³⁄₁₆in) masonry drill bit
- Spanner to fit M5 nut

1 Place your flowerpot on a piece of waste timber or board and make a pencil mark at a point on the inside of the pot roughly 25mm (1in) from the rim. Using a drill and masonry bit, drill a 5mm (³⁄₁₆in) hole through the pot from the inside. Do not use the drill's hammer action and drill with care to minimize the chances of cracking the terracotta. Place the ridge tile on a sheet of waste timber or heavy card with the outer curved surface down. Place the flowerpot in the tile – with the drilled hole in the middle of the rebate of the tile and the bottom of the pot roughly 25mm (1in) above what will be the bottom edge of the tile. (Many ridge tiles narrow towards one end: the wider end should be the top of your wall planter and the narrower end the base.) Use a pencil to mark the position of the newly drilled hole in the pot on to the tile. Remove the flowerpot and carefully drill a 5mm (³⁄₁₆in) hole through the tile where marked.

2 Place a washer on the 40mm (1½in) M5 bolt and push the bolt from the back of the tile through the drilled holes in both the tile and the pot to join them together. Place a second washer on the protruding bolt and secure with a nut, finger tightening it only. If there are no other existing holes in the tile suitable for hanging the completed planter, drill a 5mm (³⁄₁₆in) hole in the rebate about 50mm (2in) from the top edge of the tile. The wall planter may be hung from a wall on a nail or hook from this second hole.

3 Cover the hole or holes in the bottom of the flowerpot with a piece of broken crock. Fill the flowerpot with potting compost and a suitable plant. Always keep the plant adequately watered. Fast-growing plants in small and medium-sized flowerpots will soon dry out in hot weather.

Verdigris galvanized planter

Real verdigris is a bluish-green coating that forms on copper and copper alloys when the metals are exposed to damp. Recreating the effect gives an attractive antique quality and a weathered appearance to ordinary metal objects such as this old galvanized container, now transformed into an eye-catching planter.

There are expensive kits available on the market which you can use to achieve a verdigris look, but the matt emulsion paint and verdigris-tinted wax used here can do the trick in minutes for next to nothing. This simple verdigris finish not only adds colour to an item but also enhances an imperfect surface.

As an alternative to displaying your verdigris planter outside, potted with plants like the colourful geraniums shown here, you could use the container decoratively inside the house. Fill it with delicate dried rose buds or with a sculptural arrangement of long-stemmed dried lavender tied upright in a sheaf surrounded by linen ribbon.

Put the container outside again in the spring and fill it with composted soil. Plant it with nasturtium seeds and watch them climb everywhere, their vibrant splash of colour brightening up a courtyard or corner of the garden.

Materials and equipment

- Scrubbing brush or scourer
- Galvanized container
- Hot water and washing-up liquid
- 25mm (1in) household paintbrush
- Green matt emulsion paint
- Fitch
- Liberon verdigris wax

1 Using a stiff brush or a good scourer, scrub the galvanized container well with plenty of hot water and washing-up liquid. Rinse well and leave it to dry thoroughly. Place only the very tip of the household paintbrush in the green emulsion.

2 Stipple the paint on to the galvanized surface in patches, applying it to the outside of the container and for about 15cm (6in) down on the inside. Allow the paint to dry.

3 Using a fitch, stipple on the verdigris-tinted wax, again applying it in patches. Use the wax all over the outside of the container and inside at the top, allowing the painted green background to show through in places to give the greenish mottled effect. Leave the wax to set. When dry, the container is ready for use.

Patio planter

Filled with flowers, foliage, shrubs or even small trees, planters can camouflage an eyesore, act as a focal point or give added height, colour and texture to various areas of ground.

Planters can be almost any size or shape, made of innumerable materials and finished in any number of ways. Adapt the size of your planter to suit the type of plant it will contain. Few plants will thrive in small containers that restrict root growth. Plants in small containers are also susceptible to drought in summer and frost in winter.

You can fill your planter with soil, but using a container inside your planter will help protect the wood against rot and extend its life considerably. The planter here was designed to take a square plastic container inside. It is far simpler to make your planter fit an existing pot or container rather than to find an inner container that will fit perfectly after you have made the planter.

❶ Place two of the upright pieces parallel to each other on a flat surface, the outside edges 39.5cm (15½in) apart. Mark a point 25mm (1in) from the bottom of each piece and place one short side piece horizontally across the two uprights with its bottom edge on the pencil marks and its ends flush with the outside edges of the uprights. Using a 5mm (³⁄₁₆in) drill bit, drill through the side piece at both ends, drilling approximately 6mm (¼in) deep into the uprights. Glue and secure the pieces with coach screws. Before tightening with a spanner, use a try square to check that the corners are square. Next, place one long side piece across the uprights, butting it up to the short side piece already fixed and making sure the long piece overlaps the uprights that at both ends by about 12mm (½in). Drill and secure with coach screws as before. Fix seven further alternate short and long side pieces across the uprights to

reach the end of the uprights. A total of nine side pieces make up each completely assembled side section.

❷ Repeat this step, using the remaining two uprights and a further nine side pieces, again securing them with glue and coach screws. Then begin to assemble the planter by placing the two completed side sections opposite each other. Join them with the remaining 18 side pieces, alternately using long and short side pieces to match them with those on the completed side sections and create flush corners. Fix the pieces as before with glue and coach screws and leave 25mm (1in) legs exposed.

❸ Stand the planter on its legs and use a try square to check that the corners are square. Measure the distance between the uprights. Cut and mitre four lengths of 65 x 18mm (2½ x ¾in) timber to this distance to make a capping that will cover the exposed ends of the uprights and the edges of the side pieces. Leave approximately 12mm (½in) to overhang the sides of the planter. Fix the capping in place with a generous amount of waterproof glue and 40mm (1½in) annulated ring nails.

❹ Measure and mark the depth of the container or pot you intend to use inside the planter. Fix two 37cm (1ft 2½in) supports inside the planter opposite each other, using glue and 25mm (1in) galvanized cross-head screws, approximately 40mm (1½in) lower than the depth of the container to be used. When the glue is dry, place the six remaining 370mm (1ft 2½in) lengths of timber across the supports and fix with glue and more screws to provide a floor for the planter and keep the structure rigid. Paint the planter with at least two coats of preservative wood stain, making sure that all the end grain is well saturated.

Materials and equipment

- Rough-sawn softwood timber:
  Four 48cm (1ft 7in) lengths
  of 40 x 40mm (1½ x 1½in)
- About 18m (60ft) length of
  50 x 12mm (2 x ½in), cut
  into:
  18 39.5cm (1ft 3½in) lengths
  for short side pieces
  18 42cm (1ft 4½in) lengths
  for the long side pieces
  8 37cm (1ft 2½in) lengths for
  the supports and floor
- About 1.93m (6ft 4in) length
  of 65 x 18mm
  (2½ x ¾in), cut into 4 lengths
  of about 48cm (1ft 7in) for
  the capping
- Waterproof PVA glue

- 72 30mm (1¼in) long 5mm
  (³⁄₁₆in) square-head galvanized
  steel coach screws
- 40mm (1½in) annulated ring
  nails
- 25mm (1in) galvanized cross-
  head screws
- Preservative wood stain
- Plastic pot or container
- Tape measure
- Pencil
- Electric drill
- 5mm (³⁄₁₆in) drill bit
- Spanner
- Try square
- Hammer
- Cross-head screwdriver
- 25mm (1in) paintbrush

Textured pots

Materials and equipment

- Plastic or terracotta flowerpots
- Builder's adhesive or waterproof
  tile cement
- Variety of sea shells or two
  thicknesses of rope
- White matt emulsion paint
- Exterior-grade matt varnish
- 25mm (1in) stiff paintbrush

1 To decorate the pot with rope, first measure the circumference at the top and cut a piece of thick rope to this length. Decide on the position of the thin rope, measure and cut four lengths of rope to fit around the pot. Apply builder's adhesive or tile cement directly to the back of the thick rope and place it in position just below the rim of the pot. Attach the thin rope in the same way. Allow the adhesive to dry before painting. Apply two coats of white matt emulsion paint. When this is dry, seal the pot with two coats of exterior-grade matt varnish. Use a stiff brush to apply both the paint and varnish, making sure that all nooks and crannies are well covered.

2 For the shell-decorated pot, place a liberal amount of builder's adhesive or tile cement on the back of each shell and attach the shell to the pot. If you are using tile cement, you can paste a small area at a time, attaching some shells and then adding more cement and decoration as you work around the surface of the pot. Leave to dry thoroughly. Paint as in step 1.

Wooden planter

Wooden planters are simple to make and can be used in any outdoor space. A rectangular planter is particularly suitable for use where space is limited or plants are to be trained up a wall. This planter is free-standing but may be adjusted for use as a windowbox – simply trim the legs to fit the slope of your windowsill and fit securely in place. The dimensions of the planter were dictated by the size of the plastic trough to be placed in it for the plants, but they can easily be adjusted to suit different sized troughs or pots.

This planter has been made from rough-sawn softwood, but planed timber can be used for a more sophisticated planter, which can be stained or painted with gloss paint if preferred. Alternatively, try using offcut timber, complete with bark, for a rustic look, or insert tiles or slate in simple frames mounted on the side pieces. If frames or straight-edged cladding are used, it is advisable to add a mitred flat frame on the top for protection and an attractive finish. It is not necessary to clad all the sides if the planter is to be used as a windowbox or positioned against a wall.

Materials and equipment

Use either rough-sawn softwood or planed timber for a smoother finish. As you cut the wood, mark each piece with pencil so you know what it is for.

- **2.29m (7ft 6in) length of 230 x 12mm (9 x ½in) timber or exterior-grade plywood, cut into:**
  2 81.5cm (32in) lengths for the box sides
  2 33cm (13in) lengths for the box ends
- **2.42m (7ft 11in) length of 18 x 18mm (¾ x ¾in) timber, cut into:**
  4 23cm (9in) lengths for the end battens
  2 75.5cm (29½in) lengths for the side battens
- **16.5m (54ft) length of 50 x 12mm (2 x ½in) timber or exterior-grade plywood, cut into:**
  4 24cm (9½in) lengths, mitred at 45° for the corner braces
  38 28cm (11in) lengths for the cladding
  8 32cm (12¾in) lengths for the legs
  6 33cm (13in) lengths for the floor
- **Waterproof PVA glue**
- **25mm (1in) panel pins**
- **Preservative wood stain**

1 Place the two 81.5cm (32in) side pieces on a flat surface. Measure and draw a line across the width, 12mm (½in) from each end on both pieces. Apply glue to one long edge on the four 23cm (9in) end battens and then stick and nail two of these to each side piece just inside the pencil lines. Glue and nail a side batten to each side piece in the same way, fitting it between the end battens already in place. Make sure that the outer edges of each side batten and side piece are flush. Place the ends of the planter against the side pieces, butting them against the end battens. Fix with glue and panel pins.

2 Place the planter upside down so that the side battens are uppermost. Check the corners with a try square, then fit the four mitred corner braces across the corners of the box, using glue and panel pins.

3 Next make the picket posts. Using a mitre saw set at 45°, cut a 90° apex on each of the 38 lengths of cladding and the eight leg pieces.

4 To fit the cladding, turn the planter on one side with the side battens and corner braces nearest you. Starting at one end of the side piece, fix a leg piece with glue and panel pins, ensuring that its outside edge is flush with the end of the planter and leaving about 7cm (2¾in) protruding below the base of the box. Proceed around the planter, securing the cladding and checking that it is fitted with approximately 25mm (1in) protruding below the base of the box. At the corners, the leg pieces on the ends of the planter should overlap the outer edges of those on the side pieces.

5 Lastly, secure the six lengths of timber for the floor of the planter on top of the side battens with glue and panel pins. Paint the planter with preservative wood stain, making sure that all end grain is well saturated. Two contrasting stain colours were used for the planter pictured. When the preservative is completely dry, place a plastic trough inside the planter and plant up or place ready-potted flowers or shrubs inside.

Mock stone trough

Despite being attractive ornaments, stone troughs are rare, expensive and heavy. It is possible to make an authentic mock stone trough by covering a polystyrene fish box with a concrete mix. It has all the advantages of a traditional stone planter, at a fraction of the cost and weight. A fishmonger should be able to let you have a suitable polystyrene box.

1 Cut off any extraneous moulding on the polystyrene box that would otherwise ruin the shape, then cut a drainage hole in the base and insert a piece of plastic pipe or broom handle, making sure it protrudes inside the box by at least 25mm (1in). Carefully mould wire mesh all over the box and secure it by weaving the cut ends of the wire into the mesh.

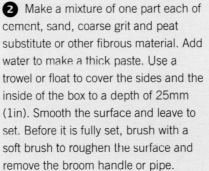

2 Make a mixture of one part each of cement, sand, coarse grit and peat substitute or other fibrous material. Add water to make a thick paste. Use a trowel or float to cover the sides and the inside of the box to a depth of 25mm (1in). Smooth the surface and leave to set. Before it is fully set, brush with a soft brush to roughen the surface and remove the broom handle or pipe.

3 When the trough is complete, you can give it a well-weathered look by brushing on a mixture of natural yogurt and liquid fertilizer. Leave the trough in a warm, moist environment to allow the mosses and algae to grow on the mixture and then plant up with low-growing alpines.

LIVING OUTDOORS

Living outdoors

Unless you use your small garden as nothing more than a convenient place to store unwanted items, you are likely to regard it as somewhere you can relax in one way or another. Children find running about and playing games exciting, and some adults find gardening therapeutic, but for most people relaxing in the garden means nothing more than sitting in the sun or shade, reading, dozing or entertaining in one way or another. A garden should be an asset to your home and an area that enhances your life.

BELOW These simple pale wood and straw chairs make ideal temporary seating in this quiet corner overlooking the lawn.

If the garden is going to mean anything at all in your life it must surely become one of the major elements in your periods of relaxation. If a garden is nothing but a chore or a millstone, this is a sign that something is wrong and needs to be put right. Change the layout and the amount of work that is required in its upkeep until you find that you have got more time to relax. Ultimately this may mean going to the extreme and completely covering the space with concrete and placing a sun-lounger in the middle. If this improves your quality of life then it is the ideal design for you.

Many people find that spending an hour or so weeding or deadheading is both therapeutic and relaxing, but do not feel guilty if you are not among their number. Your garden should reflect your own lifestyle, and that goes for the ways you choose to relax. It should not be a status symbol, and it is not the place for spending time, money and effort making something beautiful that impresses the neighbours but does not suit your needs and that you do not have enough leisure to enjoy.

Sitting around

People probably spend more time sitting around in their gardens than doing anything else, so it is worth designing or adapting the garden to take this into account. Areas in both sun and shade can be levelled so that seats and sun-loungers can be used in comfort without rocking irritatingly whenever you shift your position. Other areas might be designed to be more private spaces, where you can sit in peaceful seclusion surrounded by plants, reading or dozing, away from the activities and noise of the other members of your household and out of sight of the neighbours.

The ultimate idea of relaxation for many people would be to swing gently to and fro in a hammock, snoozing or reading, a cool drink within easy reach. For many people this represents a lifestyle they would like to aspire to, but there really is no reason why such a secluded area could not be achieved in even a small to average garden. The important thing is to make use of the space once it has been created.

ABOVE The slatted seats and backs of these wrought iron and wood chairs and table echo the roof of the arbour, which offers protection from the sunlight.

Shady business

People are becoming increasingly aware of the dangers associated with spending too much time exposed to sunlight. In the past, patios used to be sited so that they were in full sun for the maximum amount of time, but now it is regarded as not only more sensible but also more comfortable to relax in shade. Some gardens have natural shade in the form of a mature tree, but others need to have some form of shade created.

Ideas for entertaining garden features

- Barbecue
- Dining area with parasols
- Swimming pool/jacuzzi
- Children's play area
- Garden bench
- Croquet/lawn sports
- Tree seat
- Tree swing
- Climbing frame
- Putting green
- All-weather table tennis table
- Maze

Eating out

Alfresco eating is becoming increasingly popular, both for family meals and when entertaining guests. You may require nothing more than a simple flat area where you can put a table and chairs, but as people want increasingly to eat in the shade, away from the burning sun, pergolas, arbours and other shade-producing devices can be constructed to provide a dappled light. In the evening dining areas complete with soft lighting and fragrant plants provide a romantic, relaxing setting.

Cooking out

Although eating out often involves carrying food that has been cooked in the house to a table outdoors, the use of barbecues to cook the food right next to where it is to be eaten is increasingly popular. Sometimes all that is needed is a flat surface on which the barbecue can stand, but more and more often specially built structures that are integral parts of the garden are required.

ABOVE The classic simplicity of the dark Lutyens seats and the dark stone of the table and urns make this an extremely elegant formal garden area.

Fun and games

Nothing can be more satisfying on a sunny afternoon or a warm evening than having a relaxed, pleasurable time with a few friends. This may involve simply sitting around enjoying food and conversation or include activities and games.

Some games need little more than a lawn and can be brought out and set up whenever they are needed. A scratch game of badminton can be played over a temporary net on any rectangular lawn. The quality of the grass surface is immaterial. Croquet is another game that can give immense pleasure but requires little other than a smooth lawn (even a few bumps should not matter as they will present the same hazard for everybody playing). The great thing about these games is that the lawn can be cleared and another, different game played.

Some people have a love of particular games that require more of a permanent set-up. Clock golf, for example, may need one or more holes in the lawn, but others may be far more elaborate. Mazes have great aesthetic appeal as well as being fun. These may be created two-dimensionally on

ABOVE Ornate furniture would be out of place in this simple town garden. The green of the table and chairs links in with the garden's colour scheme.

the ground, simply by mowing the grass in a pattern, or by using different coloured bricks or stones sunk into the lawn. Hedges are the most usual material used to make three-dimensional mazes. In a small garden, a full-height maze would be overpowering, but one made of box clipped to about 45cm (18in) or lavender would look pretty and keep children amused for hours.

A swimming pool is something that many people would dearly love to own. It is possible to have one in a small garden, either a properly constructed one, sunk into the ground, or a less expensive one raised above. The latter often comes in kit form and can be erected by the owner, but proper pools are much more complicated and are best built by professionals. If there are children in the household, consider the safety implications carefully.

Tables and seats

Garden chairs are essential in any outdoor scheme. They come in all shapes and sizes, and the moulded plastic ones that proliferate in gardens today provide robust and affordable seating, for all their somewhat dull uniformity. Old garden seats, typically made of wood with metal frames, are often recreated in rustproof cast aluminium or plastic-coated steel. Again, these are eminently practical yet lack something of the battered charm of the original chairs. Modern technology, however, has developed a number of paints and stains that will not only allow you to revive old chairs, but also make sure that they will last long into the future.

Of course, what most of us want from our outdoor furniture is not only a collection of tables or seats but ideally ones that can be grouped together to create an area in the garden that everyone can enjoy and use to spend time relaxing, eating, drinking or simply socializing.

Siting seating areas

An area outdoors for eating or simply relaxing needs to be private, even if this means that it is sited at the end of the garden away from the convenience of the house. Choose somewhere that is out of sight of onlookers, shaded and restful, in a spot filled with flowers and herbs, fruit and fragrance.

Having chosen the site, the style of furniture must also be considered. The furniture in the garden is not an accessory: it should be an integral part of the design, harmonizing with nature so that not only are you able to enjoy a beautiful landscape, but you also become part of it. A hammock slung between two trees is the perfect place on lazy summer days. A rustic bench sculpted from figured and weathered oak or simply constructed from slabs of elm rescued from a fallen tree makes a perfect retreat for rest and contemplation.

Garden seating and eating areas need to be lit once it is dark, and for real atmosphere the most romantic lighting is candlelight. The humble household candle can be used very effectively, placed inside an empty jam jar and grouped with others on a table or around the area to be illuminated. There are many tall candle holders available, designed to be driven into the ground and surmounted by a glass cylinder to protect the flame from wind, as well as many pretty globes, lights, lamps and lanterns to choose from.

Choosing furniture

Outdoor furniture comes in very many designs and a great number of different materials. There are various types of portable garden chairs: campaign and safari chairs and deck chairs come in cotton prints, textured weaves, checks and stripes. Wood is a classic favourite for garden furniture, and teak is probably the most commonly used hardwood since it weathers to a subtle silvery grey colour, as if it has been washed for years by ocean spray. Reclaimed timbers salvaged from old buildings can also be used imaginatively. Benches and chairs can be made in softwood, such as pine, which is in plentiful supply, takes paint and stains very well and makes versatile furniture.

Cast iron, which is heavy and was fashionable towards the latter part of the 19th century, is another alternative for garden furniture and is enjoying a resurgence in popularity. Many of the original Victorian designs have also been copied in lightweight aluminium. Mild steel is another material that is used for metal chairs, tables and benches and lends itself to fences and gates bent into fanciful curvy shapes.

Furniture materials

	Advantages	Disadvantages
Wood	Usually looks good, can be folding, can be painted, can be custom made or home built	Cheap items can become loose and unstable, require maintaining and need covering or storing in winter. Some woods last longer than others
Plastic	Cheap, little maintenance, lightweight, usually comfortable	Limited colour range, looks like plastic, needs covering or storing in winter
Steel and cast alloys	Solid, long lasting, can be good looking, can be painted	Cold and hard without cushions, can rust if not maintained
Aluminium	Cheap, little maintenance, lightweight	Frequently looks cheap, fabric seats and backs are not long lasting and can become unstable. Those with fabric need storing when not in use
Stone or reproduction stone	Heavy, looks permanent, usually blends in well, easy to maintain	Cold, hard, cannot be moved. May need solid foundation
Fabrics	Wide range of colours, lightweight	Need to be stored when not in use

ABOVE Chairs and tables do not have to match exactly – it is the overall look that matters.

Furniture styles

Choose furniture that is in keeping with the style and size of your garden. Brightly coloured folding chairs, for instance, would create a jarring note in a formal garden.

Formal	Classically styled bench in teak or made of less expensive wood painted crisp white or dark green. Wrought iron seating. Fragrant bench.
Informal	Simple bench and table made from weathered bricks and planks. Wicker seats piled with colourful cushions. Sun-loungers or deck chairs.
Modern	Chairs and a table stained or painted in bold colours. Chrome seating with curved, modern lines. Mosaic table.
Woodland	Rustic carved seat. Nostalgic swing seat placed under a shady tree. Tree seat. Hammock strung between two trees.

ABOVE RIGHT Wooden garden furniture need not always be left natural or painted in muted colours: here a bold yellow helps the warm sunny feel.

Rattan and cane are frequently used for furniture in conservatories and garden rooms and conjure up nostalgic pictures of colonial verandas in the tropics. Another natural material, living willow, can be trained into bowers or arched shapes to make a screen or backdrop for a traditional timber bench. Finally, there is, of course, inexpensive moulded plastic, which looks good in shades of green, less so in white, and is arguably the most comfortable and easy to maintain of all garden furniture.

Renovating metal and wood chairs

❶ Rub down any rusty metal using a metal paint scraper and coarse emery paper to remove loose paint. When the loose material has been removed, use a wire brush to clean the metal. Treat any old painted wood in the same way, using medium-grade glasspaper. Make sure that all cracks are sanded down and any loose material is removed.

❷ Paint the metal parts of the chairs with rust cure and proofing paint, taking care to cover all the metal to eliminate subsequent water penetration. Leave the paint to dry fully before painting the wood with an oil-based undercoat. Leave the undercoat to dry overnight to ensure a good base.

❸ Paint each chair with two coats of satin finish, oil-based paint, allowing the first coat to dry fully before applying the second.

Tree seats

If you have a large tree in the garden, building a seat around it can make an attractive feature while also providing a shady place to sit on a warm day. You can buy custom-built tree seats, but they may be difficult to find and are likely to be expensive. With a little ingenuity and a few pictures, that you can decide on the style you want and see how they are constructed, it should not be too difficult to build one yourself.

Remember not to make the seat too tight to the tree, which must have room to grow. If you don't have a suitable tree, consider planting one and building a seat around it.

These seats look particularly elegant when they are painted white. Elegant they may be, however, but they are not very sociable because your companions are likely to be sitting with their backs to you.

RIGHT This classy tree seat is ideal for a young tree because the seat back prevents anyone from leaning back and damaging the tree trunk.

A tree seat kit

Create a seating area under a favourite tree with a raised planter and seat constructed from interlocking timber logs. These can be obtained in easy-to-assemble kit form. Attractive and practical, this wooden tree seat can be assembled in just five minutes, without the need for any tools. The logs, which are treated with preservative to ward off rot, have notched edges, which interlock to form the supports of the tree seat and to make the structure rigid. No other fixing is necessary.

A basic kit will contain three thin logs with notches on just one side which form the base of the seat, 24 thicker logs, with notches on both sides, which are used to build up the sides in a hexagonal fashion, six logs notched on one side only with predrilled holes for the pieces of dowel that hold the seat planks, 12 pieces of dowel (six long and six short), three narrow planks with predrilled holes right through make the in between sides up to the correct depth and six seat planks.

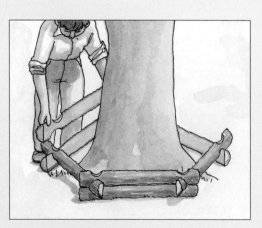

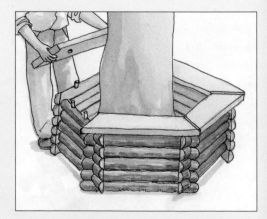

1 Lay the three base logs around the trunk, equally spaced. Arrange them so that the notches are uppermost. The logs will not meet at the ends. Move the logs around until they lie as flat and level as possible.

2 Place a thick, twin-notched log across each pair of adjacent ends to join them and form the hexagon shape. Again adjust the logs until the structure is as level and firm as possible. Then add more courses of logs until you have used them all up.

3 Fit the pieces of dowel into the predrilled holes. The shorter ones fit in the higher sides. Put the narrow planks over the dowels on the lower sides. Fit the seat planks on top so that the dowels fit into the holes on the undersides of the seat pieces.

Making a tree seat

Making a tree seat need not be complicated. First of all make sure your chosen tree is suitable. The ground around it should be fairly level and firm to make sitting comfortable and the tree seat safe and not wobbly, so avoid trees that have roots that project above the ground. The seat should not be too tight to the tree because even mature trees will continue to expand over the years and younger trees obviously need room to grow.

The seat can be made from basic planks of wood. Choose hardwood if possible, which will last much longer, or pressure-treated softwood. The seat can be of any design you like and you can use pictures of tree seats for inspiration or make up your own design. Most have six sides, but a much simpler one can be constructed with just four sides and will still look very good around a tree.

The seat is constructed from a number of basic supports – four in this case – though you could make six – are spaced around the tree and joined together with rows of planks to make the seat surface. The planks are cut with their ends at an angle of 45° so that the seat makes a neat square. If you are planning to have six sides, you will need to cut the ends of the planks at an angle of 60°. To ensure that you cut all the top pieces of wood with the angles pointing the right way, mark on each of them which is the better face, cut one of each size and use it as a template to cut the others. This will also help to get all the sides of the seat exactly the same size.

RIGHT This simple hexagonal tree seat, surrounded by a sea of gravel, should provide a shady haven in years to come.

❶ Construct four identical supports using 4 x 10cm (1½ x 4in) planed or rough-sawn timber. Attach the pieces together with brass screws.

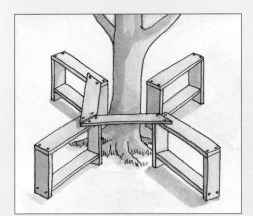

❷ Cut the planks for the seat from lengths of 2.5 x 10cm (1 x 4in) planking. Position two supports around the tree and screw the planks in place between them.

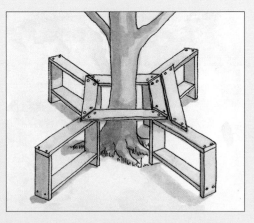

❸ The ends of the planks should come to the centres of the support tops.

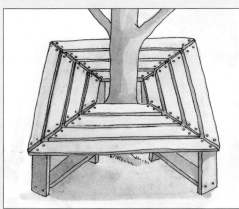

❹ Repeat with the remaining sides until the seat is finished. You will need four rows of planks in all, spaced about 1.5cm (½in) apart. The outer plank should overhang the supports.

Benches

A carefully placed bench that complements the style of the garden can be a real find in a garden, as well as being practical and providing a place to pause and soak up the atmosphere.

Positioning a bench

Choose where to site your bench carefully, especially if you are building a permanent bench that cannot be moved. Access to it needs to be good and the surface it sits on fairly hard so that a muddy patch is not created in front of it. If the bench is on a lawn or other soft area it may be worth laying a few paving slabs or putting down a free-draining material, such as gravel, where people will rest their feet. For comfort, the bench should not be in full sun or total shade for the whole of day. Angle the bench to take advantage of the best view.

Second-hand seats

For casual seating around the garden different styles of old seats and garden chairs can be bought at boot sales and from junk shops. However, they are becoming more difficult to find as they are increasingly

Bench styles

Bought wooden benches come in many different sizes and styles, from grand Lutyens-style hardwood benches, through good basic teak benches, to simple rustic benches, which are more suitable for a rural garden. Pick one to suit its position.

Lutyens-style bench

This archetypal piece of garden furniture, sometimes seen painted in glossy white, suits older, more formal surroundings, particularly areas of neat brick and tidy, colour-themed beds. It would be completely out of place in a modern garden.

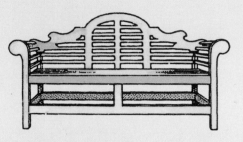

Basic teak bench

Probably the most versatile and universally popular wooden bench, this suits all but the most formal or wild of garden, but can be used in such diverse situations as wild flower meadows or patios. It should probably be avoided if you have decking.

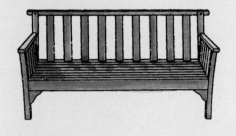

Rustic log bench

This bench is obviously ideally suited for woodland or cottage gardens, but can also look effective in a less cultivated corner of an informal garden, perhaps with climbing roses scrambling around it. It would not be suitable for modern or very formal gardens.

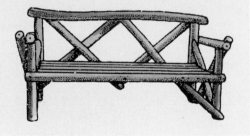

deemed to be antiques rather than jumble, but they do still turn up. They are often in a rather dilapidated state, but it is still possible to come across some pieces that can be restored and put to use, especially when you have a lot of visitors and need extra seating. Stripped and repainted or sealed, they can be very good finds and are considerably cheaper than buying examples that have already been done up, modern reproductions or even making replicas for yourself.

Cushions

Whatever style you choose for your bench, it is most probable that you will need to use cushions if you are going to spend any length of time sitting on it, as wooden

LEFT This simple wooden bench, made of reclaimed timber, has weathered to a beautiful silver with age.

planks are not the most comfortable of materials. Different fabrics can be used to complement your garden theme, either for mixing and matching or changing the style completely when you fancy an alternative. Simple foam pads are readily available and can be covered in any suitable fabric. It is also possible to buy ready-made waterproof cushions that can be left outside when the weather changes.

Maintenance

Like all garden furniture, your bench will need looking after and regular painting or treatment to protect it against damage from the elements and to ensure that it continues to look good. Check regularly that the supports, joints, back and seat are in good order, both for safety purposes and because it will start to look old and tired if it has flaking paints or becomes slightly lopsided.

Making a simple bench

It can be hard to find a bench that fits exactly in the corner you had planned for it or that suits your garden perfectly, but it is easy to make your own. The simplest bench is constructed by fitting lengths of planed timber planking over two basic brick piers. The bench can be any size you like: cut the planks to suit the space you have. The top can simply rest on the piers or can be attached with screws driven into wallplugs. Decide on the size and width of piers you will need. A base of two bricks wide and two bricks long should be about right. Build two piers for an average bench, spaced about 1.2m (4ft) apart. If you want a longer bench, build a third pier so that the planks do not sag. The piers should be about six courses of bricks high for a comfortable sitting position.

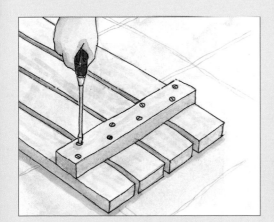

1 Build the brick piers on strip foundations (see page 36) or on a firm area of existing paving. Bed the base of the pier on mortar and lay four bricks in a rectangle shape, sandwiching them together with mortar. Spread another layer of mortar over the bricks ready for the next course.

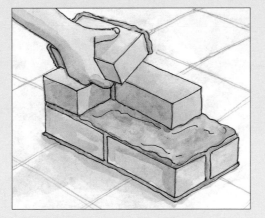

2 Arrange the next course of bricks in a different configuration to make the piers strong. Position one brick across the piers at either end and two running lengthways between them. Use a spirit level to make sure each course of bricks is level and tap the bricks down with the handle of the trowel if necessary.

3 When the first pier is complete, check again with the spirit level and adjust the top course if necessary. Next build the second pier in the same way, about 1.2m (4ft) away from the first, taking care to make sure it is accurately aligned with the first pier.

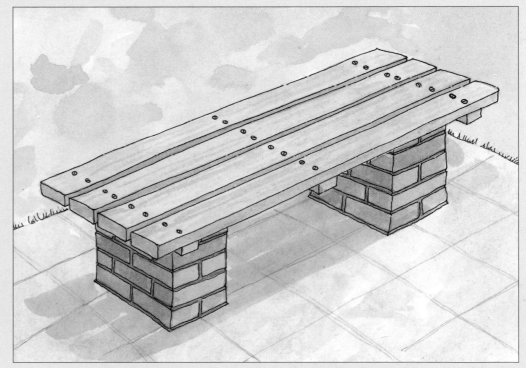

4 Cut three 64cm (25½in) battens of 7.5 x 5cm (3 x 2in) timber and four 15 x 4cm (6 x 1½in) planed softwood or hardwood planks. Attach the battens to the planks with brass screws, spacing the planks about 1cm (½in) apart. Place the wooden seat on top of the brick piers and screw it into place if you wish.

Fragrant benches

A camomile or thyme seat will produce a wonderful fragrance when it is sat upon. To make one, build a simple open-topped box of wood or brick, fill it with light, sandy soil and plant the camomile or thyme on top. Choose either *Chamaemelum nobile* 'Treneague', a tough, compact form of camomile that does not flower, or one of the low-growing creeping forms of thyme. Plant at 15cm (6in) intervals across the seat and water regularly until the plants are established. Trim the plants occasionally to keep them neat and compact.

LEFT Old railway sleepers can be used in modern settings: here they make a strong effect against the smooth gravels and stone spheres.

ABOVE Old bricks and bits of reclaimed ornamental stone make a perfect container for a simple, informal camomile seat.

Turf seats

A turf seat is an unusual addition to a garden, but one that can be enjoyable both to construct and use. In its most basic form it can simply be a rectangular block of earth that is covered with turf. The sides, front and back may need supporting, and these supports can be made out of wooden planks, bricks or thin sticks woven between uprights to form a wattle wall around the seat. The wattle can be used to create a variety of shapes of seat, including round or crescent-shaped ones. A wattle edging also has the advantage over bricks or planks in that it is easy to dismantle and rebuild somewhere else in the garden should the need arise. A similar type of seat could be cut into a bank if you have a sloping or terraced garden with wattle used to support both the edge of the seat and the back.

Making a long bench

A basic wooden bench can be made in a modular fashion, so it can be as long as you like. This type of seating would be particularly suitable along the edge of a patio or along either side of a large, formal pool.

❶ The seating is supported on a number of timber peirs spaced about 1.2m (4ft) apart and made from pairs of 10 x 10cm (4 x 4in) posts concreted into the ground. Cut the posts 75cm (30in) long and sink them 23cm (9in) into concrete foundations. Set the posts in pairs about 5cm (2in) apart.

❷ Let the concrete dry for a week, then add the timber cross-pieces. Use 10 x 5cm (4 x 2in) timber for the cross-pieces and cut them 45cm (18in) long. Use brass screws to attach a cross-piece to each side of the timber supports.

❸ Next cut nine 5 x 2.5cm (2 x 1in) hardwood battens for the seat tops. Cut them to 1.2m (4ft) lengths, butt them up close and fix them to the timber cross-pieces with brass screws.

❹ Treat the wooden seating with a wood preservative, wood stain or varnish and allow it to dry completely before use.

Making a picnic bench

This popular picnic bench and table design requires no complicated carpentry skills: the pieces are simply bolted or screwed together. The table is supported on three leg frames made from 6.5 x 4cm (2½ x 1½in) softwood, each consisting of a horizontal top batten with pairs of legs bolted to it and splayed out at the bottom. Planks of 15 x 4cm (6 x 1½in) softwood are screwed to the top of the leg frames to form the table top. The seats are made by screwing pairs of planks to horizontal battens bolted across the leg frames about 45cm (18in) above the ground.

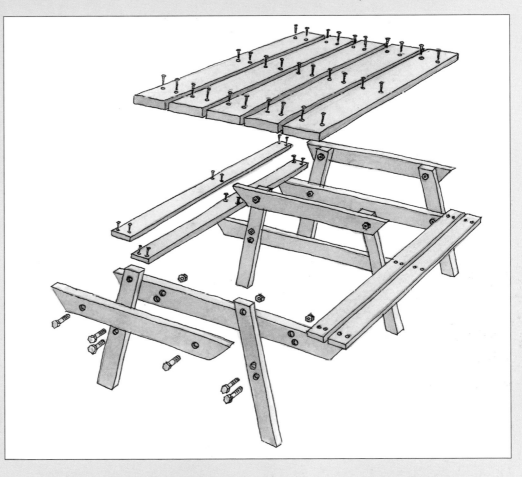

1 Start by making the leg frames. Cut six 75cm (30in) battens for the legs, cutting both ends at an angle of about 45° using an adjustable bevel as a guide. Next cut three 90cm (36in) battens for the top rails, cutting both ends at a sharp angle to prevent people sitting at the table from grazing their knees. Place the legs on the ground in pairs and put the top rails on top. Drill through both pieces at each junction using a 1cm (⅜in) bit, then bolt the pieces together with bolts and washers, leaving the nuts fairly loose.

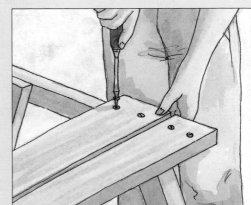

2 Add the seat formers to the leg frames. Cut three 1.5m (5ft) battens with angled ends. Lay a leg frame on the ground with a seat former so that it protrudes equally at each side and its top edge is 45cm (18in) above the frame base. Drill and bolt together and tighten all the nuts.

3 Next cut nine 1.5m (5ft) planks for the top of the table and the seats. Drill pairs of screw clearance holes in the middle of each plank and a little way in from each end. Screw two planks to the seat former of each frame to make the structure free standing.

4 Screw the remaining five planks, equally spaced, to the top rails to make the table top. Apply preservative to all surfaces of the picnic bench and allow to dry.

Sun-loungers and deck chairs

As well as conventional upright chairs, benches and reclining chairs, there are several other pieces of furniture designed specifically for relaxation. Sun-loungers can be used in both the sun and the shade. In the past they were mainly made from aluminium tubing, but now they are available in plastic as well as wood. Many are quite uncomfortable to lie on unless you spread something soft on top, but most are available with cushions or thin mattresses. Really luxurious loungers are hung from frames so that they swing gently when you sit or even lie on them. They usually have a sun shade or canopy incorporated into the framework.

Deck chairs

When deck chairs are mentioned, most people think of those stripy vinyl affairs provided in busy resorts at the height of summer. However, deck chairs have come a long way and there is still nothing to beat them in terms of portability, easy erection and style. Image is now everything, and deck chairs come in stylish canvas and other strong cloths with frames of metal, wood or a combination of the two. Usually cheaper than other garden chairs, they can provide comfortable, reasonably priced, extra seating in case of unexpected guests. Their design means they fold away and take up little space when not in use, and they can quickly

ABOVE This simple, elegant bamboo sun lounger and stool provide a perfect way to relax in this secluded area of decking and pea shingle.

be put away to protect them from the weather. If there is no room or suitable place to hang a hammock a deck chair may well be the answer.

Materials

- Sufficient deck chair fabric or canvas of similar weight: standard fabric is available in a 45cm (18in) width
- 62cm (25in) matching or contrasting fabric for pillow
- Scissors and sewing equipment
- Upholstery pins
- Hammer
- Matching sewing thread
- Stick and sew touch-and-close fastening
- Feather or foam filling for head pillow

Making a deck chair cover and head pillow

To calculate the fabric length required for the deck chair, fold the chair flat and measure the length from the front lower edge of the fixing bar, around the bar, down to the lower bar and around the lower bar to the front upper edge. Add about 20cm (8in) to this to allow for folding the fabric under the frame, and a further 62 cm (25in) of fabric for the head pillow.

1 Turn under 10cm (4in) at both ends of the fabric. Put one folded edge level with the front lower edge of the fixing bar and tack in place with upholstery pins through the folded fabric along the underside of the bar.

2 Wrap the fabric over the bar and along the length of the chair. Check that the folded edge will wrap under the lower fixing bar and fit tightly, then open out the chair so that you can tack pins on the lower edge.

3 To make the head pillow, fold the 62cm (25in) length of fabric in half with the right sides together and sew both side seams and 2.5cm (1in) at each end of the opening. Turn to the right side and press the raw edges to the inside of the cover, then insert the filling. Cut a piece of fabric the width of the pillow and 12.5cm (5in) wide. Turn under a 1cm (½in) wide double hem along the two short edges and one long edge. Attach the 'sew' half of touch-and-close fastening to the long hemmed edge, insert the unfinished edge into the opening in the pillow cover and topstitch to close.

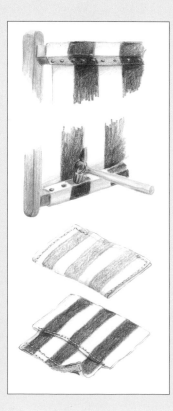

Insect nets

In areas where insects are likely to be a pest, it is a good idea to have some form of protection in the form of a net. This is especially important if you are likely to fall asleep and not be conscious of the pest until it has stung or bitten you. A fine net curtain will suffice, provided it is large enough. If you have a hammock that is hung on a frame the net may be built into it, but otherwise it must be hung from a tree or suspended on a line between the two anchor points.

Weatherproofing garden furniture

Garden furniture can be a major investment so it is worth considering how to protect it from the weather and keep it looking good. All furniture should be checked regularly to ensure it is safe, stable and that the weight bearing joints do not need replacing or repairing. That aside, the best way to maintain your furniture is to weatherproof it.

Stone furniture will not pose many problems because it is naturally built to withstand weathering, apart from some erosion. Moss and lichen can be problems in some places so make sure you remove these. Cleaning with a scrubbing brush and soapy water or a pressure washer is usually enough.

Cast-iron furniture needs regular checking for rust, and affected areas should be treated as soon as they are found. To treat the rusting areas, sand down the affected patch to the bare metal, treat with a rust-curing paint, then prime with an oil-based undercoat and paint. Regular painting will help to prevent rust in the first place.

Wooden furniture can be cleaned with a pressure washer for general cleaning, or a scrubbing brush and soapy water. Sand down any rough areas to avoid splinters and replace any rotten pieces with new wood. Old painted wood in need of a new coat of paint should be rubbed down with medium sandpaper first and then primed and re-coated. Hardwoods can look stunning if regularly oiled, and softwoods will benefit from regular coats of wood preservative to

prevent any problems. Varnished wood requires rubbing down to the base wood to provide a satisfactory surface for re-varnishing or it will prove impossible to apply a durable stain finish.

Aluminium furniture does not rust but will look better for longer if it is regularly wiped with a clean damp cloth. Fittings should be checked and oiled if necessary, and any other materials incorporated with the metal should be treated to stop them spoiling the look of the whole piece of furniture.

Plastic can often lose its brightness but this can be at least partially restored by using a proprietary cleaner, specifically for garden furniture. Accessories, such as parasols, cushions and hammocks, are probably best brought under cover in bad weather to maintain the materials, structure and colour.

Protective covers can be bought, or made to fit, and these offer temporary protection to furniture. Although not durable enough to protect over winter, if you put the covers on it means that once cleaned initially, you can use the furniture all summer without having to clean it before every use.

ABOVE The director's chairs provide bright spots of colour among the dark greens of this jungle garden.

Making a director's chair cover

For a standard wooden director's chair you will need a piece of fabric measuring 65 x 40cm (25½ x 16in) for the chair seat and another piece 65 x 20cm (25½ x 8in) for the back of the chair.

1 Make a turning of 2cm (¾in) along the top and bottom of the chair seat and repeat for the chair back. Turn under 5cm (2in) at the shorter edge of each panel.

2 Tack upholstery pins along one folded edge of fabric to hold it in place under the side seat fixing bar, then wrap the fabric over the top of the bar, over the second fixing bar and around to underside. Tack the folded edge firmly in place with upholstery pins.

3 Repeat around the side fixing bars to finish the chair back.

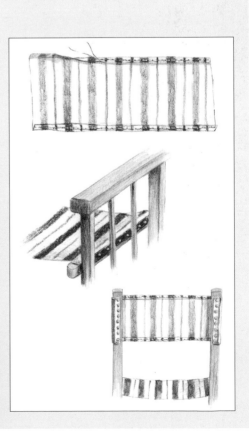

Hammocks

In the garden, the hammock, which originated in South America, is perhaps one of the most powerful evocations of lazy summer days. Garden hammocks come in a bewildering variety of designs and sizes, ranging from woven nylon aberrations to fancifully tasselled and embroidered examples. The hammock shown here is made from readily available materials. The unbleached canvas used in its construction is robust and long lasting, and it may be dyed or decorated in any number of imaginative ways. Rivets have been used to avoid the need to stitch the heavy canvas. If you have the skills, or the necessary equipment, however, there is no reason why the hammock should not be sewn. If you have difficulty in fitting the brass rings required for this project, a visit to a friendly tent or canvas awning maker might be profitable. They will have machinery designed to do this job simply and speedily.

1 Fold over 25mm (1in) at one end of the length of canvas, then fold over again to create a 7.5cm (3in) deep hem. On the folded hem, draw a pencil line parallel with, and 12mm (½in) from, the first folded edge. Holding the canvas securely to prevent the material from twisting, drill seven holes along this line, starting about 40mm (1½in) from one side and continuing at roughly 14cm (5½ in) intervals, to finish 40mm (1½in) from the other side.

Materials and equipment

- 2.5m (2¾yd) length of 90cm (36in) wide medium-weight (500g/16oz) unbleached canvas
- 4.8 x 14mm blind rivets
- M5 washers
- 12mm (½in) brass eye ring punch kit
- 1.8m (6ft) length of 25mm (1in) doweling, cut in half
- 8mm (⁵⁄₁₆in) staples
- Two 50mm (2in) galvanized metal rings
- 15m (16yd) rope, cut in half
- Twine or string
- Two 7.5cm (3in) galvanized spring (lanyard) hooks
- Tape measure
- Pencil
- Electric drill
- 4mm (³⁄₁₆in) drill bit
- Blind rivet gun
- Staple gun
- Craft knife

2 Secure the hem with blind rivets inserted through the drilled holes from the unfolded side of the canvas – each is rivet driven through the canvas with a blind rivet gun and secured on the underside with a washer. Repeat the whole procedure at the other end of the canvas.

3 At one end of the canvas and, in a similar manner to step 1, draw a pencil line on the riveted hem parallel with, and 25mm (1in) from, the first folded edge. Starting at about 10.5cm (4¼in) from one side of the hem and using an eye ring punch kit, make six holes along this line at roughly 14cm (5½in) intervals for the brass rings that will hold the rope. Fit the brass rings, inserting them from the underside. Repeat the process at the other end of the canvas.

4 Feed a length of 25mm (1in) dowelling through the riveted hem at each end and secure it to the canvas using a staple gun. Lay the length of canvas on a flat surface and choose one end of the hammock to work on first. Place a galvanized metal ring approximately 80cm (31½in) from this end. Mentally number the brass rings from one to six, running from one side of the hammock to the other. Tie a knot in one end of one length of rope and pass the rope from the underside of the canvas through ring no. 2 until it is stopped by the knot. Feed the end of the rope through the galvanized ring and then back to ring no. 1. Pull the rope through to the underside of the canvas then back to the galvanized ring, pulling the full length of the rope through each time – maintaining the 80cm (31½in) between the hammock and the galvanized ring. Now pass the rope through ring no. 6 to the underside of the canvas, then again back to the galvanized ring. Next, feed the rope to ring no. 5, passing the rope from the top of the canvas through to the underside and then passing it up through ring no. 4 to the galvanized ring. From here, pass the rope through the top of the remaining ring, no. 3, to meet the knotted end of rope on the underside of ring no. 2. Undo the knotted end and join the two ends of rope together in one knot. Repeat the procedure at the other end of the hammock.

5 At each end of the hammock, make sure all the lengths of rope leading from the brass rings to the galvanized ring are even. Gather the rope beneath each galvanized ring and bind securely using twine or string.

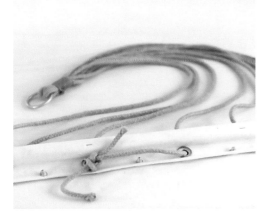

6 Finally, fit galvanized spring hooks to the galvanized rings at either end of the hammock. For safety's sake make sure that your hammock is hung from suitable secure fixings in a tree, post or wall and test it for weight before attempting to use it, especially if it will be subjected to children playing on it.

RIGHT This sturdy tree provides an ideal support for a simple canvas hammock, overlooking a sunny patch of lawn.

Hanging your hammock

It is essential to ensure that your hammock is secure. It must have strong supports. The classic position (apart from on board ship) is slung between two trees, and if this is feasible in your garden, go for it, because it is the ideal setting. However, you must practise your knots and make sure that they are secure: a bowline fits the bill and will not let you down. Most good hammocks are supplied with the means of support and instructions for tying. Avoid positioning your hammock in full sun as it is only too easy to fall asleep in one and end up being fried.

Not everyone has convenient trees in their garden, but it is possible to anchor the hammock to walls or other structures. These are not always in the right place, however, and the answer may be a frame, which can be placed anywhere in the garden. These work well and can incorporate a canopy. The problem is that they take up a lot of space when not in use. Fortunately, many modern ones can be taken to pieces or folded up.

Decorating furniture

Mosaic is a tradition as old as history. We are familiar with photographs of the ancient mosaics of Pompeii and Herculaneum, which are as invigorating today as when first made. Mosaic floors in shaded Moorish water-filled courtyards provided cool oases in a dry, sun-drenched environment. In today's gardens, modern mosaic is equally enchanting. It can be used to embellish or decorate floors, walls, furniture or smaller items like pots.

Dual-purpose tile adhesive and grout products are now available: these act as both adhesive and grout in the one material. Check before you buy tile adhesive that it is suitable for where you wish to use it as some may not be suitable for use on absorbent boards. In this case use PVA glue.

Materials and equipment

- Waterproof MDF (medium-density fibreboard), chipboard or plywood, at least 18mm (¾in) thick to fit your table
- Assorted sheets of glass squares
- PVA glue and brush
- Waterproof tile grout and grout spreader
- Pencil and paper
- Disposable rubber gloves
- Sponge

1 Mark out your desired design on a piece of paper. Soak the glass squares in water for about five to ten minutes to separate them from their paper backing.

2 Establish the centre of the table top by drawing two diagonal lines, from corner to corner. The centre is the point at which they intersect. Lay the tiles on the table following your desired pattern. (For complicated patterns, it is probably best to draw the design directly on to the table in pencil.) Make sure that the centre tile is laid over the pencilled cross. Leave narrow gaps between each piece for the grouting. This stage will take about two hours, but it doesn't need to be done all at once.

3 Once you know that all the pieces will fit, remove a small section at a time and brush the PVA glue on to the table top. Replace the tiles, checking that they are straight. Leave them to set overnight.

4 Mix the tile grout according to the instructions on the package. It should have the consistency of thick soup. Apply generously over the surface of the tiles with the grout spreader.

5 Leave the grout for 15 minutes to dry but do not allow it to set. Gently wipe the surface with a slightly moist sponge to remove excess grout until you are sure the surface is clean.

6 Glue a row of tiles around the support surface and, when dry, grout as before.

RIGHT The mosaic covering makes this pretty table ideal for outdoor living as it is waterproof and can be wiped clean easily.

ABOVE A mixture of whole mosaic tiles and broken wall tiles were used to create this bold floral top to a wrought iron table.

Garden cupboard

Matt emulsion paints in bright, primary colours will cheer up a small cupboard and a paint effect is used to give it a rustic feel. A solid plywood front door panel has been removed and replaced with chicken wire that has been stapled to the back of the door frame, so that the cupboard's contents are easily recognizable.

Ideal for use in a potting-shed or garden room, or small enough for a kitchen, this cupboard could be wall-mounted above a working top if space is at a premium. Larger versions could be used to store longer tools, such as rakes, hoes, forks and spades. Similar cupboards are readily found in second-hand shops or at auction sales and are easily converted in this way.

DIY mosaic tiles

Materials for mosaic need not be specially bought. Tesserae selected from broken china and tiles may just as easily be put to use as the ceramic tile chips. Table tops made from pieces of old patterned china discovered while digging in the garden can make interesting designs.

This project shows how fragments left over from indoor wall tiles have been broken and re-used as a mosaic.

1 Take care when breaking the tiles not to damage the surface. Use goggles to protect your eyes and wear heavy-duty gloves. The tiles are spread over the top of an existing table on a layer of tile adhesive 2–3mm (¹⁄₁₆–¹⁄₈in) thick.

2 Fill any gaps with smaller pieces then with grout, either white or coloured. Wipe off the excess and leave to dry overnight then polish with a dry cloth. If necessary, edge the table with beading fastened with panel pins to the table.

Barbecues

Allied to the growth of interest in eating outdoors is a similar growth in cooking outside. Cooking on a barbecue is fun, the food tastes different from anything cooked inside, and it is a good way to entertain both family and friends.

Visit any large DIY store or garden centre in early summer and you will see a wealth of different styles of barbecue. Some are relatively cheap and basic, while others are expensive and have many sophisticated extras. From the cooking point of view, many people find that the simplest and least expensive models work perfectly well and do exactly what they want. Although they are often left outside all year round, free-standing barbecues should be stored away when not in use and will therefore need storage space, which should be a consideration in a small garden.

Just like the free-standing type, built-in barbecues can be as simple or as sophisticated as you wish. The most basic type is little more than a brick hearth, possibly with somewhere to put tools and food, although a table will often serve just as well. If the bricks are not bonded with cement, the barbecue can be taken apart and built somewhere else in the garden, and if paving slabs are used as foundations, the whole thing will be quite mobile. For the true barbecue aficionado, a properly built structure is more likely to include a whole area devoted to alfresco cooking and eating, with built-in seats,

BELOW This brick-built barbecue is an integral feature of this modern patio garden, sited just a few feet away from the elegant dining table and chairs.

Barbecue safety

- Light the barbecue with fire lighters or barbecue lighting fuel – never use petrol or cigarette lighter fuel.
- Do not place a barbecue against a wooden fence or close to trellis or the branches of a woody shrub.
- Make sure that the barbecue is completely stable and that there is no possibility of it falling over.
- Take special care when there are children or animals in the garden.
- Leave hot coals to cool thoroughly before disposing of them.
- Keep other diners away from the barbecue because the flames can be unpredictable.
- Wear sensible clothing when cooking on a barbecue – avoid loose sleeves, ties, scarves and other clothing that could catch light.
- Don't try to move a portable barbecue once it is alight.
- Don't pour lighting fuel on to the coals once they are hot.
- Never leave a lit barbecue unattended.
- Use long-handled utensils for cooking to avoid burns.

ABOVE For really serious outdoor living in warmer climates, gas barbecues are much more practicable than solid fuel.

tables and even cupboards, and a barbecue that includes a flue.

Ready-bought barbecues are obviously made from metal, but home-made ones can often be made from scrap materials that may be to hand, such as old bricks or pieces of stone or concrete blocks. If the finished structure looks a bit scrappy and untidy, it could be roughly plastered to give it a Mediterranean or Mexican look.

Siting a barbecue

In many ways, a mobile barbecue may be the best solution because you have the flexibility to place it in the most suitable position for that particular day. The barbecue is the working centre of the party, where everything happens, and the cook will want to be as close as possible to the rest of the diners. On the other hand, barbecues have the great disadvantage of producing both smoke and cooking smells. These may be tolerable to the participants, even though they probably prefer not to be directly next to them, but remember that your neighbours might find them both a

Types of barbecue

- **Hibachi** – This is a simple cast-iron fire box with one or two adjustable cast-iron grills with handles for easy moving. It is sturdy and long lasting.

- **Brazier barbecue** – This is probably the most popular model: a sheet metal fire box on legs, which raise it to the right level for cooking. The grill is usually adjustable, and there is often a spit for cooking and turning large pieces of meat. The wind shield ensures a good cooking temperature even in windy weather. Be sure to choose a good quality model because the metal can be very thin on some cheaper ones.

- **Kettle barbecue** – This is similar to the basic brazier, but it has a large domed lid. When the lid is in place, heat is trapped within it, making the barbecue into an oven. This makes it good for cooking large pieces of meat and poultry. However, usually the grill level is not adjustable, which makes basic barbecuing more difficult.

- **Wagon barbecue** – This is a brazier barbecue built into a wheeled trolley with work surfaces on either side. Sometimes the surfaces can be folded down, which makes it easier to store when not in use. Choose a good quality model if you want it to last.

- **Gas barbecue** – Cooking on gas is easier and guarantees a consistent cooking temperature every time, but for many people it takes the fun out of barbecues. However, there is no wait for the coals to heat up. Most models use a reusable lava rock in the fire box. Choose a wheeled model as gas barbecues can be rather heavy.

- **Loose brick barbecue** – This comes as a kit, including a grill and a basic fire box (sometimes just a metal sheet), which can be built into a simple brick structure. The bricks are piled up without mortar into a circular tower, which can be dismantled and moved if necessary. Usually the grill level cannot be adjusted.

- **Built-in barbecues** – These can be constructed in any design and from any heatproof materials, including bricks, stone, cement blocks or breeze blocks. The advantage is that the barbecue can be tailored to your needs and can be a garden feature in its own right, complementing the surrounding area.

Hibachi

Brazier barbecue

Kettle barbecue

Wagon barbecue

Gas barbecue

nuisance and an intrusion. Try to place the barbecue where the prevailing wind will blow the smoke and smells where they will not worry anyone.

This is more difficult with a built-in barbecue, and if you do build a permanent structure, a chimney will help to funnel the pollutants away. Before you build, you should try to determine the direction of the prevailing winds.

Although the correct design of a barbecue is crucial to its working efficiently and safely, picking the best site for it is of equal importance. Bear in mind that the spot needs to be easily accessible from the kitchen for carrying utensils, crockery and food to and fro, so avoid a position that is too remote from the house.

Do not position the barbecue below overhanging trees, which could be seriously damaged by the intense heat. Similarly, do not place the unit too close to a timber fence or trellis.

Avoid siting the grill close to any windows that open, because curtains could billow out and catch light or because smoke and cooking smells are likely to enter the house.

If the unit is built on an existing lawn the grass will almost certainly become worn by the heavy wear it will receive as people walk to and from the barbecue. It is best, therefore, to surround the barbecue with paving slabs or brick pavers. Make sure that the surface is wide enough to accommodate several people, either standing or sitting, or if it covers a smaller area, that it is set flush with the surrounding turf so that your guests can move freely in the area.

Making a basic brick barbecue

The barbecue can be built straight on to a patio or area of paving if the base is level and solid, otherwise build it on strip foundations (see page 36). The barbecue consists of a U-shaped brick wall, one brick thick, with another U-shaped bay next to it to support a work surface. The fire box is a sheet of steel; the fire box and the grill are supported on ledges formed by turning bricks at right angles in the appropriate courses.

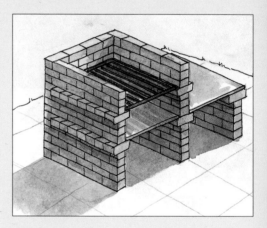

❶ The work surface can be made from a sheet of exterior-grade plywood or chipboard, a large paving slab or slats of softwood treated with a wood preservative.

Start by setting up string lines to mark the position of the first course of bricks, then trowel a 1cm (½in) layer of wet bricklaying mortar on to the prepared foundations on one side of the barbecue. Furrow the surface and lay the first course of bricks end to end. At the corner, turn a brick at right angles so that its side butts up with the end of the last brick, forming a mortar joint between the two. Continue until the first course of bricks is complete, then check it is level using a spirit level. Tap down any bricks with the handle of the trowel if necessary and check that it follows the string lines accurately.

❷ Lay the second course of bricks in the same way, this time starting with a half-brick so that the vertical joints are staggered. Continue until you have completed five courses, checking with the spirit level at regular intervals.

The sixth course of bricks makes up the ledge that supports the steel sheet on which the charcoal will go. Lay the bricks at right angles to the walls so that they overhang equally on either side. Do this on all three side walls, but position the bricks in the back walls as before.

❸ Build three more courses of bricks on top of the ledge around the barbecue unit, leaving the work surface walls as they are. Now add another course of bricks at right angles in the same way as before to form the ledge on top of which the grill will rest. Add three more courses of bricks around the cooking area to act as a wind shield, and the barbecue is complete.

When the mortar has just started to stiffen, neaten the joints by running a small offcut of garden hose between the bricks to smooth the mortar into a softly rounded profile. Leave the mortar to dry for two or three days before lighting the barbecue.

Plants near the barbecue

There should, clearly, be no plants in the immediate vicinity of the barbecue, simply because they are likely to get scorched. You might, however, want to have some herbs planted not too far away so that you can pluck a handful of fresh thyme, chives or rosemary without having to walk to the other side of the garden to find them.

Designing a barbecue

A barbecue is usually a box-shaped unit made of bricks, stone or concrete blocks, with an open top and an open front. It needs to be a stable structure with the grill set at a comfortable height for cooking; nine or ten courses from ground level is about right. The grill and the fire box can be supported on metal brackets or rods built into the brickwork, or on brick ledges sticking out from the walls. Ideally, both the grill and the fire box should be removable for cleaning and winter storage.

The design can be as simple or as complicated as you like, incorporating any number of features, such as cupboards, work surfaces and utensil hooks.

Making a loose-brick barbecue

A temporary barbecue, which can be dismantled for storage during the winter, can be made by stacking bricks dry, without mortar. Not only is the unit inexpensive and easy to construct in a matter of a few hours, but it is also a very efficient structure: the honeycomb bonding arrangement used to raise the walls ensures a plentiful supply of air to the charcoal for good combustion.

The barbecue can be built in a circular, triangular, square or hexagonal shape, as preferred. A basic circular unit will use about 100 bricks; other shapes need more. Lay the bricks in the chosen format on the prepared base with 5cm (2in) wide gaps between the bricks. Lay the second course on top, staggering the joints by half the length of a brick so that the bond will be strong. Continue to stack bricks, alternating the staggered bond with each course, until you reach the seventh course. Place a sheet-steel panel across the top of the brick wall as a charcoal tray, then add two

more courses of dry-laid bricks before fitting a slatted grill on top. Add another two or three courses of bricks around the back of the unit to act as a wind shield for the cooking area.

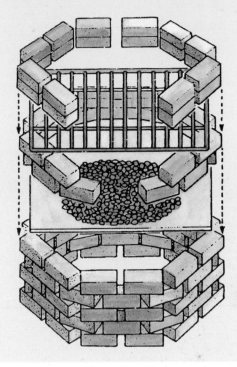

It is possible to buy a kit containing a grill, fire box and mounting brackets, and this is probably the easiest option. Buy the kit first and then design the barbecue around it so that it fits perfectly. Alternatively, make a simple fire box from sheet steel (it only needs to be a flat piece if the mounting is provided) and make use of an old slatted oven shelf as a grill.

The barbecue will probably need some sort of wind shield, so build a few extra courses of bricks around the back and sides of the cooking area to protect the coals from strong gusts, as the cooking time can be literally doubled on a windy day.

LEFT A built-in barbecue need not be intrusive in a garden. This hibachi type also has plenty of room for storing fuel.

GARDEN STRUCTURES AND ORNAMENTS

Garden structures

In many gardens it is the structures that most influence the general character of the garden. These, together with the boundaries and paved areas, make up the framework (hard landscape) of the garden, around which the planting (soft landscape) is designed. Garden structures include everything from bowers, pergolas, summerhouses and gazebos to greenhouses and sheds. They also include the small items like cold frames, compost bins and water butts.

ABOVE Decorative bird boxes can add a charming note to a flower border, although these are unlikely to attract nesting birds.

LEFT A delicate arbour provides both a focal point at the end of a garden and a sheltered spot to sit quietly and read.

Creating shade

Shade is an important element in any garden, offering a comfortable place to sit, relax or dine alfresco in warm weather, and the purpose of many garden buildings is to create shade. Many structures, including arbours, gazebos and pergolas, simply provide a framework over which climbing plants can be grown, and it is these, rather than the structure itself, that create the shade. Many climbers are suitable, especially those like vines with large leaves, which will create dappled shade under the structure. Clematis, jasmine and honeysuckle are good examples of climbers with fragrant flowers that will quickly provide cover.

To make a simple shady bower, construct a sturdy framework of wood treated with preservative, sinking the bases of the uprights into the ground to a depth of at least 45cm (18in). Plant climbing plants on three sides, leaving the fourth side open. This creates an enclosed, intimate space. For a wider view, you could plant on one or two sides only – it is up to you. A seat underneath will make a great place to sit and dream.

For a permanent bower you should concrete the supports into the ground, using the least amount of concrete that is

Making an awning

An awning can be permanently attached to the house or garden wall and pulled out when required, or it can be hung from hooks on one side, with poles to support it on the other. A simple awning can be made from a split-bamboo blind.

1 Measure the distance between the fittings on the blind and mark the position on the wall for the two hooks (included with the blind). Using a masonry bit, drill two holes and insert rawl plugs. Screw in the hooks and hang the blind up.

2 Push the bamboo poles deeply into the planted flowerpots. Unroll the blind to its full extent and position the flower pots at an equal distance away from the wall, making sure that the bottom of the blind reaches the top of the poles. Push the poles carefully through the slats in the blinds, then secure the guy rope to the bottom of the blind; this will keep the blind resting on the poles. However two guy ropes – one at each corner attached to the blind – would be needed for use in a high wind.

ABOVE This wooden pergola frames the classical urn at the end of the walkway and provides support for climbers, including roses and wisteria.

RIGHT An overgrown arbour provides useful shelter from the prevailing wind while still allowing you to sit in the fresh air.

needed to support the posts safely, so that climbers can be planted as close to them as possible. If possible, provide a hard area beneath to make sure that there is a good, stable surface on which tables and chairs can stand.

Temporary shade

Awnings and garden tents are a popular and quick way of creating shade. They have several advantages over natural vegetation, the chief of which is that they can be packed away when they are not in use, so that light and sun can be allowed to return to the area when you are not in it. This is particularly valuable in a small garden, where there will not be enough room to have both a sunny and a shady

sitting area. Another advantage is that you can choose the colour of the fabric, perhaps even having reversible fabric, that has bright, cheerful colours on one side and cool, soft ones on the other. Virtually any fabric can be used, although with more permanent awnings a weatherproof material, such as canvas, should be used. Ready-bought split-bamboo cane blinds can also be used to create excellent dappled shade.

Garden tents are also becoming more widely available. These are usually erected on a simple framework consisting of four poles, and they have a top and a pelmet, but no sides. If you wish, one or two side panels can be attached to keep out wind and even rain.

Arbours and gazebos

What is the difference between an arbour and a gazebo? The answer lies mainly in their use. Both are fairly small structures that offer some protection from the worst of the weather, but arbours are hideaways while gazebos have a view.

Arbours

Arbours are one of the greatest inventions in gardening. They allow you to create a room that is enclosed and 'safe' and yet at the same time open to the air and to the elements. They also enable you to grow some of your favourite plants in close proximity, especially climbing ones, which are allowed to clamber over the structure.

An arbour should be big enough to accommodate a seat or, preferably, a bench.

Gazebos

A gazebo is defined as a summerhouse or turret with a wide view but is often regarded as more of a hideaway – a (usually) small, enclosed area, often with a seat. They are generally made of wood or a screening material, although they can be of wrought iron or any other material you can fashion into an acceptable shape. Gazebos are places to sit and view the garden to meditate or simply to take cover from the

ABOVE A willow arbour with a seat is both informal and intriguing as the planted twigs will continue to grow, making a living piece of garden furniture.

RIGHT This tiny lilac-painted wooden gazebo is designed to be seen as well as to watch the garden from. It also serves to mask the shed behind.

Making an arbour

1 Set the supporting uprights in concrete, or use fence spike or bolt-down plates to hold them securely. Make sure you position the notched end at the top, with the notch correctly aligned.

2 Slot the two cross-beams into the notches in the tops of the uprights. The cross-beams should run parallel to each other. For extra strength, drive long nails through the sides of the uprights into the cross-beams.

3 Space the rafters evenly along the length of the cross-beams and at right angles to them. Fix them in place using special galvanized brackets that are first nailed to the cross-beams.

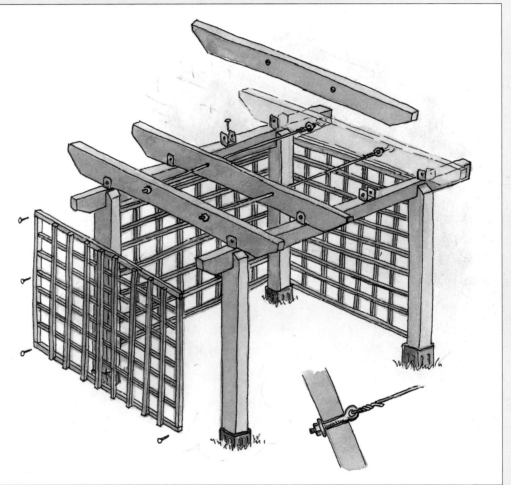

elements. They provide a sheltered haven in the garden all year round.

Site them so that the wind and rain do not blow in the opening and in a part of the garden with little through traffic and away from sheds, stores and greenhouses. Gazebos can be covered with climbing plants or left bare – whatever you feel is appropriate to make a private place within your garden.

Building a wooden arbour

A classical arbour is a simple wooden structure, often a flat-backed arch, but arbours can be built in any shape or size, for instance with uprights and cross-beams like a Japanese-style pergola. A simple arbour is fairly easy to build, especially if you buy ready-shaped uprights and cross-beams that fix together easily. First, mark out the position of the structure using string and pegs. Drive in a

peg where each upright will go and link the pegs together with string. When you are happy with the position, start to build the structure.

The posts need to be at least 10cm (4in) square and 3m (10ft) high. For simple fixing, choose posts with notched tops into which the cross-beams slot. Make sure they are treated with preservative to prolong their life span. Set the supporting uprights in concrete, or use fence spikes or bolt-down

Post support options

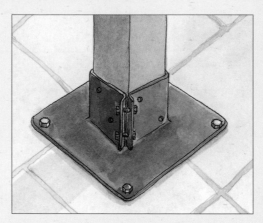

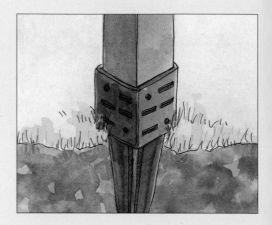

Concrete foundations

To concrete a post into place, dig a hole about 70cm (28in) deep and set the post in compacted hardcore to 15cm (6in) below ground level. Fill the rest of the hole with concrete and bevel the surface to repel rainwater from the post.

Bolt-down plates

When erecting a post on a hard surface, such as a patio, use a bolt-down plate to hold it upright. The post fits into a metal collar which usually tightens around it with screw fixings. The post is held down by a wide metal plate that is bolted to the patio.

Fence spikes

Alternatively, use a fence spike, which consists of a long metal spike, topped by a collar into which the post is inserted. The post can be 60cm (24in) shorter if you use a spike rather than concreting the post into position, but the structure may not be as strong.

plates to erect them securely (see Post support options box, above). Use a spirit level to check that they are vertical.

Link each pair of uprights together with cross-beams, which run parallel to each other, one on either side of the arbour. If you have used notched posts, the cross-beams will simply slot into position, but they can be attached to the tops of the posts using galvanized brackets, specially designed and available with the posts.

Next add the rafters that go across the top of the arbour at 90° to the cross-beams. These are fixed to the crossbeams at regular intervals with galvanized brackets. The brackets are first nailed to the cross-beams, the rafters are positioned, then nails are driven through holes in the brackets into the sides of the rafters.

The trellis side screens can then be firmly nailed in place on the uprights on three sides of the arbour. Use ready-made trellis panels for speed.

If the rafters are widely spaced and you intend to grow climbing plants right over the

LEFT This large arbour, built in the form of a Japanese-style pergola, provides ideal screening from the buildings behind.

top of the arbour, you could, perhaps, consider adding some wires between the rafters, running parallel to the cross-beams, to which the plants can cling. Fix the wires to the end rafters with threaded eyes, stretching them tight, and pass them through a hole drilled in each of the rafters between.

Now add a seat and you have the perfect arbour. You can paint or stain the structure and seat but make sure that whatever you use is not toxic to plants. Choose your favourite scented climbers to create a pleasurable place to sit and relax. Small arbour-shaped structures can also be used as niches for framing statues.

RIGHT The classic arbour, with climbing roses scaling the sides, suits the symmetry of a formal garden planting style.

Attaching an arbour to a wall

An arbour can be fixed against a wall on one side if you do not have the space for a free-standing structure. The arbour is built in the same way, but on one side, instead of supporting the cross-beam with two uprights, it is screwed to the wall.

First, make a series of holes in the cross-beam that will be attached to the wall. Drill 2.5cm (1 in) diameter holes in each end of the cross-beam about 45cm (18in) from each end, then at roughly 45cm (18in) intervals in between.

Use a spirit level, a long plank and chalk to mark a line on the wall where the top of the cross-beam should go. Get someone to help you lift the cross-beam into position, aligning its top with the chalk line, then make a chalk mark on the wall through each of the holes in the beam. Remove the beam and drill a hole at the position of each of the marks, using a 35mm (1⅜in) masonry bit, to a depth of about 11.5cm (4½in).

Position the cross-beam again, then insert a 16.5cm x 16mm (6½ x ⅝in) steel anchor bolt through each of the holes. Tighten the bolts with an adjustable spanner until the beam is held securely against the wall.

Fix the galvanized brackets along the length of the cross-beam to take the rafters, then slot the square-ended rafters into the brackets and nail them into place.

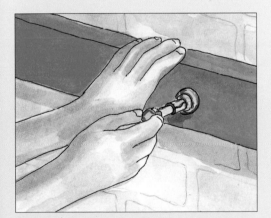

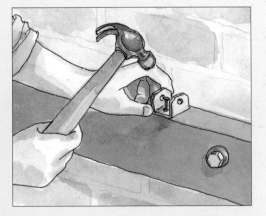

❶ Secure the cross-beam on one side of the arbour to the wall using steel anchor bolts at 45cm (18in) intervals. Remove the outer casing of the bolt and insert it into the hole, then push the bolt into position and tighten it.

❷ Use U-shaped galvanized brackets to attach the rafters to the cross-beam in the usual way. Attach each bracket to the cross-beam with a galvanized nail.

❸ Lower the end of a square-ended rafter into each U-shaped bracket and fix in place by driving a galvanized nail through the hole in each side of the bracket.

Archways and pergolas

Arches and pergolas are among the most popular garden features you can build. They can be made in a variety of different styles – very sturdy or more delicate – and a variety of different materials, which should be chosen to complement the overall style and scale of your garden. They may be purely decorative, such as an archway linking one part of the garden with another, or, in the case of pergolas, provide shade. On the other hand, they may also have a more practical purpose, such as providing support for climbing plants. Arches and pergolas frame a view of the garden as you pass underneath and may even form the entrance to the garden, and so the initial view. Consider the view framed by the entrance. It may be the path and front door or it may be the garden itself. No matter what is framed, it gives an immediate impression of your space. An archway, whether it is solidly made of brick, wood or iron, or is living, in the form of a hedge, is the best sort of frame.

LEFT A classic yew-covered pointed arch. If it is allowed to, the yew will eventually grow round the wood and conceal it.

ABOVE A modern take on the Gothic arch. Made of wrought iron, such structures look delicate but are quite strong enough to support climbing roses.

Arches

Archways are the ultimate way of framing entrances and exits as well as linking different areas of the garden. A glimpse of what lies beyond is often tantalizing enough for people to abandon the area they are in and move on to the next.

Whether wooden or metal, simple or lightly ornate, arches add considerable charm to any garden. Not only do they form a decorative support for a profusion of climbing plants, such as clematis, honeysuckle and roses, but they can also be used as an informal division between various areas of the garden, for example, to separate the lawn from the patio or vegetable plot. Build a series of arches close together and you have a pergola.

Regardless of type, a wooden arch is relatively straightforward to build, and in most cases the various wooden sections are simply held together with galvanized nails.

If you are unsure of the size and design of arch to build, it is a good idea to sketch your ideas on paper first. Then take photographs of the archway's position

Ideas for arches

You can build various styles of arch, depending on the style of your garden. In fact, whatever the style of your garden, you should be able to devise an arch that will fit in with it.

- In a country garden build the arch in a lattice-work pattern from rustic poles with the bark still in place.
- For a more formal garden build a less rustic structure using square-planed timbers.
- For a grand design erect pillars made of brick with square sections of wood at their corners and panels of trellis in between.
- A simple arch leading from an Oriental-style part of the garden could consist of large sections of wood with a single crosspiece at the top, its ends cut at an upward-sloping angle.

Simple joints for creating an arch or pergola

When you build an arch or pergola out of rustic poles, there are a number of simple joints that can be used to join the poles together. The joints must be close-fitting and strong; use large galvanized nails or screws to secure them.

Use this type of joint to join lengths of timber.

To make a right angle, fix the horizontal and vertical pieces as shown.

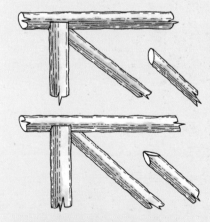

To attach a timber into the crook of the right angle cut it at 45°. Alternatively, make a V-joint by cutting a V-shaped notch in the cross-beam and shaping the end of the other pole to fit.

Diagonal corner brackets should be used to strengthen the structure and add to the decorative effect.

from both sides and use tracing paper to produce overlays that will show what your ideas would look like if they were built in the garden.

Plastic and metal archways

The simplest way of creating an archway is to buy one of the many plastic or metal ones that are available from garden centres and the larger DIY stores. Plastic usually looks like plastic and does not last long, so metal is a more economical choice for the long term. Be sure to check its dimensions before you buy, however, as many of the ready-made arches are too narrow to walk through comfortably. When you are buying an arch, always imagine what it will look like when it is covered with roses and how much space will be left between the posts for you to pass comfortably through and under it.

Clothing an arch

Depending on the situation, arches can be left bare or clothed with climbing plants. In a small garden, where space is at a premium, an archway can be used as an excuse to grow a few more plants. Roses are popular choices for this type of situation, and you may want to look for a thornless variety, such as 'Zéphirine Drouhin'. Many

ABOVE This rustic arch frames the view into the garden beyond and positively invites passers-by to explore along the path.

roses will produce flowers all summer through, but by running a clematis up through the rose you make sure of a double season. Both the rose and the clematis should be planted in spring and tied to the uprights. Keep the shoots inside the arch trimmed or tied back so that the plants do not become an obstacle.

Making a rustic arch

Making your own arch is often cheaper than buying a ready-made one from a garden centre, and it can be more fun and is certainly more rewarding. The simplest style is a rustic archway; although the construction must be sound, accuracy is not quite as essential as it would be with wood of uniform section. Slight variations in the sizes and arrangement of the frame's pieces are all part of the attraction of the final appearance.

As a guide, an arch should give about 2.4m (8ft) of headroom and be at least 1.2m (4ft) wide. When you are happy with the design, you can order the materials. As a general rule, wood with a diameter or width of 7.5–10cm (3–4in) will be needed for the main supporting framework of an arch. Sweet chestnut poles are the most satisfactory to use, but any timber that has been treated with preservative is suitable. Make sure you stand the feet of the uprights in buckets of preservative for several days so that it really soaks into the endgrain. Rustic poles with the bark left in place should be treated on their ends only because the bark will prevent absorption of the preservative.

Pergolas

Pergolas are formed by building a series of arches in a row. Whether attached to the house or boundary wall or free-standing, pergolas are an attractive means of providing shade to a walkway or patio as well as acting as a support for climbing plants. They are invariably built from wood, although some may have brick or block columns supporting thick wooden cross-pieces.

As with arches, pergolas can be built in many styles to suit different types of garden, so it should not be too difficult to

Rustic arch

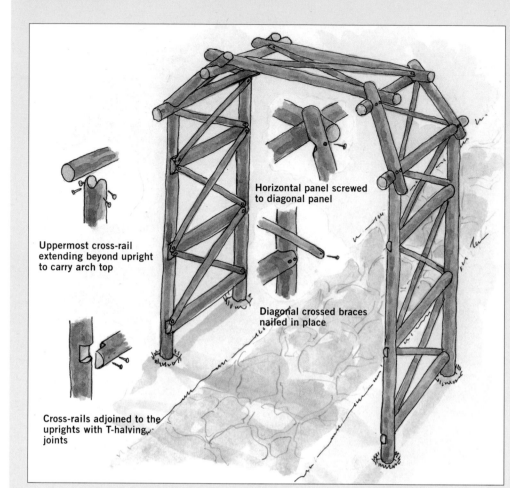

Uppermost cross-rail extending beyond upright to carry arch top

Horizontal panel screwed to diagonal panel

Diagonal crossed braces nailed in place

Cross-rails adjoined to the uprights with T-halving joints

Rustic arch

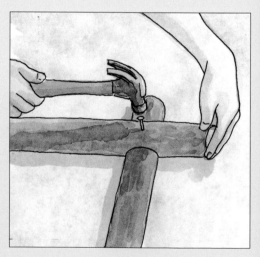

1 Before starting, lay out the sides. The sides should be made from 7.5–10cm (3–4in) diameter poles. The cross-rails should be 5–7.5cm (2–3in). The diagonal cross-braces should be half the diameter of the cross-rails.

2 You can use cross-halving joints for the top cross-rails. The diagonal braces can be nailed in place directly, since they are more for decoration than support.

3 Make sure that all the joints are secured with angled nails. They should be long enough to connect both pieces of wood but not show through on the other side.

come up with something that fits in exactly with your own plot. It is a good idea to take a number of photographs of the area where the pergola is to be built and use tracing paper overlays to try out various designs until you find the right one.

Similar sizes of wood should be used for a pergola as for an arch, and the minimum width and headroom apply also.

Erecting a free-standing pergola follows the procedure for a wooden archway. Individual arch frames are nailed together and set in holes in the ground with concrete collars. When the concrete has set, additional cross-pieces and rails can be added to tie the structure together.

To help plants run up and across the pergola, you could add trellis on the sides or wires on the top. To fix trellis, either nail the trellis directly to the uprights or attach battens to the uprights and use panel pins to fix the trellis panels. Wires can be threaded through screw eyes or holes drilled in the wood or even stapled to the wood.

RIGHT An arch need not necessarily be curved or pointed. The straight lines of this example are softened by the gentle lines of the rose.

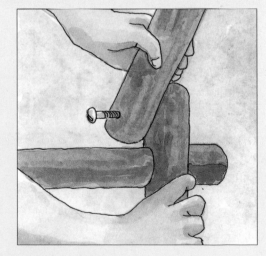

4 For a neater joint on the other cross-rails, cut a V-shaped notch in the upright and arrow the ends of the cross-rail to the same dimensions. Nail the joints securely.

5 Erect the sides first and secure them with temporary supports while the cement foundations of the uprights dry. Check the measurements before constructing the top of the arch.

6 Fix the top of the arch either to the side uprights or to the cross-rails with heavy-duty screws.

Summerhouses and treehouses

Summerhouses come in many designs, shapes and sizes. They range from little wooden huts tucked away out of sight, to large, full-scale brick buildings. Choose a style that will be in harmony with the rest of your garden. As it is a relatively small building you can have fun with the design and build your summerhouse in the style of a thatched cottage, classical temple or wood cabin, for example.

ABOVE This sturdy treehouse would be suitable for older children who are capable of climbing up the steep ladder without falling off.

RIGHT This pretty, simple summerhouse at the end a walk through overgrown shrubbery is a perfect place to sit quietly.

Summerhouses

The most common role of a summerhouse is to provide an undercover sitting area for taking in a view of the garden or even dining in relaxed surroundings. What you have in your summerhouse largely depends on its intended use. Summerhouses can double up as storage rooms for furniture, pool equipment and so on. Unwanted items can be tucked away on shelves, under built-in seats or even in the roof space in some summerhouses, leaving more space to enjoy meals and socializing. Summerhouses can even be made into offices or workshops, but you should check with your local authority as to the uses allowed.

When you decide on a summerhouse make sure its size and design suit the garden. Play around with shapes and sizes on a plan of the garden, putting different shapes in different spots until you have found the ideal site and size you want.

Siting a summerhouse

Where you position a summerhouse can have an effect on the rest of the garden. For example, a summerhouse placed close to the house in a small garden can dominate the scene; tucked in the bend of a shrub border, it will be far less obtrusive. Summerhouses are, of course, a focal point and where you use them to draw the eye is important. At the end of a path or to one side, hidden in a shrubbery or in full view, the same structure can have different effects, which is why you should spend some time at the design stage deciding on the right one. Better quality summerhouses tend to look more effective, so if you are going site it prominently you will probably benefit from spending a bit more. If it is going to be hidden away you can get away with a slightly less up-market model.

You could install power to provide electric lights, or you can use candles, with care, or lanterns. In a small garden a summerhouse may be the only focal feature, and you can create the illusion of space by placing shrubs and plants in front of it so the summerhouse is glimpsed through them. It will be an intriguing feature and invite you to explore further.

Treehouses

Treehouses are perhaps more appropriate for older children, but adults often get fun out of them a great deal, and you may wish to build a simple platform around a tree to provide an additional and novel seating area.

A treehouse can really be built in a tree if there is one, but it can equally well be above ground in some other way, such as being built on sturdy stilts. Choose a style that suits your garden: rustic logs would look right in a woodland garden or plain timber in a garden with decking. In a children's garden, it would even be possible to make one look like a ship.

Safety

Before you build a treehouse, check the planning regulations in your area to make sure that you do not need planning permission.

Your style of treehouse can be as original as you want as long as it is safe. If you build one actually in a tree, it will be harder to provide adequate support and you will need to make access safe, so a tree house like this needs to be made with the help of a professional. It is not worth risking serious injury by going ahead without proper guidance.

Good quality materials are vital in a weight-supporting structure. Thin planks can break and cause serious splinters as well as depositing the unfortunate person hard on the ground. Good paint will cover better and offer longer weatherproofing, while strong supports are obviously vital to keep the structure safe. Steps or a ladder to get up and down must be securely fastened and strong.

However, if the thought of making a tree house within the branches of the tree itself is daunting and not for you, then an equally inviting treehouse can be built around the trunk itself, in the form of a simple raised platform.

Making a simple tree platform/hideaway

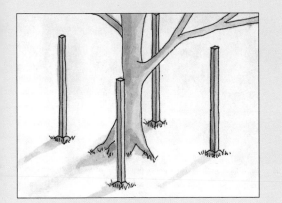

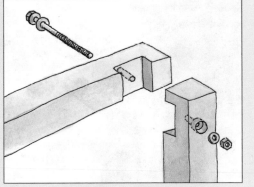

1 Measure and mark out the positions of the posts, then set them in concrete, avoiding the roots of the tree. Alternatively, use fence spikes to erect them.

2 Join the rails to the uprights with cross-halving joints, then drill holes and bolt them together using hexagonal bolts, nuts and circular washers. Recess the heads of the bolts and nuts.

3 Make two rows of rails, one to support the platform and the other as a handrail above it. Set the two opposite pairs of rails at the same height as each other, checking them with a spirit level.

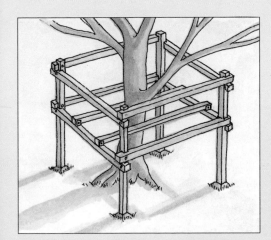

4 Next add two or more joists, joining their ends to the two lowest rails using U-brackets.

5 Make a platform from 2.5cm (1in) thick exterior grade plywood or chipboard sheets. Screw them to the joists at regular intervals. A fun child's hideaway can be made by screwing on decorated plywood or chipboard side panels and securing the steps.

Sheds and storage

Storage is often a neglected area of garden planning. However, without adequate storage your garden will quickly become cluttered and your tools will soon rust and rot. The trusty garden shed is the classic outdoor structure, and provides not only storage space but also a useful haven for DIY, potting and other garden maintenance. There is, of course, more to garden storage than just the standard apex-roofed shed. Bunkers, cupboards and more innovative shed designs should all be considered when planning your outdoor space.

Bunkers

Although sheds are the ideal form of storage for almost everything connected with the garden, bunkers or large boxes will take up less space and may provide enough space for the few tools that you need in the garden. As long as it is not too heavy to lift, even a mower can be stored in it. Old coal bunkers are ideal. Storage space could also be built into other features. For example, if you want a permanent barbecue with a built-in sitting area, the seats could be constructed as lockers so that there is storage space beneath

them. Building a raised wooden deck instead of a patio might allow you to create storage space below it.

Camouflage

If your objection to a shed is not so much the space it takes up but its dominant presence, which makes it appear to be too large for the garden, think about ways of disguising it. Painting it dark green will help to make it merge into the background of the garden, and covering it with climbing plants will make it even less noticeable.

TOP A basic garden shed can be made to look more attractive by painting it dark green, so that it blends in with the background.

ABOVE This tiny shed will hold only a few basic tools but would be perfect for a small garden.

ABOVE LEFT Rather than being hidden away, this shed makes a virtue of its workmanlike nature.

The plants will soften the edges and break up its surface. If there is space, placing a trellis in front of it, again covered in climbers, will help to hide it.

Assembling a garden shed

A good foundation really is the most important part to erecting a sound and long-lasting shed.

1 Mark out the area for its foundation, making it a little larger than the base of the shed. If you want a hard area in front or to the side of the shed, include this in the area you mark out. Use taut pegged string lines, making sure the width is uniform by measuring with a steel tape.

2 In order to make the concrete pad on which the shed can rest, first build a wooden framework (form work) to hold the concrete in shape while it sets. It needs to be as deep as the combined thickness of hardcore, sand and concrete (see step 4).

3 Support the timber frame using pegs and use a builder's square to make sure the corners are perfectly square.

4 Lay a 10cm (4in) layer of hardcore and compact well. Then lay a thin layer of sand

(2cm/¾in) to bind the hardcore, then add the concrete. A general-purpose concrete mix made up of 1 part cement to 2 parts sharp sand and 3 parts coarse aggregate should be suitable for this purpose. It needs to be about 7.5cm (3in) thick for lighter sheds and 10cm (4in) for heavier ones.

The concrete for a small base can be laid as one unit, but larger one will need to be laid in two units separated by a contraction joint, which helps to prevent cracking. This consists of a piece of hardwood filler strip, which is placed midway between the two sides of the form work for the base. A piece of softwood about 2.5cm (1in) thick is laid next to this and held in place using pegs. The concrete for the first section is laid, overlapping into the second section by about an inch. The softwood support is removed but the hardwood filler strip is left in place. The concrete from the second section is pushed up against it and the concreting is finished.

Most sheds are fairly easy to assemble but you will usually need the help of another person, as the timbers are heavy. Follow the manufacturer's instructions carefully. Make sure that all corners are flush to allow as little water in as possible. If the roof is felted, make sure the felt is well secured so that water cannot get underneath and cause rot. Add another coat of creosote or preservative once the shed has been erected, or you can paint it with one of the wood stains available in a range of colours.

Changing use

If you have young children, their use of the garden is likely to dominate the layout until they have grown up. Thinking about the long-term use can make the transition easier, however. For example, a playhouse could subsequently be used for storage purposes and could be positioned, designed and constructed or specially purchased with that in mind.

Inconspicuous sheds

In a little garden, a small lean-to tool shed can be built against a wall or against a fence if it is substantial enough. (If it is your neighbour's fence you should ask for permission.) This shed can be big enough to contain the mower and a few tools but will take up little room. A simple frame of 7.5 x 5cm (3 x 2in) timber can be constructed. The sides and the door can be made either by cladding the frame with feather-edged boarding or by buying some fence panels and cutting them to size. The door can be made in a similar way but will need a 5 x 2.5cm (2 x 1in) frame around the

edge to strengthen it. A simple sloping roof can be made from a sheet of cheap plywood covered with roofing felt. Where the top of the roof meets the wall or fence, fill the gap with a flexible filler so that rainwater cannot trickle into the shed. Surround the shed with shrubs so that it cannot be seen.

Choosing a garden shed

Sheds are extremely useful, not only for storing materials and tools but also for working in, as a temporary place to put items that you need to lock away or for placing seed trays near windows.

Sheds can be made from hard or soft wood, metal or concrete. There are advantages and disadvantages to all materials but the most commonly used, largely due to its price, is softwood that has been treated with preservative to withstand rot. When you choose a shed, make sure you see one already erected at the garden centre or wherever you buy it. Make sure it is sturdy and large enough for your purposes and that it is secure.

As a shed is likely to be a permanent structure choose the site carefully. Make sure it is accessible but will not dominate the garden. If it is impossible to hide it, consider screening it with trellis and climbing plants or shrubs. You can even train plants up and over the shed itself.

Storage

Storage is always a problem, especially if you have limited space and want to use all space that is available for the garden itself. By introducing storage ideas with a practical side you will solve both the problem of where to put things and add character and interest.

You can buy benches that have a hollow base that is designed for storage or very large wooden boxes made for the same purpose. These can either be stained with one of the many shades of wood colour or you can even paint them.

If there is really not room for a shed, a garden store might be the answer. These come in many different sizes and materials and can often be erected against a wall. They take up much less room than a shed but, of course, will hold less, so you need to think very carefully about why you need the store. Lean-to storage units can be used where there is no space for a shed or garden store, and you can make your own from wood if you are creative enough. Many carpenters will gladly make you a storage unit to your own specifications, and it is not as costly as you think. Old coal stores make good storage units, and very individual stores can be created using barrels, spaces cut into grassy banks or built into walls. Small, lockable chests make good storage too, although they are rarely large enough for the bigger tools.

A really easy idea is to use plastic bins with lockable lids, like those used for children's toys. Lay them on their side in

ABOVE Simple battens with nails in provide a good way to keep larger tools such as spades, forks and hoes tidy and out of the way.

Shed maintenance

Good quality sheds are expensive, so once you have gone to the trouble of buying and erecting one, make sure you don't just let it rot in the corner of the garden. Sheds, like all structures, need regular maintenance, and a little attention will prolong the life of a shed for many years.

Weatherproofing.
A quality weatherproofing or preservative solution should be applied to the wooden parts of your shed every two years. Choose a fine, sunny day for your weatherproofing and wash the shed down thoroughly first.

Repairing rotten timber
Check your shed annually for signs of rot. A darkening and softening of the wood is the most obvious indicator of rotten timber. Small areas of wood rot can be removed and filled once the remaining wood has been treated with wood hardener. For larger areas, damaged wood should be cut away and replaced with fresh timber. Any new wood should be immediately coated with preservative.

Roof repairs
Shed roofs should also be checked regularly for signs of wear and leaks. An annual coating of bitumen paint can help to prolong the life of your shed's felt roof, but once leaks start to appear, you will need to patch or even renew the roof. A complete roof renewal should only be attempted if you have either DIY experience or a commercially produced shed-roofing package. Patching a roof is more straightforward. First you must remove the damaged area of felt and the relevant retaining nails. Next cut the new felt (which must be kept relatively warm to avoid cracking), allowing an overlap of 10–12.5cm (4–5in) with the old felting plus 2.5 cm (1in) in order to overturn the edges. The new felt should be secured in place using galvanized nails at intervals of 11.5 cm (4½in).

Guttering
Modern plastic guttering is relatively inexpensive, and so it is usually easier and cheaper to renew damaged areas rather than to repair them. Check your shed's guttering at the end of each summer.

rows and use them for storage. They will hold plenty of things, like trowels, tape, string, seed packets and lots more, and are waterproof and come in a range of colours. Plastic drainpipes can also be used, cut into lengths and laid on their side.

A very individual idea is to make your own 'tube' out of wood. This will fit, stood upright, into any corner. You slide your hoe, fork, spade and so on inside the tube. Quirky and original storage ideas can be used to add another feature to the garden rather than trying to tuck them away.

Shelving offers a huge range of possibilities. You can put shelving around the outside buildings like sheds and stores if there is no room inside. Painted in a complimentary colour, the shelves will look very effective against a background wall.

They do not have to be the traditional shape either, and you can create patterns with shelving and have large, curved shelves or angular ones and therefore get both originality and practicality into the garden.

A series of shelves placed at an angle with containers on them makes excellent use of a small area and can introduce greenery and flowers to a previously dull wall. Decorative screen walls offer the perfect place for storage. The shelves can be used for ornaments as well as other items you need to store. The only limitation to the use of shelves in the garden itself is that you cannot store items that are susceptible to the weather.

Hooks and hanging spaces open up a range of possibilities. Hooks can go almost anywhere on the outside of buildings, on walls and fences and even on the trunks of trees. The range of sizes and styles is very large, and they are available from DIY shops and hardware stores. Large hooks are a very practical way of storing garden hoses.

You can buy hooks for hanging baskets that suit the theme of your garden. Large gold ones for a formal theme or black and white ones for a minimalist garden. Alternatively, you can buy hooks that are interesting intrinsically, such as large, brightly coloured ones or florally decorated ones. You could even paint them yourself for even more individuality.

Constructing a storage bench

A storage bench will prove very useful in the garden, especially where space is limited. They make the best of what space is available in balconies or roof gardens.

They are suitable for storing everything that is not adversely affected by the cold and damp, such as bags of compost, plastic toys and trays – all those things, in fact, it is hard to find a place for. Plus, of course, they offer the dual role of providing a comfortable seat.

The bench does not have to be large, but the larger the size you can fit into the garden, the more it will hold, so you need to decide what to store to determine the size. The bench needs to be very strong because it will be taking the weight of people sitting on it, plus the lid will be raised and shut often, which puts a strain on the joints and timbers. You can buy ready-made benches with hinged lids that are intended for indoor use and weatherproof them by treating the wood yourself, but to get the right size it is probably better to make one.

The timber needs to be 5cm (2in) thick at least. Measure the area for the bench and decide on the width and length of the timbers needed for the sides and ends. The bottom piece needs to be a little thicker. The top piece (lid) should overlap the front and ends by about 1cm (½in). All the timber must be thoroughly treated with preservative or your bench will have a very short life.

Carefully put the pieces together to make sure they fit. The end-pieces should butt squarely to the sides and bottom so that there is no room for damp to seep in.

Join the pieces together using either Lok joints, square-section wood battens or dowel joints.

It is a good idea, if possible, to have the bottom of the bench raised a little, and in this case, you can use corner joints in the gaps at the sides to add extra stability and strength. A raised base is not vital but it will keep the bench off the ground.

When you have joined the main pieces securely, position the bench in its final place. Use butt hinges or continuous (piano) hinges cut to size to attach the lid.

It is a good idea to fix two chains to either end from the lid to the front piece of timber so that the lid cannot topple backwards when it is opened.

Once your storage bench is made, you can paint it in any colour you like, or leave it with a natural look.

Large cushions will make the bench comfortable to sit on, while allowing easy access to the lid

Other ideas for using benches for storage include making use of the space under an ordinary garden bench by fitting lengths of timber over the ends and back to hide the space underneath. A drop-down front can be fitted with a stay to prevent it from unintentionally falling open.

BELOW Wall-mounted shelving is a perfect way to provide storage for small items, such as pots, without taking up vital floor space.

Dustbin screen

❶ Build a brick structure with three walls and roof it with paving slabs. Put another course of bricks round the top to create a bed.

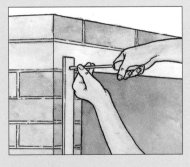

❷ Screw vertical battens on either side of the opening and attach trellis doors.

❸ Once completed, the doors hide the dustbins and the plants disguise the unsightliness of the structure.

Greenhouses

Most gardeners hanker after a greenhouse in which to raise a variety of plants. Greenhouses are not only expensive, however, but also take up quite a bit of space, especially as the rule of thumb for buying one is that you work out the size you need and double it, because you will always need more space than you think. Although it does not have quite the same prestige as a greenhouse, a cold frame can do almost anything a greenhouse can do, apart from keeping the gardener dry in wet weather. It takes up far less space and can be made more easily and cheaply by the gardener than a greenhouse.

ABOVE A greenhouse can be built next to the house, where it will benefit in winter from the warmth from the main building.

LEFT A classic wooden greenhouse in a working garden, with concrete flooring in the middle to make it easier to use during wet weather.

Heating in cold weather will depend on whether your greenhouse is intended to be warm or temperate, but some kind of heating is generally needed, even if it is only to provide undersoil heat for seedlings. Paraffin and other free-standing heaters are good buys if the area is small, but they need watching and constant care. Other models that you can set using a thermostat are excellent but will add a lot to your heating bills. Lean-to greenhouses sited close to the house will get some warmth and shelter from the house wall, so they can be cheaper to keep frost free.

Size and model

Versatility is essential if you are serious about maintaining thriving plantlife in a greenhouse. A green house 3 x 2.4m (9ft 9in x 8ft) would give ample room for cultivating seeds, fruit growing and protecting plants in winter. However, work out exactly what you will use your greenhouse for before buying and estimate the size accordingly. Naturally, the size of greenhouse also depends on what you can afford and the size of your garden. A 2.4 x 2m (8 x 6ft 6in) model will suffice in a small urban garden. Anything bigger will be too dominant.

You will also need to anchor the structure and provide a firm base, so bear in mind

Siting

The site of your greenhouse is important. Avoid overhanging trees and nearby buildings, which may cast shadows, and windy, exposed sites, which will cause a loss of heat. Your greenhouse should also be near some sort of water and electricity supply, and it must be easily accessible.

If you are going to have a greenhouse, it is worth considering other practicalities.

Shade will be necessary when the weather is very hot. Even the great sun-loving plants do not like the high humidity created on some days, so shading in the form of blinds, whitewash or mesh will be necessary.

If you want your greenhouse to have one shady side and one sunny side, position it so that the door faces east. If you want both sides to receive direct sunlight, place it so that the door faces either north or south.

Types of greenhouse

There are many types of greenhouse to choose from, including free-standing and lean-to models. They may be built of wood, metal or PVC. Wood tends to look more attractive than metal, and it is marginally warmer, easier to repair and better for fitting shelves. However, it is heavy to construct, while steel and aluminium are light and easy to handle. Because they are stronger than wooden ones, metal frames can be fitted with larger panes of glass, which results in better light penetration.

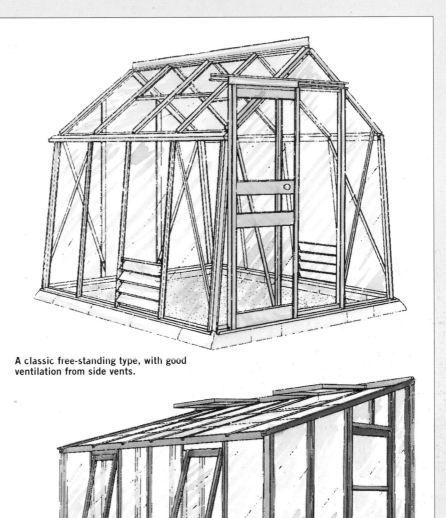

A classic free-standing type, with good ventilation from side vents.

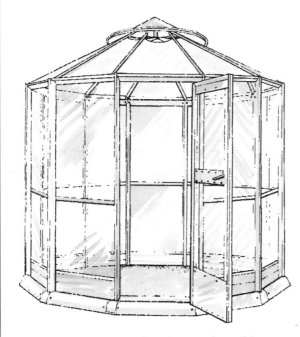

A circular model gives plants maximum light from all sides

A lean-to-type, built against a wall.

what sort of foundations are needed. Go and look at a number of greenhouses before deciding which type will be appropriate. A variety of styles of greenhouse is on sale, including Dutch light, span roofed, lean-to, three-quarter span and mansard, so choose which will suit your garden best.

Ventilation

Ventilation is another thing to think about. Vents and fans can be incorporated into the frame of the greenhouse itself and, again, these can be timer-operated or programmed to react to particular levels of heat and humidity. Remember that a greenhouse will need ventilation even during winter months to avoid damp-related problems such as fungus and mould.

Water

Watering requires serious thought if you are going to buy a greenhouse. Unless you want to keep going back and forth with a watering can, some sort of irrigation system might be a good investment. Whether you decide on a drip, automatic or mist system, you need to weigh up the costs and relative effectiveness for your type of gardening.

If you are going to need an electricity or a water supply (or both), this needs to be considered when you plan the greenhouse. Always get work checked by a professional as safety is very important.

Installing a heater in your greenhouse

Keeping your greenhouse at the right temperature is very important. This may mean you need a heater for the coldest months. If the greenhouse is large, heating only part of the area will save money and use energy efficiently. You can buy thermal screens, which are plastic sheets that you suspend from wires across the greenhouse to keep heat in the lower part. They can be drawn at night or at other times during the day. The screens can also be used hung vertically to divide the greenhouse into smaller areas, thereby reducing the area to be heated.

A thermometer is a good investment so that you can efficiently control the warmth and avoid overheating the greenhouse. Using a form of insulation material such as 'bubble' plastic sheeting or double-glazing will also help to save costs.

Replacing a window in your greenhouse

Accidents do happen and at some time you may need to replace a pane of glass in your greenhouse.

1 Put gloves on and carefully remove the glazing clips holding the broken pane. You can re-use these for the replacement pane.

2 Gently remove the broken pane. If the glazing strip is damaged, you need to remove it, cut a new one to the right length and press it down into the grooves in the glazing bars, which form the framework that holds the glass.

3 Carefully place the new pane in position. Make sure it fits securely, leaving a gap of about 2mm (1/16in) on all sides to allow room for the glazing clips. A higher pane of glass should overlap the one underneath by about 1cm (1/2in).

4 Use overlay glazing clips to secure the pane safely to the lower one. Then use ordinary glazing clips to hold the new pane in place. Push it gently but firmly until the pane sits securely in place.

In older greenhouses, the panes may be embedded in putty. This should be carefully chipped away to leave a smooth surface then cleaned. Any exposed or old wood should be primed. When the primer is dry, replace the pane using a bed of putty or mastic and glazing tacks to it in place.

ABOVE A thermostatically controlled greenhouse heaters are a good idea if you cannot check on the greenhouse regularly, but they are expensive to run.

LEFT This modern aluminium greenhouse has integral shelves on one side that are far enough apart to allow salad vegetables to be grown in pots.

Deciding on the kind of heater you need is the next step. The three likely candidates are electric, gas or paraffin. If there is a ready supply of electricity or gas, the choice is easy but, if not, you need to look at the heaters available and the installation costs along with the maintenance involved.

If you decide on a free-standing heater, make sure that you have a flat, hard, level surface for it, away from inflammable items. The heater should ideally be placed towards the middle of the area to be heated, to make the best possible use of energy and to avoid draughts near the door.

If you are using electric or gas heaters you may need to install a supply. Electricity can be run overhead in outdoor cables or the wires can be buried in a trench from the main supply to the greenhouse using armoured cable and waterproof fittings. Gas may be supplied from the mains or in bottles. Either way, installation must be done by a qualified electrician or gas fitter.

Electric heaters are usually controlled by a thermostat, which gives you a lot of control. Little heat is wasted and the heaters require little maintenance. Fumes and water vapour are not a problem.

Several types of electric heater are available. Fan heaters are effective and some models can be used to cool the greenhouse in summer. Fan heaters also keep the air circulating, which reduces the chance of many diseases occurring. Tubular, waterproof heaters can be fitted to the sides of the greenhouse about 30cm (12in) off the ground and are very effective.

Gas heaters are less convenient than electric ones and adjustment is needed to obtain the correct setting. They need regular checking and the gas bottles need changing. For safety, it is best to have a spare bottle and an automatic change-over valve so that the new bottle is switched to as soon because the old one is empty.

If propane gas is used, ventilation is necessary as the heater produces water vapour and fumes.

Paraffin heaters are popular because they are relatively cheap and they are easily transported. However, they can be expensive to run and they are not very efficient. The fuel needs to be stored somewhere and the fuel level, flame and wick of the heater must be checked daily to make sure they are burning clean.

Introducing heating to your greenhouse can bring tremendous advantages, but it does need careful thought.

Greenhouse maintenance

- Regular checks will ensure that any problems are picked up before they become major ones.
- Clean the glass with water or a proprietary window cleaner. To get between the panes, use a small plastic knife to loosen dirt and debris and then hose off.
- Replace any damaged panes as soon as possible.
- Check and replace any rusty door hinges.
- Check the staging and shelves to make sure they are in good order.
- Treat any wooden areas with preservative and replace rotten pieces.
- Check that ventilators are watertight and the mechanism works.
- If you have guttering and down pipes, keep them clear of debris, especially in autumn.

- Regularly check plants for any sign of pests and diseases as these can rapidly spread in the confines and warmth of a greenhouse.
- Rake gravel regularly and keep the floor clear of weeds.
- In autumn clean shading with a soft cloth.
- In autumn, on a breezy but warm day, take out all the plants and disinfect all the surfaces inside the greenhouse. Replace the plants and use a smoke fumigator to destroy all pests.
- Regularly take five minutes to walk around the greenhouse checking doors, glass, ventilators and so on. Then go inside and check there are no leaks in any irrigation system, that the plants are healthy and that there are no gaps in cladding or thermal screens. Check the insulation is secure and the staging is safe. Regular checks take only a few minutes but can prevent disease and major problems.

ABOVE Spray door hinges with lubricant and check that the door has not warped and closes properly.

ABOVE Clean the windows in spring or autumn to allow as much light through as possible.

ABOVE Brush all shelving with a stiff brush to get rid of dried soil, cobwebs and leaves.

ABOVE Lubricate window hinges so that they move freely, especially if they are in awkward-to-reach places.

Frames and cloches

Cold frames and cloches are most useful for hardening off plants in spring before they are transplanted and for protecting plants over winter. Being portable, cloches are mostly used in the vegetable garden to protect plants already growing or to warm up the soil planting, while cold frames are used mainly to overwinter tender plants and to protect young seedlings.

The most popular cold frames are made of metal with glass sides and glass tops. You can also get these with wooden sides and glass tops, and there are also ones with brick sides. Some of the tops are hinged so you can wedge them open when gradually hardening off plants, while others have sliding tops. The hinged types are best because they protect the plants from rain, but they do have a tendency to blow shut in windy weather.

Types of frames and cloches

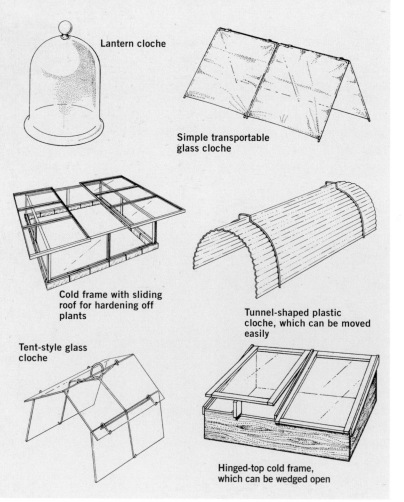

Lantern cloche

Simple transportable glass cloche

Cold frame with sliding roof for hardening off plants

Tunnel-shaped plastic cloche, which can be moved easily

Tent-style glass cloche

Hinged-top cold frame, which can be wedged open

How to make a portable cloche

You can quickly and easily construct a portable cloche for little expense using some strong wire and polythene sheeting. Make sure that the polythene is thick enough to resist easy tears but not so thick as to reduce the light getting to the plants or soil below.

First, cut the polythene sheet to size. To work out the length required, measure the area you want to cover and add about 3m (9ft 9in) to allow plenty of excess at the ends. The width of the polythene should be about three times the required height of the cloche.

❶ Cut and bend the wire into hoops of the required size, making a small loop at either end.

❷ Run two bits of straight wire through the loops until the structure forms one complete unit.

❸ Lay polythene over hoops, and anchor the frame using staples made from the wire. Secure polythene with string.

❹ Tie the polythene at either end. If it gets too hot, one or both ends can be unfastened.

Compost bin

A ready supply of organic matter is very important for the creation and maintenance of healthy, fertile soil. Compost is useful for lining planting holes and trenches and for conditioning the soil. It will help improve all types of soil: dry to sandy soils will retain water better and heavy clay soils will have better crumbly structure with the addition of organic matter such as compost. Compost also attracts the beneficial soil organisms that play a huge part in improving the texture of the soil by breaking down organic material and metabolizing it into nutrients that plants can absorb easily.

Regularly buying compost is expensive and means extra transport, packaging and fuel is used, so it makes environmental and economic sense to make your own compost heap so that you have a regular supply you can use when you need it. The ideal compost bin consists of two compartments, each at least is 1m³ (39 cubic inches). One will hold the compost you are currently using, while the other is filled with organic material and kitchen waste and breaking down to form new compost.

You can buy ready-made compost bins, but building your own means you can make them the size you need. The compartments should be a minimum of 1m³ (39 cubic inches) to ensure that the compost maintains the required heat for the breakdown of material.

You can start to fill your compost bin with waste from the garden and kitchen (but not meat or cooked food, as these attract vermin). To help the breaking down process you can add nitrogen in the form of manure feed. Do this in a layer over each 15cm (6in) or so of compost.

Turning the heap with a garden fork to introduce air will ensure that breakdown is aerobic (anaerobic micro-organisms are not beneficial and tend to make unpleasant smelling compounds) and help speed up the process. The compost should be ready to use in 3–4 months. It should have a good consistency, be dark in colour and have a pleasant smell. Do not put compost bins where air circulation is poor and do not use polythene to weigh material down as this stops air getting in.

When one side is ready, start to use it and fill the other side. When the bins are empty let them rest for a while before adding new material. This will ensure that any anaerobic organisms have a chance to be killed off. Once this compost system is up and running you should have a cheap, reliable source of organic material at little cost and little work.

Making a compost bin

❶ Mark the area you are going to use for the compost heap. A foundation is not needed because it is best placed straight on the ground where earthworms will be encouraged to come and start work. Mark places for six 1.5m (5ft) posts to form a double square. Drive the posts a third of their length into the ground. They need to be stout to support the weight of the bin and compost. Make sure they are level using a spirit level and plank.

❷ Secure batons along the bottom and sides to make the structure temporarily secure. Nail the boards in place. Cut the top boards into shape and nail them in position. Nail a long board to the backs of each panel at the bottom. Make sure the middle panel is central and check the angles. Continue nailing boards to the backs until the back of the bin is complete.

❸ Make runners for the front slats by nailing 25mm x 25mm (1x1in) lengths of wood along the front edges of the three posts. Cut the front boards to fit so they slide up and down the runners and fit into place. Small blocks the same width as the the runner sit between the slats. Paint the wood with preservative. You can make a wooden lid or cover the top with sacking and weigh it down with bricks.

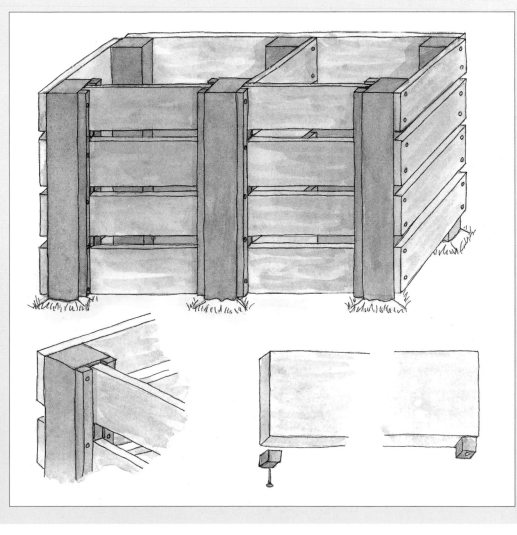

Making a sundial

The earliest known sundial was discovered in Egypt and dates from some 5,000 years ago. Before the advent of mechanical clocks, primitive water clocks and sundials were the only means of accurately recording time. Although many European churches show evidence of early vertical sundials on their walls, the need for measuring time was largely unimportant for agrarian people. Dawn and dusk dictated the passing of their days and there was little need for hours or minutes.

This sundial is made from slate, but various other materials, including concrete, are acceptable. Once positioned, your sundial should not be moved, so the weight of materials are relatively unimportant. Although simple sundials can be purchased, they will not be accurate unless made for your locality. The time depicted by your sundial (local time) will differ from zone time by its longitude east or west of the zone's meridian – somewhere 10° west of Greenwich, for example, will have local noon 40 minutes later. To make a working sundial for a particular site, a little work with paper and pencil is required.

RIGHT This simple, dark, stone sundial provides a point of interest among the pale coloured flowers clustered around its base.

Materials and equipment

- Tracing paper
- About 50 x 50cm (20 x 20in) square of 25mm (1in) thick slate slab
- Right-angled triangle of slate, about 18mm (¾in) thick x 35cm (14in) base length, for the gnomon – the height of the slate will be dictated by your location
- Two-part exterior stone adhesive
- Metal Roman numerals I to XII including 2 no. VIs (optional)
- Tile adhesive
- Pencil and sheet of paper
- Ruler
- Pair of compasses
- Protractor
- Carbon paper
- Masking tape
- Angle grinder
- Thin stone-cutting disc
- Safety goggles and dust mask
- Straight edge

The mathematics

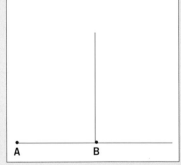

1 Draw a horizontal line towards the bottom of the paper. In the centre of the line draw a vertical line perpendicular to the horizontal line. Mark the left point of the horizontal line as **A** and the point where the lines intersect as **B**. The larger the piece of paper you use, the easier it will be to draw accurate angles and the more accurate your sundial will be.

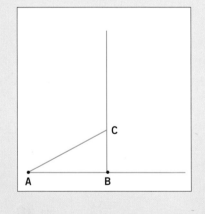

2 Draw a line from point **A** at an angle that is equal to the latitude of the location of your sundial (how many degrees north or south of the equator), to intersect the vertical line at point **C**. This angle will be the angle for the construction of your gnomon, the triangular piece that casts the shadow on the completed sundial.

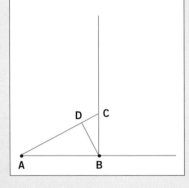

3 Draw a line from point **B** that is perpendicular to the line **AC**, joining **AC** at point **D**.

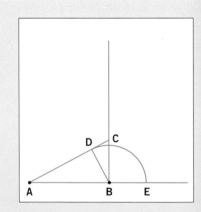

4 Measure the distance from **B** to **D**. Mark this same distance on the horizontal line to the right of **B** to make point **E**. Centre the compasses on point **B** and join points **D** and **E** with a curved line.

Making your sundial

1 Use a photocopier to enlarge or reduce your plan for the sundial to the size of your slate. Place carbon paper on the slate and your drawing on top. Secure the plan with masking tape and draw over the pencilled lines, transferring them to the slate. Make sure that all the angles are accurate.

2 Carefully cut the marked lines in the slate using an angle grinder and a thin-gauge stone-cutting disc. A metal straight edge can be used to help you cut accurate lines.

3 Cut the triangle of 18mm (¾in) slate using the angle grinder with one 90° angle and one angle as calculated in step 2 below. If you do not have an angle grinder ask a stone mason or floor tiler to cut the triangle for you with a large disc diamond cutter.

4 Place the triangle of slate on the 12 noon line of the sundial base, making sure that the calculated angle positioned on the horizontal base line of the grid, and fix it in place with two-part stone adhesive. If you have chosen to use Roman numerals on your sundial, secure them with tile adhesive at the ends of the hour lines, as shown in step 7 below.

5 Your sundial should be situated in an open position and not overshadowed by any trees or buildings. If you live in the northern hemisphere the gnomon (12 noon line) of your sundial must point towards true north. Remember that true north is not the same as magnetic north so do not use a compass. You can locate true north in one of three ways:
i) Use an accurate large-scale survey plan of your location with longitude marked on it to locate north.
ii) Choose a clear night and locate the North (Pole) star. Set the gnomon of your sundial to point at the star.
iii) On a clear sunny day, place a vertical rod on the place you wish to locate your sundial. When the shadow thrown by this rod is at its shortest (in the middle of the day) the shadow is pointing at true north. This will be most accurate on 15 April, 14 June, 1 September and 25 December.

6 When you have located true north, secure your sundial in position on the top of a wall or a plinth, using sand and cement or builder's adhesive.

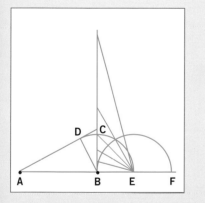

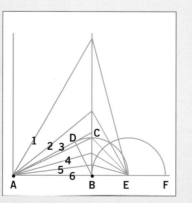

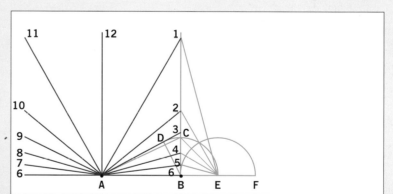

5 Centre the pair of compasses on point **E** and draw a semicircle from point **B** to point **F**. Using a protractor, divide the left half of the semicircle into five 15° sections – accuracy is most important here. Draw lines with a pencil and ruler from point **E** to intersect the vertical line through each of the 15° marks.

6 Connect the points where the lines intersect your vertical line to point **A**. You have now created the afternoon hours for your sundial. Draw a vertical line from point **A** to represent your noon line.

7 To create your morning hour lines, you need to recreate lines, a mirror image of the afternoon ones, to the left of your noon line. The easiest way to achieve this is to make a tracing of the afternoon lines on a sheet of tracing paper. Turn over the sheet so that the lines are repeated to the left of the vertical line at point **A**. Go over the tracing in pencil in order to transpose the markings on to your original plan.

Making a bird box

Nesting boxes come in all shapes and sizes, but this one is a simple closed box, which has been designed to attract a wide variety of garden birds. A 25mm (1in) hole will attract smaller birds, while a 35mm (1¼in) one will appeal to larger nesting birds. The box can be modified to suit birds that prefer an open nesting site by eliminating the hole and cutting away 5cm (2in) from the top of the front panel. It is a misconception that nesting boxes should be fitted with a perch, because most birds will cling to the hole itself or to the rough wood surrounding it. Perches can, in fact, provide access for unwelcome predators to attack the nest.

The box has been constructed from rough-sawn softwood timber and offcut timber, complete with its original bark, obtained from a local sawmill. This barked timber is the largely unwanted side product of many sawmills and can often be secured at little or no cost. The box can as easily be made entirely from rough-sawn softwood timber, planed timber or waterproof plywood.

Materials and equipment

- 35cm (14in) length of 15cm x 12mm (6 x ½in) rough-sawn softwood timber [back]
- About 56cm (22½ in) offcut timber complete with bark, trimmed to 15cm (6in) wide [front and sides]
- 23cm (9in) length of 18cm x 12mm (7 x ½in) rough-sawn softwood timber [roof]
- About 15cm (6in) length of 12cm x 12mm (5 x ½in) rough-sawn softwood timber [base]
- Medium-brown water-based non-toxic preservative wood stain
- Waterproof PVA glue
- 40mm (1½in) cross-head screws
- 2 40mm (1½in) no. 8 round-head solid brass screws
- 15cm (6in) length of 12 x 12mm (½ x ½in) softwood plus three 25mm (1in) cross-head screws, or 15cm (6in) length of 5cm (2in) rubber seal plus 12mm (½in) steel tacks
- Nails or screws, for positioning the box
- 25mm (1in) or 32mm (1¼in) hole cutter
- 2mm (⅙in) drill bit
- Cross-head screwdriver, 25mm (1in) chisel, electric drill, try square, tape measure and hand saw

1 First, cut out and shape the components. Take the back piece and cut off 25mm (1in) triangles from the corners of one short end. Saw the barked timber into three sections: one front piece 16.5cm (6½in) long and two side pieces 20cm (8in) long. Angle the top edge of each side piece, so that there is a slope from 16.5cm (6½in) at the front to 20cm (8in) at the back. Take the roof piece and on one long side cut out a strip of timber, measuring 15cm x 20mm (6 x ¾in), 40mm (1½in) in from either end, using a saw and chisel.

2 Cut the end grain on the top edge of the front section at, approximately, a 15° angle to match the sloping angle of the side pieces. Drill a 25mm (1in) or 35mm (1¼in) hole in the middle of the front piece, 10.5cm (4¼in) from the base. Stain the pieces with non-toxic preservative wood stain making sure that all the cut edges are saturated.

3 Insert the front piece between the two side pieces. Pre-drill two screw holes through each side, then glue and screw the front in place using 40mm (1½in) cross-head screws and making sure that the 15° angle on the top edge of the front is flush with the sloping angle of the sides, to ensure that the nesting box is water- and windproof. Drive the screws into the solid timber so that the heads are concealed within the bark.

4 Fit, glue and screw the back piece within the sides of the box in exactly the same manner, allowing for its straight bottom edge to be flush with the base of the nesting box.

5 Fit the 15 x 12.5cm (6 x 5in) base piece of rough-sawn timber inside the nesting box, flush against the front piece and butting up to the bottom edge of the back piece. Pre-drill screw holes, then glue and screw into place, using two 40mm (1½in) cross-head screws on each side. Fit the roof piece to the top of the box, placing the cut-out over the back piece. Pre-drill one hole in the centre of each side of the roof and, without using glue, screw the roof to the box, using two 40mm (1½in) no. 8 brass screws. To make a waterproof seal between the back and the roof, fit the piece of 12 x 12mm (½ x ½in) softwood on top of the roof using three 25mm (1in) cross-head screws, or secure a 5cm (2in) rubber seal in place with 12mm (½in) steel tacks.

Bird box maintenance

Empty bird boxes should be cleaned out in the autumn or winter. A flip-top lid or sliding base will make this easier. Throw away all the nesting material and brush out the debris with a stiff brush. Leave it open to the air for a few days if possible.

In winter, if there are any signs that birds are roosting in the box – for instance, small birds spotted near the box regularly late in the afternoon, or signs of recent visitors when you open it – wait until they have left in early spring before cleaning out the box.

Reapply preservative wood stain in autumn every couple of years to keep the wood in good condition.

6 To fix your nesting box, use nails or screws. Nesting boxes should be sited in a sheltered position, at least 2m (6ft 6in) above the ground on a wall or tree and away from any overhanging branches, which might otherwise allow cats or other predators to raid the nest. Ideally, a nesting box should be hung facing away from prevailing winds and from the heat of the midday sun.

Making a bird table

The bird table for this project has been designed to fulfil a number of important functions. It is dual-purpose in that it provides a useful nesting box in its roof, it is designed to be suspended in order to keep it out of the reach of marauding cats and it is roofed to keep food dry in wet weather and moist in hot weather.

Its size should prevent it being raided by larger and often unwelcome birds, which will not be able to get in it, and its design ensures that it will be an attractive addition to the garden. In addition, it has a hole in the base to simplify cleaning.

This project calls for a number of different dimensions of timber. Whether you use rough-sawn timber or plywood, you will find that an electric saw table will prove particularly useful in allowing you to cut pieces of wood to the same size accurately.

Materials and equipment

Rough-sawn softwood timber:
- 2.4m (7ft 10in) length of 18cm x 12mm (7 x ½in), cut into:
   4 40cm (15in) lengths [base and roof support frame]
   2 lengths about 38cm (1ft 3in) [roof ends]
- 2.21m (7ft 3in) length of 40 x 12mm (1½ x ½in), cut into:
   Four 23cm (9in) lengths [uprights]
   Two lengths about 34.2cm (13½in)
   Two lengths about 300cm (12in)
- 6.2m (20ft 6in) length of 25 x 12mm (1 x ½in), cut into:
   8 lengths 35cm (14in) [edging for base and roof support frame]
   4 lengths 23cm (9in) [uprights]
   2 lengths 25cm (10in) [roof end supports]
   4 lengths 20cm (8in) [roofing strips supports]
   4 lengths of about 29cm (11½in) [barge boards]
   75cm (2ft 6in) length of 10cm x 12mm (4 x ½in) [decorative frieze]
- 2.76m (8ft 6in) length of 10cm x 6mm (4 x ¼in), cut into 6 lengths of approx. 42cm (1ft 5in) [roofing strips]
- Waterproof PVA glue
- 25mm (1in) panel pins
- Four 40mm (1½in) brass- or zinc-plated steel screw eyes
- Four 915mm (3 ft) lengths of 10mm (3/8in) ramin doweling
- Eight 40mm (1½in) brass- or zinc-plated steel cup hooks
- 65mm (2½in) galvanized metal hook
- Water-based non-toxic preservative wood stain

1 Make up the base of the table by gluing together, side by side, two of the 40cm (16in) lengths of timber. Secure them with four of the 35cm (14in) long edging pieces, glued and nailed with their edges flush to the edges of the base, to form a 40 x 35cm (16 x 14in) base frame. Repeat with the other two 40cm (16in) lengths of timber and the remaining four pieces of edging to make the roof support frame. Drill a 35mm (1¼in) drainage hole 40mm (1½in) away from one of the base frame's corners.

2 Join the frames at each corner, the flat unframed sides facing each other, with corner supports made from the four 23cm (9in) lengths of 40 x 12mm (1½ x ½in) and the four 23cm (9in) lengths of 25 x 12mm (1 x ½in) timber, using glue and 25mm (1in) panel pins. Fit the 25mm (1in) wide upright pieces on the long sides of the frames, flush with the corners, and overlap the 12mm (½in) width with the 40mm (1½in) wide upright pieces pinned and glued to the short sides of the frames so that the face of each corner support is roughly 40mm (1½in) wide.

3 Fix a 25cm (10in) length of 25 x 12mm (1 x ½in) timber on top of the edging on the two short sides of the roof frame (the one without the drainage hole) with glue and 25mm (1in) panel pins. Measure between the newly fixed corner supports (about 35cm (14in) for the long sides and 30cm (12in) for the ends of the frames) and cut 40 x 12mm (1½ x ½in) timber to fit. Fix to the four sides of the base frame, using glue and panel pins to conceal the edging.

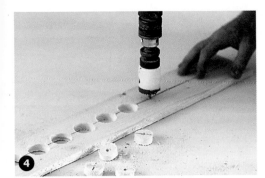

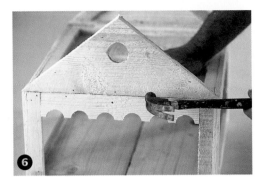

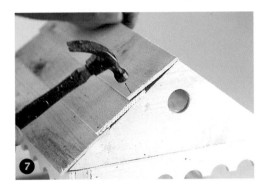

4 To make the decorative frieze, take the 75cm (30in) length of 10cm x 12mm (4 x ½in) timber and draw a line lengthways along the centre of the timber. Mark points along this line at 5cm (2in) intervals starting about 25mm (1in) from one end. Drill holes through the timber using a 35mm (1¼in) hole cutter.

5 Saw along the line through the holes to make two 75 x 5cm (30 x 2in) strips. Cut each strip in two (making four lengths) to fit between the corner uprights, flush with the roof frame. Secure the decorative frieze with glue and panel pins.

6 Cut two triangles approximately 38cm (15in) long by 15cm (6in) high from 175 x 12mm (7 x ½in) timber to make the two roof ends. Drill a 35mm (1¼in) hole in one piece 6.5cm (2½in) from the apex of the triangle. Fix two 20cm (8in) lengths of 25 x 12mm (1 x ½in) timber to the sloping sides of each triangle, flush with the edges and mitred at the top of the triangle to fit the apex – these will be inside each roof end to provide support for the roofing strips. Fix the roof ends to the roof frame, gluing and nailing them to the 25cm (10in) roof end supports previously fitted.

7 Measure the length of the bird table between the roof ends – about 42cm (17in) and fit three lengths of 10cm x 6mm (4 x ¼in) timber or plywood for the roofing each side of the roof, fixing them to the roofing supports with glue and panel pins. Starting at the bottom, fix the first strip to overhang the bird table edge by approximately 12mm (½in); overlap the remaining two roofing strips to finish flush with the apex of the roof. Repeat on the other pitch of the roof, making the final strip overlap the top strip on the first side for a tightly sealed roof, which will keep out the rain.

8 To conceal the gaps where the roof strips overlap, fix two barge boards, about 29cm/11½in long each end, made from 25 x 12mm (1 x ½in) timber and mitred at the apex to fit. Secure these to the roof ends with glue and panel pins. Cut two decorative finials from offcuts of timber and use to cover the joint in the barge boards at the apex at each end of the roof, securing them with glue and panel pins. Use your imagination to decide on a pattern for your finials to give your bird table an individual look.

9 Lastly, insert four 40mm (1½in) brass- or zinc-plated screw eyes into the corners of the bird table roof. Take the four lengths of ramin dowelling and drill a 3mm (⅛in) hole in the end grain of each. Dab glue on to the eight cup hooks and insert one in each end of the lengths of dowelling. Allow the glue to dry.

10 To complete your bird table, paint it and the dowelling rods with a preservative wood stain. Allow to dry and then attach each piece of dowelling to the bird table by placing the cup hooks through the screw eyes fixed to the roof.

11 Finally, screw a 6.5cm (2½in) galvanized metal hook into a suitable branch or overhang, where the bird table will be well out of the way of any cats or other predators. Hang the bird table from the cup hooks, fed through the galvanized metal hook. Chain may be used instead to hang the bird table but dowelling does help the stability.

WATER
FEATURES

Choosing water features

Very few of us have a natural stream or spring just waiting to be landscaped into a pond: most of us have to start from scratch, but it's well worth the effort. Whether it be a formal raised pond on the patio, a wildlife pool at the foot of the garden, a bubbling cobble fountain or a rocky waterfall, a water feature is guaranteed to add another dimension of enjoyment to your garden.

From a design point of view water is an amazing surface to use, since it varies constantly. A still sheet of water gives a peaceful air to the garden and provides mirror images of the changing sky, but when a breeze stirs the surface of the pool, the whole picture changes. Moving water gives varying patterns and colours as sunlight plays upon it, as well as introducing sound. From a slow steady drip on to rocks to a roaring torrent from a fountain or waterfall, the possibilities for creating sound with water are endless.

Choosing a style

The most important thing to do before any earth is turned is to sit down and think why you want a water feature, the style you want, where you want it and the shape. Once you have an idea clearly in your mind, go ahead and create the feature you want.

The shape and style of your water feature will depend on the garden design you have chosen and should reflect the theme of your garden, enhancing its overall style, rather than introducing a new element. A symmetrical pool can really add to the austere serenity of a formal garden while an asymmetric pool will enhance an informal design. Interlinking circles, a single large rectangle, small pools linked by streams: it is up to you. As long as the water feature you choose suits the garden and is safe, the only limit to its design is your imagination.

Formal pools

A formal pool is often the ideal option for a small garden where there is little or no lawn and the surface is dominated by paving. The formal pool has clearly defined, crisp edges, which are generally paved and form regular, geometric shapes. The planting is restrained, confined mainly in aquatic planting containers, and dominated by specimen plants that have bold upright leaves, such as irises, which create a strong vertical contrast to the even, horizontal surface of the water.

Informal ponds

The priority in planning an informal pond is to blend it into the style of the garden, whether it is an existing one or a new creation. This type of pond would have strong appeal to the plantsperson, offering considerable scope for lush planting that may not be possible in other parts of the garden. The boundaries of the pond could be extended to a bog area, so allow space for this at the planning stage.

Raised pools

These are similar to formal pools in their suitability for small spaces and being surrounded by paving. For small or patio gardens surrounded by high fences or walls, they introduce reflected light to counteract any feeling of claustrophobia. One of the great pleasures of a raised pool is to be able to sit on the pool surround and enjoy the

Types of liner

- **Rigid liners** are made from fibreglass in a fairly wide range of shapes and sizes. They are very tough and, if installed properly, virtually leakproof.
- **Semi-rigid liners** are made from vacuum-formed plastic. They are cheaper than rigid liners but are nowhere near as strong. You would probably be better off using a flexible liner.
- **Flexible liners** may be made from PVC reinforced with nylon or from butyl rubber. Of the two, the butyl version is the stronger and will often be guaranteed for 20 years, although it may last much longer than that – perhaps for as long as 50 years.

LEFT A brick-edged circular pool with a classical fountain would usually be thought of as formal, but here it strikes just the right note nestling in front of a vibrant mixed border.

prey on them, while also increasing the scope for planting. Animals that come to visit your pond will often reward you by devouring pests. Hedgehogs, toads and frogs eat slugs, snails and insects, while birds that come to bathe and drink also rid the garden of harmful soil pests and insects.

A pool can be large or small. Even the tiniest pool in a barrel will attract insects and allow you to grow some aquatic plants. A large pool allows you to create areas for marginals and bog plants, deep-water plants, free-floating aquatics and oxygenators. You can even create a beach area to allow animals to come and drink and also allow them an escape route if they fall in. Hedgehogs and badgers can swim but some drown because they cannot escape.

Pools and children

If you have young children or pets, it may be better to build a raised pool or a bubble fountain. Avoid pools with overhanging rims with deep water below. Instead, have a shallow 'beach' of pebbles in a more natural-looking pool. If you really want a formal-edged pool, probably the easiest solution is to place bricks or blocks near the edge just below the surface of the water to form steps.

water at close quarters. Raised pools combined with a fountain are very suitable for fish because the fountain spray oxygenates the water in the summer months.

ABOVE This simple rectangular pool makes a perfect link between shrubby border and stone-edged lawn.

BELOW A carefully sited cascade leading into a pool can add interest to a garden by introducing different levels of planting and the sound of water.

Ponds for fish

If you aim to keep fish in a pond it is important to resolve the practical issues of good fish husbandry at the initial planning stage in order to avoid problems when the fish are introduced. The serious fish-keeper's requirements are vastly different from those of the plantsperson. The design needs to allow for an increase in the amount of equipment, such as pumps and filters as the fish increase in size and number, as well as easy cleaning on a regular basis. Small fish grow into big fish, particularly if koi carp are chosen, and large koi are not the most suitable partners for ornamental water plants. Oxygenating plants that may be adequate for a small ornamental pond will not supply the needs of big fish.

Water and wildlife

Nothing attracts wildlife and appeals to all ages quite like a water feature. Water is the essence of life and brings to a garden vibrant insect visitors and the animals that

Safety measures

The question of whether it is safe to have a pond if young children use the garden poses a serious dilemma for parents or carers. No area of open water, no matter how shallow, can be considered entirely safe and a pool may have to be deferred for a while. In the meantime, this postponement can be made easier and more interesting by creating a water-sympathetic feature that could be developed to incorporate water at a later date. A dry scree bed leading into an area of cobbles would simulate a watery environment, which could subsequently become a stream and pond. Similarly, a sand pit could be built on the site of the future pond. Inexpensive polythene used to line a shallow excavation could be recycled as an underlay for the pool.

ABOVE Safety grids need not be dull: this striking modern example is on a waterlily theme.

BELOW This large ceramic urn is a safe water feature as there is little opportunity for an infant to fall in.

A more difficult situation is faced by a family with very young children that has moved to a new home where an existing pool makes an outstanding contribution to the garden. Draining the pool and filling it with sand to provide a safe play area may provide a temporary answer, but a more aesthetic solution may be to fence off the pool with an attractive picket fence and a lockable gate. In either case, the time will soon come when it is considered safe enough to fill the old pool with water or remove the fence. Even so, some safety measures may still be prudent. In this situation, there are a number of ways to make a pond a safer feature.

Grading edges

Many pools in rural areas are remnants of old dew ponds, which are pools formed by puddling clay or digging out to the water table. These pools often have edges that fall sharply into the water, particularly in the summer months as the pool level sinks. This type of edge holds significant danger, with youngsters running towards the pond and losing a foothold at the water's edge. This hazard can be reduced by regrading the edge to a gentle slope, so that the water surface can be seen from some distance away rather than being hidden from view until the very last moment.

Play features

A cobblestone fountain with a gurgling jet is a great source of fun for children as well as making an attractive garden feature. Construction is explained in detail on pages 178, and provided the supporting mesh for the cobbles is strong enough, there is no danger of falling in. A simple spray fountain that children can run through is a further refinement of the cobble fountain; in this instance the grid for the reservoir is fine enough to support a smaller grade of rounded pebble, which it is easier to walk and run on. On a modern note, other visually exciting features, like water running in a sheet down a perspex wall into a concealed reservoir, or a shallow rill of less than 2.5cm (1in) of water in the lawn in which paper boats can sail are also child-friendly.

Gentle gradients around a pond leading to shallow, sloping submerged margins not only make it safer but more inviting by creating a greater sense of space. The pond will appear less deep and forbidding with no shadow at the water's edge. The design of any new informal pool surrounded by grass should allow for this restful grading for a short distance beyond the edges rather than a level area that suddenly changes to a steep edge at the pool's edge.

Something else to avoid is mounding the soil excavated in the making of the pool around the immediate margins, thereby leaving a distinct hump. This not only looks unnatural but, more importantly, creates the danger of a steep slope immediately next to the water.

Surfacing edges

The surface of any hard edge around a pool should be non-slip for the safety of all age groups. The most lethal edging is old, reclaimed stone paving slabs, which attract algae and become slippery when wet. If natural stone must be used, choose a stone with a riven surface for any paving slabs and keep them clear of algae. Many concrete paving slabs are manufactured with roughened, non-slip surfaces, and these can make good surrounds for the immediate edges of a formal pool.

Timber decking is now more widely used, but always make sure that it has a non-slip, ribbed surface. Wet timber is just as hazardous as natural stone, and smooth-planed surfaces are not intended for walking on. Decking tiles, which are laid with ribbed timbers in order to create a chequerboard effect, are also helpful in reducing the danger of slipping on wet, slimy wood.

Plant barriers

A natural physical barrier can be created by thick planting in the pool margins and around the sides, to help prevent a fall into the water. This planting may limit the view of the pool while it is in place but it can be moved when the children grow up. The vegetation is most effective if it is thick and woody at the outer edges up to the pond margins, where the sappier, softer leaves should then predominate.

Dogwoods (*Cornus*) and bushy willows (*Salix*) make good barriers where the soil is moist, but the range can be extended to other thicket-forming shrubs in drier soils. The design of wildlife pools, with their shallow beaches and thick vegetation around the sides, makes them good examples of relatively safe pools for gardens where children will be playing.

Using a protective grid

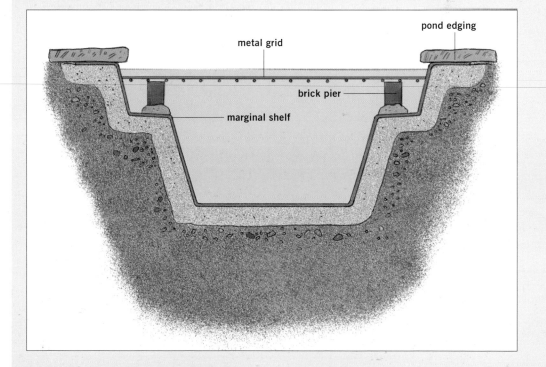

A very small pond can be covered with a strong galvanized metal grid, which can be disguised by growing several marginal plants through it. These grids are available at builder's merchants, where they are sold primarily for reinforcing concrete floors and paths. Their average size is approximately 2 x 1.2m (6½ x 4ft), so they are adequate for a pond smaller than this where the grid will overlap the edges.

For larger ponds, a grid can be supported on piers inside the pool, enabling several panels of the grid to be butted together. If there are marginal shelves around the pool, the piers supporting the grid can be inside the pool, built on the marginal shelf, and need be no higher than two or three bricks. Longer piers would be necessary inside the deeper areas of the pool.

An alternative way to conceal a protective grid if it is sited just below the water surface is to arrange cobbles on it in the same way as a cobblestone fountain – see page 178 for full instructions.

Raised and semi-raised ponds

In a raised pond, the whole body of the pool sits above ground level, whereas in a semi-raised pool the lower part is sunk into the ground. Semi-raised pools are particularly useful on sloping sites, where one side can nestle into the hillside while the other stands above it as the ground slopes away.

For raised ponds, in particular, you must bear in mind that the walls will have to be able to withstand the entire outward pressure of the water. For example, a pool with internal dimensions of 1 x 2m (about 3 x 6ft filled to a depth of 50cm (20in) will contain 1000 litres (220 gallons) of water weighing 1 tonne (more than 2000lb). This means that any structure surrounding a raised pool – whether timber, brick or concrete – must be supported by strong foundations and be well built. If you are in any doubt, get an expert to help.

Flexible liners can easily be used in raised pools, but preformed units are not really practical for any but the smallest because they are prone to cracking if not completely and evenly supported.

ABOVE While this garden would not be particularly practical for either children or elderly people, its broad coping stones make ideal seating.

In semi-raised ponds, more of the outward pressure of the water is absorbed by the ground, so rigid units do become a more practical proposition for small pools on level ground.

The materials used to build raised or semi-raised pools depend largely on the style of the garden, but there are some practical considerations to bear in mind. Brick, concrete or railway sleepers would suit a pool on a patio, as long as proper foundations could be laid. Always use a double thickness wall. Log roll is not usually used on patios because the pointed stakes that support it have to be driven deep into the earth and it is, in any case, a more appropriate material for an informal pool.

Semi-raised log roll surround ponds

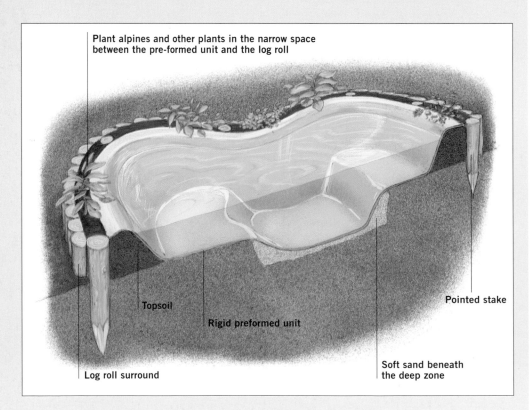

Plant alpines and other plants in the narrow space between the pre-formed unit and the log roll

Topsoil

Rigid preformed unit

Pointed stake

Soft sand beneath the deep zone

Log roll surround

Electricity and water

There is an understandable reluctance to introduce cables carrying mains current to a pond. However, the risk of electrical shock has been almost totally eliminated by the application of residual current devices (RCDs), also known as contact circuit breakers, which are fitted to any electrical equipment outdoors where there is a danger of accidentally earthing mains voltage. These are extremely sensitive trip switches that are able to cut off the supply within 30 milliseconds of a possible earth leakage.

Although there are a number of electrical pond accessories, such as pond lighting, which are made safer by operating on low voltage using a transformer, the reduced voltage is not powerful enough to operate pumps for fountains more than 1m (39in) in height, and the majority of these still operate on mains voltage. It is therefore advisable to note the following guidelines before installing electrical equipment.

- Use a qualified electrician for advice on both equipment and installation.
- Protect against accidental shock by installing an RCD at the connection to the mains voltage in the house, even if low-voltage accessories are used. If mains cabling is to be taken across the garden, use armoured cabling sunk to a depth of 30–60cm (12–24in) under the soil and mark the position of the cable by covering it with roof tiles and warning tape.
- Use only approved waterproof junction boxes or switches to connect the mains cable to the cable supplied with the equipment. Position these where they are unlikely to be flooded.
- Keep a record of where any underground cables are located.

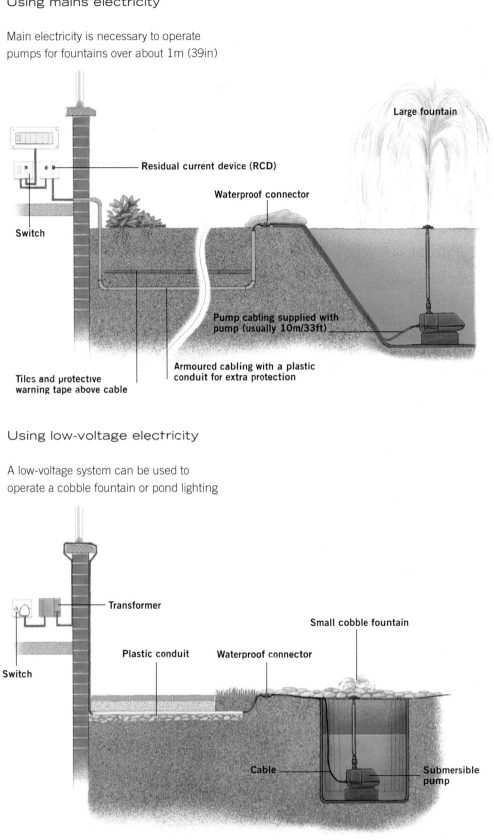

Using mains electricity

Main electricity is necessary to operate pumps for fountains over about 1m (39in)

Large fountain

Residual current device (RCD)

Waterproof connector

Switch

Pump cabling supplied with pump (usually 10m/33ft)

Armoured cabling with a plastic conduit for extra protection

Tiles and protective warning tape above cable

Using low-voltage electricity

A low-voltage system can be used to operate a cobble fountain or pond lighting

Transformer

Small cobble fountain

Plastic conduit

Waterproof connector

Switch

Cable

Submersible pump

Siting a water feature

Before taking the final step of choosing a site for a pond or other water feature, there are some guidelines relating to its size, relative dimensions and profile that need to be considered.

Size

The general rule with a pond is the bigger, the better. This is because the larger the pool, the easier it is to manage as time goes on. In addition, most pool owners will admit to wishing they had built a larger pool because they do not have room for new plants or their fish have outgrown the pool.

The smaller the pool, the more likely it is to have problems of green water, excessive temperature fluctuation and inadequate oxygen for the fish. If possible, try to achieve a minimum surface area of 4.5–5.5 square metres (50–60 square feet).

Proportions and profile

Size is linked to depth. No matter how large the surface area is, if the pool is only 15cm (6in) deep, it will be a disaster. The ideal depth for a medium-sized pond with a surface area of 4.5–18.5 square metres (50–200 square feet) is 60cm (24in). Ponds less than 4.5 square metres (50 square feet) in area may be 38–45cm (15–18in) deep. Ponds larger than 18.5 square metres (200 square feet) would benefit from a depth of 75cm (30in). The reason for these guidelines is related to the needs of green algae. Algae thrive in warm, shallow water in full sunshine. Deeper water allows for a greater volume of water that is not in the susceptible top 15cm (6in), where the algae thrive in the warmer and lighter conditions. The larger water volume also acts as a buffer to rapid and frequent temperature fluctuations, which are detrimental to many forms of pond life.

The relationship of depth to surface area is valid only when a pool has almost vertical side walls. Pools with a saucer-shaped profile or marginal shelves all the way round the sides have a reduced volume, so increase the depth of the centre to compensate.

Siting the feature

With the concerns of size and profile in mind, the process of selecting the site for your water feature can begin. It might appear obvious to put a formal pool on the patio near the house or an informal pool at the lowest point of the garden, but to ensure that the best possible location is identified, the following points should be taken into account.

Shade

The pond should receive enough sunshine to warm the water and bathe the submerged plants in adequate light. The range of aquatic plants that can be grown in shaded pools is quite limited, and waterlilies are reluctant to flower in these conditions.

Shade from overhanging trees is particularly troublesome because it is associated with leaf fall, which leads to a thick layer of decomposing vegetation on the pond bottom. As this vegetation decomposes, methane gas is produced, and this is harmful to fish. It is especially important to prevent the leaves of yew, holly and laburnum sinking to the pond bottom since they are poisonous to other plant and animal life in the water. Although conifers may seem to be less of a problem, their leaves are constantly falling and depositing fine dusty bud scales on the water surface.

Wind

Wind cools the water surface, blows fountain spray and damages the soft, succulent stems of marginal plants. In an attempt to capture the maximum amount of sun in a small garden, the pool is often sited in the centre of the lawn, where it is more prone to wind exposure. Shelter can be provided by a trellis or planting on the pool's windward side.

ABOVE These elegant twin ponds are staggered to lead the eye across to the far end of the garden and encourage you to walk up the flagstone path.

Frost

Cold air accumulates in low-lying pockets, making plants more susceptible to browning by spring frosts. Informal ponds are often sited in low-lying areas because that is where they look more natural, making them more liable to frost damage. The pond should be sited slightly higher up the slope.

Sloping ground

A steep slope need not be too much of a constraint if the pond is partially dug out of the bank and partially banked up on the lower side. The outline of the pool needs to be slender and follow the contours of the slope.

A pond at the bottom of a slope is prone to frost damage and to run-off from the slope in heavy rain. If the surrounding grass has been treated with fertilizer, which then leaches into the pond from the run-off, it can result in a sudden and dramatic growth of green algae in the pond as a consequence of the increase in nutrients. Drainage channels should be constructed where prolonged heavy rain or flash flooding is common.

Water table

The water table is the level at which water will stand in a ground hole or well. Most water tables are well below the level at which a pond will be dug, but occasionally it may be a problem on wet, heavy land. A test to check if there is a high water table can be carried out by digging a hole 60–90cm (24–36in) deep and leaving it for a day or two to see if water appears in the hole. If water lies near the surface, there could be problems, since pond liners can billow up to the pool surface as a result of water pressure from the water table beneath.

Underground hazards

Once you have narrowed down your siting options, it is vital to ensure that the pool will not be positioned over the route of underground services such as drains, gas pipes, water pipes, electricity cables and telephone cables. If there is any doubt over their route, contact the appropriate supply company, which will have the equipment to pinpoint the underground line.

Where to site your pond

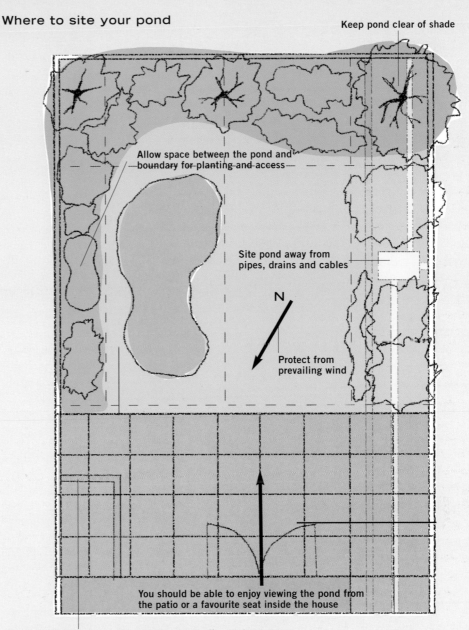

Keep pond clear of shade

Allow space between the pond and boundary for planting and access

Site pond away from pipes, drains and cables

N

Protect from prevailing wind

You should be able to enjoy viewing the pond from the patio or a favourite seat inside the house

Some services (such as electricity) can enter the garden from a different source and may make right angle turns

Fine-tuning the site

The ideal site will probably be a compromise. For instance, high on your list of priorities may well be the ability to see the feature from a frequently used window of your home. Your choice may also be influenced by the desire to position the pool so that features, such as garden ornaments and trees, are reflected in the water. Sketching a siting plan that identifies shade, prevailing wind direction, services and viewing lines from the windows is a useful step towards preparing a shortlist of possible sites before taking out a hosepipe to lay on the ground. Place a full-length mirror laid flat on the ground inside the circumference of the pipe to simulate the effect of the water surface and see what reflections appear. A movement of 60–90cm (24–36in) on the ground makes a great difference to the angle of reflection and how well the feature is framed.

Having identified the optimum site, decide how important an electricity supply is at the pool side. If a pump is vital and the distance makes this prohibitive in terms of cost, it may mean a final alteration to the site.

Preformed ponds

A preformed pond is the ideal choice for creating a pool with a symmetrical shape. There are two types of preformed pond – the rigid forms, which are made of fibreglass or reinforced plastic, and the thinner semi-rigid forms, made from a cheaper plastic, which is moulded into sophisticated shapes under a vacuum process. Both types are more effective when prefabricated into simple shapes rather than having over-fussy or narrow outlines. Square, rectangular and circular shapes make it easier to pave around the edge and disguise the unit. The stronger units are easy to clean out and repair if necessary, and their shiny surfaces make it a simple task to remove algae.

Rigid and semi-rigid pools are relatively easy to install compared to installing a flexible liner, which involves folding in tight corners. Rigid pools are also very useful on a sloping site where one end of the unit is strong enough to be partially raised and disguised with either soil or a retaining wall. Semi-rigid pools are not suitable for sloping sites.

Most rigid pools have preformed shelves, usually 23cm (9in) deep, around the sides, and these enable aquatic planting baskets to be housed in the shallower water. When the containers are closely packed together on the shelves, the plants blend with each other, giving an informal and established appearance in a short period of time.

In general, preformed ponds are less appropriate for informal pools, particularly those versions that have irregular, slender outlines and several shelves at different heights, because these reduce the overall volume, making the water prone to

ABOVE The broad coping slabs both conceal the unit and provide an attractive finish to this formal pool surrounded with plants.

greening. It is vital to ensure they have a minimum depth of 45cm (18in); units shallower than this will be vulnerable to rapid temperature changes and unsuitable for fish in hot summers or cold winters.

Preformed ponds become extremely heavy when full and are subjected to considerable water pressure. If the

Excavation

1 In order to mark out the site for a symmetrically shaped preformed pool, invert the unit on to the proposed site and run a line of sand around the edge of the rim.

2 For asymmetrical shapes, stand the unit upright on the proposed site and temporarily support it with bricks or walling blocks to prevent it from falling over. Push canes from the rim into the soil directly beneath the unit at about 1m (39in) intervals. Run a length of string around the canes to mark the outline, which can then be marked out using sand.

3 Measure the depth of the unit from the rim to the bottom of the marginal shelf. Remove the soil down to this depth from 5–7.5cm (2–3in) outside the outline.

4 Lightly rake and level the dug surface. Place the unit in the prepared hole and press it down firmly on to the raked surface so that an impression is made of the base. Lift out the unit, then dig from 5–7.5cm (2–3in) outside the area marked by the unit base.

5 When the depth of the unit plus an extra 5–7.5cm (2–3in) for a layer of soft sand has been

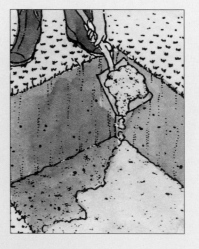

reached, lay the straight-edged length of wood across the width of the hole and with a tape measure check that the hole depth is correct. Make sure that the base of the hole is level by using a spirit level.

6 Rake over the base and sides of the whole to remove tree roots and sharp stones, and firm the base evenly. Then spread a layer of sand across the bottom.

Installing a preformed pond

Materials and equipment

- Sand, bamboo canes and string for marking out
- Preformed pool unit
- Bricks or walling blocks for temporarily supporting an asymmetrically shaped unit
- Tape measure
- Spade
- Wheelbarrow
- Rake
- Soft sand or sifted soil
- Straight-edged length of wood, long enough to straddle the sides of the unit
- Spirit level
- Flat-ended length of wood, 5 x 5 x 60cm (2 x 2 x 24in), for tamping the soil
- Suitable edging materials

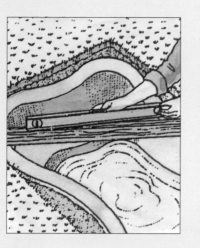

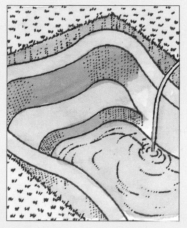

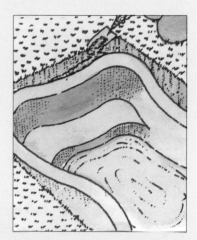

1 Enlist help to lower the unit into the hole. Check that it is sitting level by laying the straight-edged length of wood across the unit sides and using a spirit level.

2 Gently pour water into the unit to a depth of 10cm (4in), then backfill with sand or sifted soil between the sides of the unit and the sides of the hole to the same depth as the water. Use the flat-ended length of wood to ram down the backfilling. This process is known as tamping.

3 Repeat this procedure by adding a further 10cm (4in) depth of water to the unit, then 10cm (4in) of sand or sifted soil around the sides at a time, ensuring that no air pockets are left in the backfilling and the unit continues to remain dead level, until the pool is nearly full and the weight of the water will keep it stable. After this the edging can be put in place.

excavation does not support their shape evenly the varying stresses in different parts of the unit can cause hairline cracks in the cheaper versions, which are difficult to detect once the pool is filled with water. Bear in mind that preformed ponds look deceptively large when displayed on their sides at a garden centre and much smaller once sunk into the ground.

Preformed pond units, especially the semi-rigid types, are vulnerable to cracking if ice is allowed to form over the whole surface. A solid layer of ice will also trap poisonous gases underneath it, which if they are not allowed to escape, might kill fish. To prevent this, use a floating pond heater or, if ice does form, make a hole it by placing a pan of hot water on the ice until it melts. Do not try to crack the ice.

RIGHT Simple shapes of preformed pond work better than fussier outlines, especially for informal pools, where the emphasis is on the planting.

Flexible liner ponds

Flexible liners provide the greatest scope for different shapes and designs of pool. They can be used entirely on their own to create informal ponds on heavy soils, or in combination with concrete or walling blocks to secure the sides of the excavation for formal pools. Flexible liners are also invaluable for waterproofing old concrete pools that have sprouted hairline cracks.

Flexible liners are available in a variety of materials, colours and thicknesses, sold from rolls of varying widths or welded to specific sizes for larger applications. The choice of material will depend on available resources and the style of the pool. The most expensive is butyl and the cheapest is polythene, and between these two types there is a range of excellent materials

ABOVE Flexible liners are particularly suitable for use in creating natural-looking wildlife ponds, like this small stone-edged example.

LEFT Interestingly shaped informal pools can be created using butyl rubber, which is easier to mould into corners than older plastic types of flexible liner.

suitable for most applications. Reducing the size of the pool in order to buy the most expensive liner is not recommended. If the liner is to be covered with soil or other materials, such as cobbles, the more inexpensive varieties are perfectly adequate since they will not deteriorate through exposure to ultraviolet light.

Where different colours are available, choose black – it looks more natural and gives the illusion of greater depth.

Underlays

Protective underlays for pond liners are now widely available in the form of rolls of non-woven geotextiles, which are impenetrable by even the sharpest of stones. These have replaced sand or newspaper, sand being unstable on the sides of the excavation and newspaper eventually rotting under the liner and exposing it to sharp objects as the weight of the pool settles the soil underneath.

Using flexible liners

Flexible liners offer the maximum amount of flexibility in the construction of ponds and other water features. There is a good case for completing all the necessary excavations before purchasing the liner. By completing the digging first, there are no limitations on making last-minute adjustments to the shape and depth of the pool, although if you wish to avoid going to the trouble of getting the liner welded or stuck together you should bear in mind the size of liner you are intending to buy (see How much liner? below). After the excavation, move well away from the site and view it from as many angles as possible to see if any adjustments would be an improvement.

One rectangle of liner can provide a variety of pond shapes, including designs with narrow waists to make a crossing point for added interest. Where the wastage of liner would be excessive for very narrow sections, smaller pieces can be welded together at specialist suppliers or taped together on site using proprietary waterproof joining tape. While large creases in the corners of rectangular pools or sharp curves in informal shapes are inevitable, they can be made to look less conspicuous if the liner is carefully folded before the pool is filled. With time, the covering of algae and submerged planting will disguise the folds of the liner even further.

How much liner?

Measure a rectangle that will enclose the outline of the pool. Measure the maximum length and breadth of the pool, then add twice the depth of the pool to each measurement. This is the bare minimum of liner required, so add 30cm (12in) to each measurement to provide a small overlap. For brimming pools, add a little more than the width of the paving or bricks that surround the pool so that the liner can extend beneath the edging to create a vertical lip behind it.

Types of flexible liner

	Pros	Cons
Polythene (Polyethylene)	• The oldest type of pool liner, developed in the 1930s • Available in different thicknesses (only the thickest grades are suitable for lining ponds) and roll widths • Cheap	• Deteriorates in ultraviolet light by hardening or cracking, making it the least durable liner • Unwieldy to handle • Easily torn • Separate pieces cannot be joined • Cannot be repaired • Life expectancy of 3–5 years • No guarantees usually given
Low density polythene	• A recently developed and improved form of polythene that is becoming more widely available • More flexible than standard polythene • Difficult to tear • Can be repaired • Extremely slow deterioration in ultraviolet light, giving a life expectancy of 15–30 years • Guarantees available for 15–30 years • Cheaper than alternative liners	• Separate pieces cannot be joined
PVC	• Developed from a new generation of polymers in the 1960s • Available in different thicknesses and densities • Certain grades laminated and reinforced with nylon netting for extra strength • Separate pieces can be joined • Can be repaired • Longer durability than ordinary polythene, with a minimum life expectancy of 15–20 years • Most grades supplied with guarantees • Variable in cost	• Heavy-duty types are not very malleable or flexible
Butyl	• Developed about the same time as PVC and still remains the most commonly used liner for the professional • Available in various thicknesses • Its elasticity gives it more strength than other liners and it fits awkward shapes more easily • Easily extended by welding, which can be done on site if required • Easily repaired; bicycle inner-tube repair kits can be used • Resistant to ultraviolet light • Long life-expectancy – at least 50 years • Most suppliers give a guarantee of a minimum of 20 years	• Costly

Constructing a pond using a flexible liner

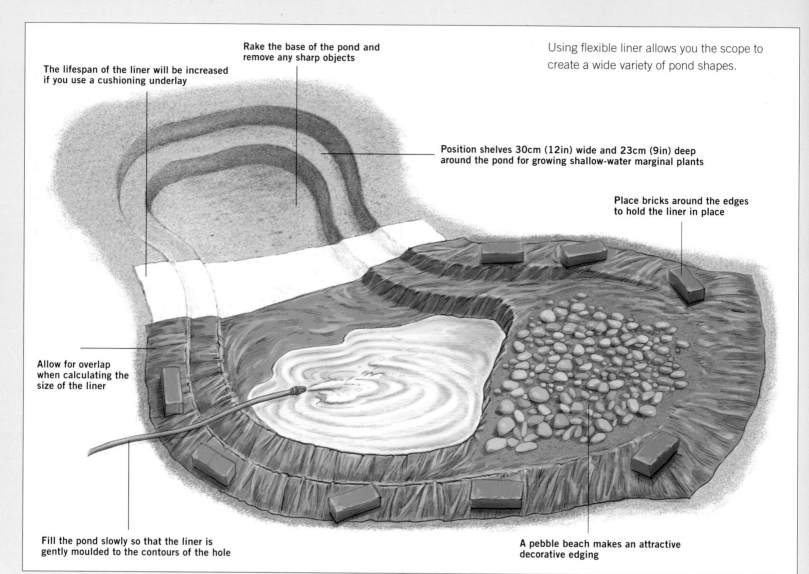

The lifespan of the liner will be increased if you use a cushioning underlay

Rake the base of the pond and remove any sharp objects

Using flexible liner allows you the scope to create a wide variety of pond shapes.

Position shelves 30cm (12in) wide and 23cm (9in) deep around the pond for growing shallow-water marginal plants

Place bricks around the edges to hold the liner in place

Allow for overlap when calculating the size of the liner

Fill the pond slowly so that the liner is gently moulded to the contours of the hole

A pebble beach makes an attractive decorative edging

Excavation

Mark the pond outline using a hosepipe or string and pegs. If the pond is to be sited in a lawn, remove the turf and use a lawn edger to make a neat edge to the remaining turf. Knock in a series of wooden pegs around the pond about 15cm (6in) out from the outline at 60cm (2ft) intervals. The pegs need to be sufficiently close so that a straight-edged length of wood can straddle the adjacent pegs.

Make a mark on one peg at the desired level of the surface of the finished pond. This is known as the datum peg. Use the straightedge and a spirit level to mark the other pegs to match, so that any variations in level around the outline can be seen and

adjusted by adding or removing topsoil. Begin digging the hole 15cm (6in) inside the pegs to a depth of 23cm (9in), angling the sides inwards slightly. This reduces the risk of damage to the pool by expanding ice in severe winters and of the walls subsiding. Rake the base of the excavation, then use sand to mark the position of any marginal shelves around the perimeter of the hole. These shelves should be 30cm (12in) wide and positioned where you want to plant shallow-water plants.

Dig the inner or deeper zone inside the sand marks, avoiding the marginal shelf outlines, to the full depth of the pond – a further 23cm (9in) if the pond is to be

45cm (18in) deep or a further 38cm (15in) if the pond is to be 60cm (24in) deep.

Rake the bottom of the pond to level the surface and gently rake over the sides and bottom to remove any sharp stones or protruding objects. Line the hole with a 2.5cm (1in) layer of damp sand if the ground is rough or rocky.

If you are planning a grass edge to the pond where people might walk, it might be an idea to strengthen it by making a wider marginal shelf and mortaring a course of walling stones on top of the liner under where the grass edge will be.

RIGHT This eclectic pond, with a Japanese water feature echoing the sphere on the plinth behind, has been given a variety of edging materials. The liner has been disguised on the far side by rocks and around the sides by planting.

Liner installation

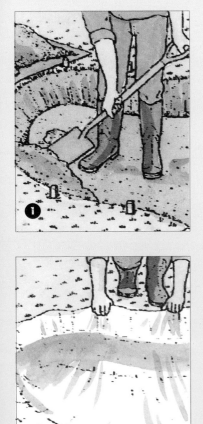

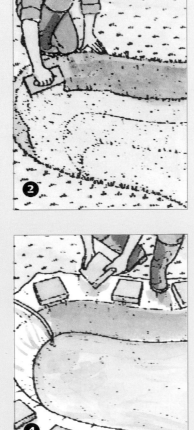

1 Mark out the pool and use a series of wooden pegs to determine whether the site is level (see Excavation, opposite). Dig down in even layers, incorporating a marginal shelf if you like.

2 Using a plasterer's float, line the hole with a 2.5cm (1in) layer of damp sand, making sure it sticks to the walls of the hole.

3 Spread out the liner on any lawn area adjacent to the excavation to warm up in the sun, thereby smoothing out any creases and making it more pliable to work with. Then drape the underlay across the hole and surrounding shelves, leaving an overlap of approximately 30cm (12in) all round the pool. Arrange the liner in position on top, making sure it is centred and overlaps the sides of the pool.

4 Drape the liner into the pond, working it carefully into the shape of the hole and making sure it overlaps the edges all round. Creases inevitably appear, but try to keep them to a minimum. Place bricks or heavy stones around the edges to hold the liner in place and prevent the wind from blowing the edges into the pool. Then fill the pool three-quarters full with water and remove the bricks or stones holding the edges of the liner.

5 Build or add any edging before filling the pond with water to the final level. Trim the surplus liner with scissors only after you are absolutely satisfied that the water and edging are satisfactory.

Rigid stream units

Small streams and waterfalls are ideal candidates for using preformed fibreglass stream units and header pools. Larger and more ambitious watercourses using flexible liners and rocks to create the waterfalls require considerably more skill, since mortar is required to make the waterfalls watertight.

As with preformed pools, the disadvantage of rigid stream units is that they limit the size of the stream. Some of the colours used are extremely difficult to disguise and make look natural. But, on the plus side, installation is relatively quick and easy.

ABOVE This cascade has been linked to the rest of the garden by using materials of the same colour.

Tips

- Make sure that the base pool is large enough to charge all of the stream units and the header pool without the water level falling too seriously in the base pool.
- It is also a good idea to make sure that the header pool is deeper than the stream units.
- A small flow-regulating valve inserted into the delivery pipe near the point of entry into the header pool will provide an easily accessible means of controlling the rate at which the water flows over the stream.
- Since water flowing over shallow units in summer is prone to allow the development of blanketweed, try using a proprietary electrical blanketweed controller, which has an electrical coil that wraps around the delivery pipe, and acts to reduce the problem.

Constructing a stream with rigid units

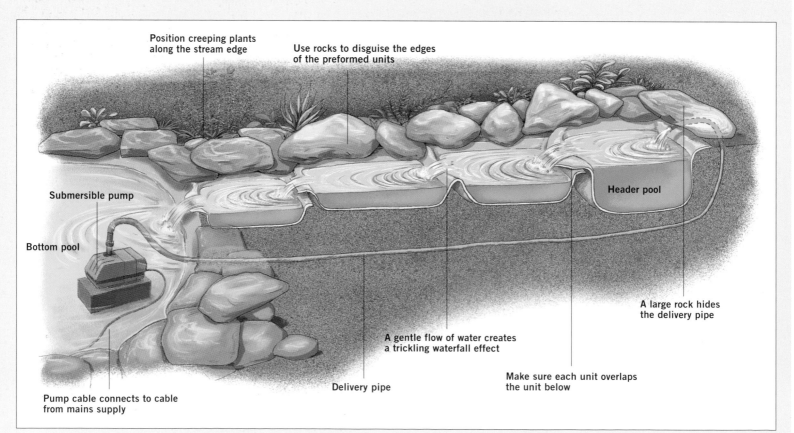

Position creeping plants along the stream edge

Use rocks to disguise the edges of the preformed units

Header pool

Submersible pump

Bottom pool

A large rock hides the delivery pipe

Pump cable connects to cable from mains supply

Delivery pipe

A gentle flow of water creates a trickling waterfall effect

Make sure each unit overlaps the unit below

The best rigid stream units are the fibreglass variety, which are strong, have a long life-expectancy and are resistant to ultraviolet light. Stream units and rock pools are also made in PVC and vacuum-formed plastic moulds, which, while cheaper, have a limited life expectancy and are much more easily damaged. All rigid stream units can be obtained in various finishes, such as pebbledash, textured rock and grit. They are best used among rocks on a sloping site where they are more easily blended into the scheme. If you are using several stream units, which are designed to overlap one another to form a longer stream, vary their direction to give a natural look, since water seldom travels in a straight line down a slope.

Unlike natural streams, the soil immediately surrounding moulded stream units is dry and therefore not suitable for marginal and moisture-loving plants that thrive in wet soil. There are, however, a number of creeping alpine plants that will grow in these dry conditions and help to disguise the artificial edges of the stream units.

Preformed rock pools are excellent for creating small pools at the top of the watercourse, known as header pools, which make a natural point of origin for a small stream. These rock pools contain a small reservoir of water even when the pump is not working and prevent a surge of water directly into the stream when the flow is turned on.

LEFT The essence of making any artificial stream lies in making it look as natural as possible.

Excavation and installation

Materials and equipment

- Tape measure
- Rigid stream units and header pool
- Wooden pegs and string for marking out
- Spade
- Trowel
- Wheelbarrow
- Soft sand
- Spirit level
- Length of plastic corrugated or reinforced flexible pipe or hosepipe 2–2.5cm (¾–1in) in diameter to act as delivery pipe from the pump; use a 2.5cm (1in) pipe if the distance to the top of the stream is more than 3m (9ft 9in)
- Medium to small rocks
- Submersible pump
- Approved waterproof connector
- Contact circuit breaker
- Selection of creeping plants

1 Having measured the stream's length and purchased the necessary number of stream units and a header pool, mark out the route for the stream on the sloping soil next to the pond. Dig a level trench approximately 15cm (6in) deep and the same width and length as the first or bottom stream unit. Line the trench with a 5–7.5cm (2–3in) layer of soft sand. Position the unit firmly and level it on the sand, with the outlet projecting over the bottom pool by 7.5–10cm (3–4in) and add enough water to keep the unit stable. Bury the delivery pipe from the pump 15cm (6in) deep alongside the stream.

2 Install as many intermediate sections as required in the same way until the top of the stream is reached. Make sure that the outlet for each of the units overlaps the unit below.

3 Dig the hole for the header pool and line it with a 5–8cm (2–3in) layer of sand. Insert the unit, taking care to keep the sides level and the outlet lip overlapping the section below.

4 Use a backfilling of sand or sifted soil tamped around them to secure the units in place. Run the delivery pipe from the pump into the header pool and disguise it with rocks. Keep the end of the pipe above the water line of the header pool to prevent it siphoning water to the bottom pool when the pump is turned off.

5 Make the connection of the integral cable from the submersible pump to the cable from the mains supply with a waterproof connector. Ensure that the mains supply cable to the pond is protected by an RCD device (contact circuit breaker). Turn on the pump to check that the stream is flowing satisfactorily and then make any final adjustments to the levels of the units.

6 Position a few strategic rocks throughout the watercourse and plant creeping plants along the stream edge.

Fountains

Another attractive water feature is a fountain, which can be added to a pond to introduce movement and a pleasant sound or can be built into a wall to make a small-scale feature on a patio. A fountain is operated by a submersible pond pump, which sits on the floor of the pool or on a platform of bricks or blocks if the water is very deep. Some pumps combine a fountain with a flexible hose outlet that can feed a waterfall as well.

Choosing a fountain

The important thing is to choose a fountain that will not overpower the effect of your pool. It should not be over-elaborate if the pool is small nor should it shoot the water so high that wind-blown spray falls outside the pool. Fountains are ideal for formal pools but should be used with care in natural surroundings as they tend to look out of place.

Installing a fountain

In most cases, the fountain outlet simply projects above the pump and can usually be fitted with a range of different heads that vary the pattern of the water jets. The pump should be positioned so that the head just projects above the level of the water in the pool, if necessary raised on a paving block.

Electric pumps

The water for a fountain or waterfall is circulated by a submersible electric pump, which usually takes its power from a transformer connected to the normal mains electric supply.

Water is delivered to the fountain head direct from the pump below or, in the case of a waterfall, water is delivered to the top of the waterfall by a hose connected to the pump in the pool. Conceal this hose under the ground alongside the waterfall, with its open end concealed by a rock.

BELOW Box (*Buxus*) in containers emphasizes the striking shape of this modern water feature.

Fountain sprays

Make sure the fountain head you choose will create the right effect for the water feature.

- **Tier:** a traditional fountain that produces continuous tiered circles of water gently falling in a pyramid-shaped display.
- **Plume:** seething and foaming plumes produced by this head create an architectural feature, best operated from a simple but substantial pool.
- **Bubble:** this head makes a natural looking, low fountain of water which bubbles up gently as if issuing from a spring.
- **Bell:** a fountain that produces a sculptural, almost semicircular sphere of water that falls in a bell shape from a central pipe.
- **Column:** two or three columns of white water shoot up in a neat and stylized manner. This works well with modern designs.
- **Geyser:** the geyser fountain forces water up into the air, sometimes to a great height, to give a natural-looking rush of foaming white water and a gushing sound.

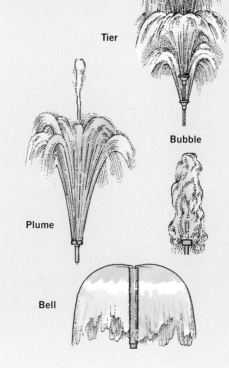

Tier

Bubble

Plume

Bell

Installing a pump

Ornamental fountains
Connect the pump to the fountain jet with a length of tubing or hosepipe. If the fountain plinth is hollow, hide the pump inside it.

Simple fountains
Place the pump in the pool at the right height so that the fountain head comes just above the level of the water. Use bricks or paving blocks to support it at the right height.

ABOVE An old farmyard pump can make an interesting form of fountain.

RIGHT In this modern formal pool, the swimmer appears to be balancing on the water as it gushes from the fountain.

The power cable for the pump runs along the floor of the pool and then up the side. Run it under one of the edging stones and then take it to a waterproof connector and link it to the transformer with a cable. Although the low-voltage electricity carried by the cable between the pump and transformer will not give you a serious electric shock, you should protect the cable from damage. Do not leave it lying on the ground where, if nothing else, it could trip someone up. By far the best idea is to run it through a plastic conduit 60cm (24in) underground, making sure it does not run under flower beds that may be dug over in the future.

To calculate the pump capacity you need for any moving water feature, you need to know the following: the fountain height, or the stream height and length, the flow rate, the overall size of the feature, whether it will run constantly, and whether it will have a filter. This information should be on the pump box, but your stockist will help.

Reservoir features

The variety of efficient submersible pumps and the increasing range of larger containers have led to more and more innovative ways of creating moving water features for the smallest space in the garden or conservatory. The basic requirements are the proximity of an electricity supply and a reservoir large enough to cope with the recirculation of water where there could be evaporation loss. Once installed and filled, these features place little demand on the mains water supply other than occasional topping-up. They also require little maintenance, unlike pools, which are dependent on plants or filtration to maintain clear water, and are surprisingly inexpensive to run.

ABOVE Millstones make attractive reservoir features and suit both modern and traditional gardens.

LEFT In this unusual take on a cobblestone fountain, paving slabs radiate from the water like the spokes of a wheel.

The cobblestone fountain is a simple feature suitable for both formal and informal settings and can be as small or as large as the garden dictates. Its effect can be varied considerably merely by changing the arrangement of cobbles at the outlet or by raising or dropping the level of water in the reservoir, which influences the sound of the water falling in from the cobbles.

Wall fountains

Small enclosed town gardens, courtyards, patios and conservatories make ideal sites for wall fountains where there is often insufficient room for a free-standing pond or fountain pool. The various forms of wall fountain outlet, mainly masks and gargoyles, work well as small architectural features. They should be chosen with care, since they tend to dominate, even when the fountain is off. A wall fountain can make a strong focal point at the end of a path, particularly if caught by sunlight and seen from the house.

Design features

As with all fountains, a reservoir is needed to act as a sump for the pump. This may take the form of a wall-mounted container a short distance beneath the spout or a pool at the base of the wall. Generally it is better to have a base pool with ample reserves of water to combat evaporation and splashing loss. A wall-mounted reservoir capable of holding adequate water reserves is likely to be heavy and require strong supports.

The design of the base pool allows for variation. A raised pool with a wide coping offers a place to sit and enjoy the sound and feel of the water. If the walls of the raised pool are made of the same material as the wall on which the spout is mounted, it will appear as if it has always been part of the wall design.

Self-contained wall fountains are sold complete with a very small pump and require no more than screwing to the wall and the pump cable connecting to a

RIGHT This lion mask is mounted on a false wall in front of the main wall. This hides the pipework and cabling from view.

Installing a wall fountain

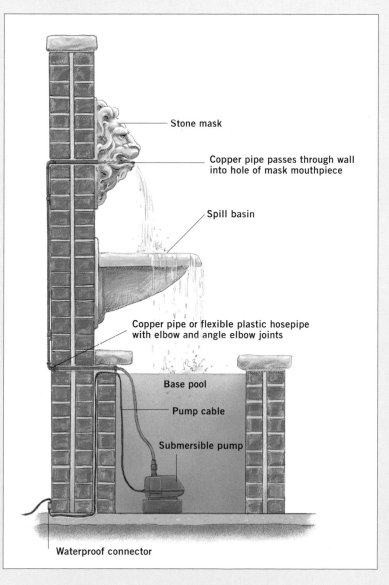

- Stone mask
- Copper pipe passes through wall into hole of mask mouthpiece
- Spill basin
- Copper pipe or flexible plastic hosepipe with elbow and angle elbow joints
- Base pool
- Pump cable
- Submersible pump
- Waterproof connector

❶ Mark the position of the mask mouthpiece on the wall and drill a hole through the wall. In order to hide the delivery pipe behind the wall, drill a second hole in the wall just above the water line in the base pool.

❷ Cut a piece of copper pipe long enough to pass through the wall into the hole of the mouthpiece. Put the pipe in place to provide temporary support for the mask, leaving at least 2.5cm (1in) projecting from either side of the wall.

❸ Spread a thin layer of mortar over the back of the mask, and position it on the wall, sliding the mouthpiece over the copper pipe for support until the mortar dries. Once the mortar has hardened, make any adjustments to the length of the copper pipe to create the best spout.

❹ Attach the end of the copper pipe to an elbow joint. If you are using flexible hosepipe, attach the elbow joint to a vertical length of hosepipe, then attach the

other end to a second elbow joint, using hoseclips to tighten the hosepipe on to the elbow joints. Join the bottom elbow joint on to a short length of copper pipe that feeds back through the lower hole in the wall and connects with the submersible pump in the base pool. If you are using copper pipe, use angle elbow joints to fix the copper pipe to the elbow joints. Secure any pipework by screwing brackets to the back of the wall.

❺ Connect the submersible pump to the mains electric supply with the waterproof connector, then test the system for the rate of flow. Adjust the flow adjuster if necessary.

socket. They are generally small features and could look out of scale on a large expanse of wall.

Technical considerations

One of the main technical problems to be overcome with larger wall fountains is how to disguise the delivery pipe from the pump to the wall spout. If the wall has an adequate cavity, the hose can be pulled through after making the entry and exit holes. If access is possible behind the wall, the method below can be used.

Where neither of these options is possible, the pipe will need either to be disguised with wall trellis and climbing plants, or hidden behind a terracotta tile drainpipe cut in half and mortared to the wall, in a vertical line from below the spout to the base pool. The plumbing can be hidden by building a false wall in front of the existing wall, in between them, with a small gap at the same time providing a more secure construction to support any heavy wall basin. Never mount a wall fountain on a house wall. The water will eventually penetrate the wall.

RIGHT Larger stones can also be used in cobblestone fountains. To create such a feature, it is better to buy a pre-drilled stone rather than attempt to drill the hole yourself.

Installing a cobblestone fountain

1 Choose a site that can be easily seen from a favourite viewing window and clear an area of ground approximately 1–1.2m (3–4ft) square. Measure the diameter and depth of the tub or bin and dig a hole slightly larger than these measurements.

2 Lower the reservoir into the hole so that it is just below ground level. Check that the rim is level with a spirit level on a straight-edged length of wood. Firm the surrounding soil by tamping it into the gap between the reservoir and the perimeter of the hole. Once the reservoir is secured, create a saucer-like depression 7.5–10cm (3–4in) deep extending to a radius of 1–1.2m (3–4ft) in the ground around the rim.

3 Drape a polythene sheet over the prepared area and temporarily secure with cobbles. Cut out a hole over the top of the reservoir slightly smaller in diameter than the reservoir rim.

4 Place a paving stone in the bottom of the reservoir to prevent any debris from clogging the intake strainer on the pump and lower the submersible pump on to it. Connect the length of pipe to the pump outlet.

5 Place a galvanized metal or wire mesh, 10cm (4in) wider than the diameter of the top, over the reservoir. Cut a small hole in the centre of the mesh and thread through the outlet pipe.

6 Lodge the pipe between cobbles, then arrange more cobbles around it on the wire mesh. If the pipe is flexible, ensure that the arrangement of cobbles maintains the pipe in a vertical position in order to achieve the effect of the water falling back on itself. If a rigid pipe is used, the cobbles play less of a role in keeping the spout of water upright. Position just enough cobbles at this stage to assess the effect when the pump is turned on, since any adjustment required to the flow adjuster on the pump will involve removing the cobbles and mesh. Partially fill the reservoir and turn the pump on to check the effect.

7 Once you are satisfied with the rate of flow, fill up the reservoir. If the outlet pipe is too conspicuous, trim it to the required length, then finalize the arrangement of cobbles depending on the effect you want. Mounding the cobbles over the outlet dissipates the water into several small sprays, while leaving it clear results in a single plume of water. Finally, arrange the remaining cobbles over the surrounding mesh.

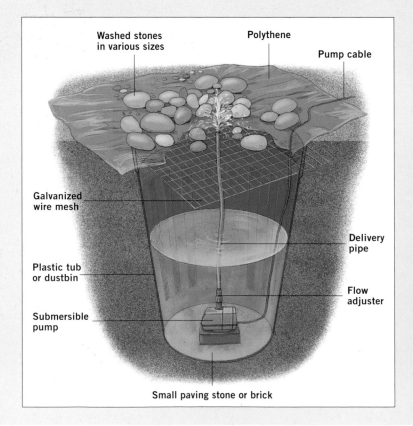

Washed stones in various sizes

Polythene

Pump cable

Galvanized wire mesh

Delivery pipe

Plastic tub or dustbin

Flow adjuster

Submersible pump

Small paving stone or brick

Installing a slate fountain

Materials and equipment

- Plastic water reservoir tank, about 60cm² (24in sq) and 40cm (16in) deep
- Concrete mix
- Sand
- Polythene pond liner
- 4 75cm (30in) lengths of 15cm x 18mm (6 x ¾in) shuttering board or plywood
- 4cm (1½in) cut or oval nails
- 81.5cm (2ft 8in) length of 18mm (¾in) copper or galvanized steel piping, cut into: 20cm (8in) length and 60cm (24in) length
- 18mm (¾in) copper or galvanized steel L bend elbow joint
- 18mm (¾in) metal-to-plastic pipe connector
- 18mm (¾in) plastic water pipe
- Submersible water pump (60 watt is ideal)
- 2.5cm (1in) galvanized metal mesh
- Quantity of slate
- Waterproof mastic
- Quantity of cobbles

1 Dig a trench for the electrical power supply leading to the site. (Use an outdoor socket or waterproof junction box for the power supply.) Dig a 15cm (6in) deep hole with gently sloping sides, the base to be about 1.3 x 0.9m (4ft 4in x 3ft). Inside the hole and about 15cm (6in) from one corner, dig a second hole the size of your reservoir tank. Adjacent to this hole, dig a 15cm (6in) deep hole, approximately 40cm (16in) square. Insert the plastic reservoir tank in the second hole, leaving about 2.5cm (1in) above the surface. Fill the third hole with concrete mix to make a base for the slate fountain structure. Level the surface and leave the concrete to set.

2 Line the sides and base of the 1.3 x 0.9m (4ft 4in x 3ft) hole to a depth of 2.5cm (1in) with sand and cover with a polythene pond liner. Cut a hole in the liner over the top of the reservoir, ensuring that the liner overlaps the reservoir tank sides by at least 5cm (2in). To form the concrete base for the fountain, construct a simple 30 x 30 x 15cm (12 x 12 x 6in) square or angled box from shuttering or plywood. Drill a hole in the centre of one side using a 20mm (⅞in) spade bit. Using a handsaw, cut out a 2cm (⅞in) wide U section below the drilled hole to allow the shuttering over the pipe to be removed once the concrete within it has set. Place the box on top of the existing concrete base with the U section facing down and towards the reservoir. Join the two lengths of metal piping with an L bend elbow joint and place the whole piece in the box with the shorter length passing through the U section and over the reservoir. Fill the box to its surface with more concrete mix, making sure the longer metal pipe remains vertical in the concrete. Leave it to set.

3 Remove the wooden casing from the set concrete. Place the water pump in the reservoir and connect the plastic pipe to the metal pipe. Connect the pump to the electrical supply and place the metal mesh over the top of the reservoir. Using the 20mm (⅞in) masonry bit, drill holes to take the copper piping in the centre of the slate slabs. Build the fountain by sliding each slate slab over the vertical metal pipe on to the concrete base and securing with a generous application of waterproof mastic.

4 Fill the large lined hole with loose cobbles to just above the surrounding surface level and fill the reservoir with water. Turn on the pump and enjoy your creation.

Canals

Canals are perfect in formal gardens for linking water features, such as raised pools or fountains, with shallow, refreshing movement and for drawing the eye to sculptures, urns and other decorative features. Keep the canal width to the scale of the garden, erring on the narrow side rather than the wide. A canal 30cm (12in) wide will have quite a dramatic impact, particularly if accentuated by columnar plants or clipped hedges and topiary.

Canals (sometimes known as rills) and canal pools should harmonize with the surrounding walls and paving, providing a perfect setting for restrained planting and containers. Explore the range of suitable materials available. Concrete is an ideal choice for construction, given the shallowness and rigid design of a canal, while glazed tiles, whether plain or patterned, used for edging create a wonderfully cooling effect.

This type of feature requires a great deal of care in its construction, with close attention paid to checking levels, depths and proportions. Maintaining the same level throughout the canal is vital if you are to maintain an even depth of water all along it.

Using a paving slab base

Another method of constructing a canal is to use a paving slab base instead of concrete, as this requires fewer building skills. For short canals, paving slabs 90 x 60 x 5cm (36 x 24 x 2in) should be adequate placed either singly or side by side along the length of the canal, with a sufficient skimming of cement between the joints and over the total surface area of the slabs and walls to render them waterproof. Concrete walling blocks 46 x 23 x 7.5cm (18 x 9 x 3in) could be used to form the canal sides instead of bricks and decorative paving stones 5cm (2in) thick used for the edge. If this method is employed for long stretches of canal, the skimming should contain reinforcing fibres in order to strengthen the seal between the joins in the paving.

OPPOSITE ABOVE The small fountains in this simple canal echo the tiered fountain at the end.

OPPOSITE BELOW This complex of geometrcial shapes, together with the symmetrical planting, serves to lead the eye to the seat under the arbour.

Tips

- Reinforcing fibres will prevent the concrete used in the canal from cracking if there is any ground movement in the future.
- The more traditional method of incorporating galvanized mesh into the concrete base will also help to prevent large cracks, but this is not such a reliable method.

Excavation and installation of a canal

Materials and equipment

- Bamboo canes and string for marking out
- Spade
- Wheelbarrow
- Soft sand
- Heavy-duty polythene sheet
- Straight-edged length of wood
- Spirit level
- Sharp sand
- Cement
- Reinforcing fibres
- Flat-ended length of wood, 5 x 5 x 60cm (2 x 2 x 24in), for tamping
- Common bricks
- Bricklayer's trowel
- Ready-mix mortar
- Coping bricks (engineering bricks or brick pavers)
- Plasterer's steel float

1 Mark out the width and length of the proposed canal on a level site. Excavate the area to a depth of 15cm (6in) for the canal plus a further 5cm (2in) for the base layer of soft sand. Add the sand, then drape the polythene sheet across the excavation to provide a protective base on which to bed the concrete.

2 Check that the sides of the excavation are level using the straight-edged length of wood and spirit level. Mix the concrete using 2 parts sharp sand and 1 part cement, adding reinforcing fibres during the mixing following the manufacturer's instructions. Pour on to the polythene sheet and level by tamping with the flat-ended length of wood.

Cross-section of a canal

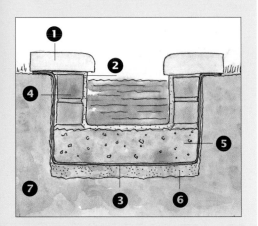

1. Coping bricks
2. Cement mix with reinforcing fibres
3. Polythene sheet as a protective base
4. Common bricks
5. Concrete
6. Soft sand
7. Soil

3 After the concrete mix has hardened in a day or two, construct the side walls using common bricks mortared on to the base. If brick pavers are to form the surrounding edge, two courses of bricks will provide an adequate depth. Make sure that the brick courses are absolutely level as construction proceeds.

4 Once the mortar has hardened, lay the coping bricks at right angles on top of the side walls and mortar into place, allowing an overlap over the water of 5cm (2in). After the mortar has hardened, skim the inside of the canal with a cement mix containing reinforcing fibres, using a plasterer's float. The thickness of the skim should be 5mm (¼in) on the side walls, with two layers each 5mm (¼in) thick applied to the base.

Stepping stones

Stepping stones offer an attractive method of crossing water, even if it is only to linger midway to enjoy the sensation. They make any expanse of water more interesting and lead the eye from one part of the garden to another. Stepping stones should not be used in deep water or approached from steeply sloping ground. Their placing should ensure that people can take easy, gentle strides without having to watch their step too carefully. If in doubt as to how far apart to put them, err on the side of caution and place them closer together. Once the crossing place is finalized, a sturdy foundation should be provided, preferably before the liner is inserted.

Paving slabs

These make good stepping stones, particularly reconstituted slabs with riven or non-slip surfaces. Although used mainly in formal garden schemes with square or rectangular outlines, manufactured concrete stepping stones are available in round or irregular shapes with riven surfaces for more informal schemes. Circular paving slabs make a dramatic impact in modern designs, echoing the roundness of waterlily leaves. Whatever shape is used, make sure that the individual stones are wide enough to allow comfortable standing room.

Bricks

Bricks make good piers for supporting paving slabs used as stepping stones. In pools no deeper than 60cm (24in), courses of four bricks butted at right angles to each other allow a paving stone of 46cm (18in) square to be placed on top with a slight overhang, without any bricks having to be cut. When the brick courses reach above the water line, the paving stone can be placed squarely on to mortar dabbed onto the top of the pier and checked for level with a spirit level as it is tapped into the soft mortar.

Boulders

Large round-topped or flattish natural boulders are ideal in informal water features such as streams, wildlife pools and bog gardens. Choose non-porous boulders, such as granite, because softer, porous stones, such as some freshly quarried sandstones, may crumble in time with the action of frost and attract slippery algae. Rounded boulders look good when they are partially submerged and are most appropriate at narrow points in a stream, where subtle placing gives no hint of deliberate bridging and so looks natural. The tops of

ABOVE Large flat-topped boulders link areas of decking on either side of this large, open pond. Stepping stones are an ideal means of providing direct access to more remote areas of a garden.

LEFT In this naturalistic stream, surrounded with butterfly-friendly flowers, the same type of stone is used for the stream bed, stepping stones and wall, making a unified scheme.

Making a bog garden

Although not necessarily aesthetically pleasing, a bog garden next to a wildlife pool can be a fascinating pond feature for the nature lover. The bog garden should be constructed at the same time as the pool, using one large piece of liner for both features.

Excavate a 30cm (12in) basin next to the pool. Its edges must be the same height or a little higher than the bank of the pool, but the interconnecting lip must be a little lower. Spread a layer of coarse grit or gravel over the soil in order to aid drainage.

When the pool is lined, continue the liner over the lowered band and across the bog area, and then tuck in the edges in the same way as for the pool. Puncture the liner in a few places and cover the floor with a layer of gravel to prevent the holes becoming clogged up.

Add a layer of well-rotted farmyard manure before filling the basin with a mixture of loam and leaf mould.

ABOVE RIGHT The pebble beach provides a gradual transition between lawn and pond, providing an ideal way for frogs and toads to get in and out of the pond.

waterfalls also make excellent places to introduce a few stones in the clear, shallow water before the water tumbles over the fall.

Stones need to be bedded on to a mortar base to prevent any danger of wobbling. Ordinary soil, although initially appearing to help stabilize the stone, will become soft mud very quickly. The larger the stone the better, so enlist help to install them. In a pond lined with a flexible liner, use spare offcuts of liner or underlay where the stones will be mortared into position. After installation, regularly remove any algae from stepping surfaces with a wire brush.

Wood

Wood can be used to make stepping stones provided every precaution is taken to remove slime and algae from the surface. Where it is possible to stabilize large log rounds in boggy soil, staple chicken wire over them to reduce the risk of slipping. Sections of round hardwood trunks, embedded in concrete to prevent them floating and to give extra stability, look effective and will last several years in shallow woodland ponds.

Pebble beaches

By making a portion of the edge of a pool into a beach or shallow gradient, wildlife is always ensured access to the pond, despite the various fluctuations in water level in summer and winter. Pebbles or round cobbles make an ideal covering for shallow beaches, preventing the edges from turning to mud and the water from becoming cloudy through the activity of birds.

Use a mixture of different sizes of cobble to make a more interesting and natural-looking beach, and grade the sizes so that they increase in diameter from below the water line to the drier margins. In order to prevent them from rolling to the bottom of the pond, mortar a small retaining wall of larger cobbles at the point where the shallow edge finishes and the deeper zone begins.

Pebbles disguise liners very effectively and prevent any deterioration through the action of ultraviolet light. The liner can also be protected from puncturing by dogs' claws if the cobbles are secured underneath the water line with concrete.

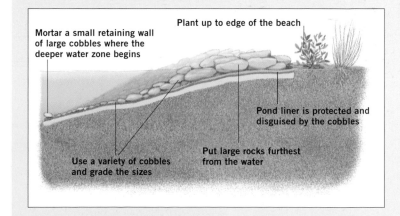

Plant up to edge of the beach

Mortar a small retaining wall of large cobbles where the deeper water zone begins

Pond liner is protected and disguised by the cobbles

Put large rocks furthest from the water

Use a variety of cobbles and grade the sizes

LIGHTING

Lighting

Lighting can make an ordinary garden look spectacular, highlighting its best features and leaving the rest masked by darkness. With careful placing, lights reveal a side of the garden that is invisible in the day – the silhouettes of tree branches, textures in bark and brickwork and the play of shadows on a path or wall. It can create illusions too, both of space and intimacy. For example, a seat facing towards brightly lit borders will feel more private for being in the dark even if by day it is marooned in the middle of lawn. Coloured lights give illuminated features a two-dimensional effect, making it difficult to work out how large or distant they are. Lights shining across the surface of water have a similar effect, disguising the bottom of even the most shallow pool and making it appear unfathomably deep.

Outdoor lights also send a clear message. The harsh glare of halogen security lamps shouts 'we can see you so keep away' while soft lighting along a path or outside a door can be inviting to visitors or suggest that they have arrived, directing people to a parking space or to a doorbell.

TYPES OF LIGHTING SYSTEM

There are three types of lighting systems available – mains powered, low voltage and solar powered.

Mains power

Mains-powered lights can either be connected to an existing lighting circuit in the house or garage or run off their own outdoor circuit with a separate fuse on the consumer unit. The method you choose depends on how many lights you intend to have and how far they are away from the house. Elaborate schemes with multiple lights should be wired to their own separate permanent circuit. This should be carried out by a qualified electrician, although you can save money by preparing trenches for the cables before the electrician arrives and backfilling them once the lights are connected.

Low voltage

Low-voltage systems are connected via a transformer to a mains socket in the house, garage or garden shed. The transformer 'steps down' the mains electricity supply to a very low voltage before it is run outside into the garden, meaning that even if you cut through one of the cables accidentally there is no risk of electric shock. Because the voltage is so low, the cables don't need to be buried in the soil or protected within armoured conduit-making them simple to lay and very easy to adjust and move around. This flexibility is one of the main advantages of low-voltage lighting systems as it allows different parts of the garden and plants to be illuminated as the seasons change. Also, the light fittings tend to be

ABOVE This garden incorporates both uplighting and downlighting, using the former to emphasize areas of the garden and the latter to illuminate the steps.

smaller than mains-powered lights and are easier to hide. On the down side, power is lost with distance from the transformer (the average cable run is just 30m/100ft) and with the number of lights on a single cable. For this reason, often more than one transformer will be necessary to light an average sized garden adequately.

Solar power

Solar-powered lights work by capturing the sun's energy during the day and storing it in a battery for use at night. They are very simple to set up, requiring little or no

Considerations when installing security lighting

Badly placed security lights can annoy neighbours, cause false alarms or even remain inactivated as an intruder approaches, so it is well worth taking the time to make sure they are positioned and adjusted properly.

False alarms can be avoided by adjusting the sensitivity control on the infrared detector to activate only when a person approaches and not a domestic animal. Also, ensure that the detector doesn't point towards public paths or alleys that run along the side of your property – a security light should come on only when someone steps on to your land.

If you are using a light with a remote infrared sensor, make sure that the sensor is positioned away from central heating flues or other heat sources that could activate the lights and that it doesn't point directly at the lamp. This is to avoid the bright halogen beam fooling the photo-sensitive cell that it is day time, causing it to flicker and reducing the life of the bulb.

Installing a low-voltage lighting system

❶ Position the transformer next to a mains socket outlet near an outside wall of the house or in a garage or shed that is protected from the weather.

❷ Drill a hole through the wall or through the corner of a wooden door or window frame at a downward angle to run the low voltage cable out to the garden, sealing around the cable with mastic or silicone sealer.

❸ Where the cable crosses a path, it has to be buried beneath it both to prevent tripping and to avoid the cable being damaged under foot. For grass paths, make a slit with a spade and push the cable into it. Where there are flag stones, lift a small section, lay a plastic pipe in the footings for the cable to run through and re-lay the paving.

knowledge of electrical wiring and can be used independently of a power source. However, their use is limited as they are not powerful enough to light large areas.

SECURITY LIGHTING

Even decorative lighting will enhance the security of your home, but on its own it is impracticable, because you have to remember to switch it on each evening and off every morning. For security, it is better to choose lights that either sense when it is dark and switch on or activate as someone approaches.

Security lights are available in a range of styles, and which you choose depends on where the light is fitted. For doorways and porticos, choose softly glowing porchlights or globes that will illuminate the front of the house without dazzling visitors; for paths running down the side of the house use wall-mounted spots, bulkheads (bulbs encased in frosted plastic covers) or globes that will draw attention to intruders and provide practical lighting, allowing you to move about your garden safely at night. For large areas, such as front and back gardens, floodlights are the best option.

Fitting a wall-mounted spotlight/security light

These instructions are for UK standard electrical connections. For other systems consult a manual or qualified electrician. Never attempt to do any wiring unless you are completely sure of what you are doing and get a qualified electrician to check the wiring before connection.

❶ Switch off the electricity at the consumer unit and remove the lighting circuit fuse.

❷ Mount the spotlight and drill a hole through the wall at a slight downwards angle, running the spotlight cable into the house. Seal the hole with mastic to prevent moisture entering the house.

❸ Locate the lighting circuit near to where the security light cable comes into the house and screw a four-terminal junction box to a nearby wall or joist.

❹ Cut the lighting circuit cable, prepare the ends and fit to the respective live, neutral and earth conductors in the junction box.

❺ Position the light switch in a convenient place, for example, by the back door, and run its cable to the junction box. Attach a small piece of electrical tape to this last conductor to identify it.

❻ Prepare the end of the cable running from the spotlight and connect the red/brown conductor to the switch terminal, the green and yellow conductor to the earth terminal and the blue/black conductor to the neutral terminal.

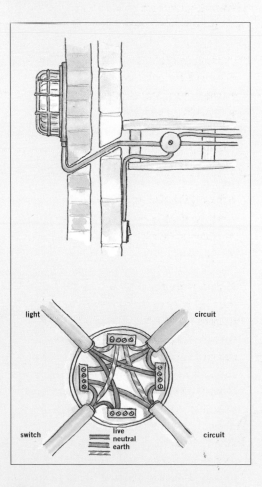

❼ Check the connections are tight and screw the junction box cover in place. Replace the lighting circuit fuse and switch the power on.

ABOVE Candles and flaming torches provide instant light wherever it is needed without the need for an electricity supply.

Many security lights have infrared sensors that detect the body heat of an approaching person and activate the light, startling intruders and making them conspicuous. The sensors can be integral to the light or placed in a remote unit. They have sensitivity controls to prevent them being activated by small animals such as cats, or foliage as it moves in the wind. They are also fitted with photo-sensitive cells so they do not switch on in the day. Lights with remote infrared detectors are more complicated to wire but can be positioned to detect intruders anywhere in the garden and activate the security lights accordingly. If multiple security lights are required, they be connected on their own separate outdoor circuit with their own fuse and RCD protection – a job best left to a professional electrician. However single security lights can be wired to an existing house lighting circuit (see Fitting a wall-mounted spotlight, page 187).

Whether you choose mains-powered lighting, low voltage or a combination of the two, the opportunities for creating atmospheric pictures in light are limitless. But to get the best effects, you'll need to buy appropriate fittings and position each light with care, taking aesthetics and practicality into consideration. Remember, it's usable light you want to see and enjoy not the light fittings or the source of the light. For example, a garden bench cross-lit by spotlights may look stunning but it is unpleasant to sit on because the lamps glare like the headlights of a car. Likewise, an outdoor dining table may feel unpleasant to dine at because of strong shadows cast across it when people sit down to eat.

Another key element is flexibility. Spotlights in borders should have enough slack in their cables so that they can be repositioned if summer foliage covers them or redirected as the seasons change, to illuminate the garden's best features such as the bright, white winter bark of a birch tree or the high summer silhouettes of canna lilies.

CHOOSING THE RIGHT LIGHTS AND MOUNTINGS

Spotlights and spread lights The most adaptable type of light is the spotlight. Spotlights direct a beam of light in one direction making them useful for highlighting garden features, such as statues, trees, walls and borders. They are particularly good for lighting established gardens where the hard landscaping is complete because they can light features from a distance without being fitted to them, saving the considerable disruption of, for example, fitting recessed lights in an existing path or deck. The drawback is that their beam can be dazzling and cast dark shadows. However, this problem can be largely overcome by using lights with frosted lenses or by lighting features such as steps and benches indirectly by bouncing the beam off a nearby wall or planting, which has the effect of making their light more diffuse.

Spotlights are available with wall mountings, floor-stands and spikes, which can be pushed into the soil or in among the foliage of pot plants on a terrace or patio.

Spread lights are similar to spotlight but produce a wide arc of light, which is useful when downlighting paths, backgrounds and borders.

Recessed lights Elegant and adaptable, recessed lights can be used to create both crisp and professional lighting schemes as well as magical effects. When evenly spaced along walls or next to steps, they add an air of rhythmic formality, which is ideal for highlighting existing symmetry or giving the approach to a house a smart and tidy look.

When set into decking or gravel paths, the effect is more magical, inviting you to walk among the light. If a thin layer of gravel or, better still, rolled glass chippings are spread over their top, the path will appear to glow from beneath.

BELOW The covers on these lamps ensure that as much light as possible is thrown on to the path without shining into the eyes of anyone walking past.

Colour

The colour and quality of different lighting systems varies according to the type of bulb fitted in the lights. The two main types are halogen, which produces a sharp, magnolia light excellent for illuminating detailed features such as statues, and tungsten, which produces a warm, diffuse yellow light, good for background and mood lighting. Mercury lights are available too: these produce a chilly green light, and it is advisable to leave them to a professional garden lighting designer to place them to get the best effect.

Coloured filters add extra theatre to a lighting scheme, particularly for parties and in combination with water. Because they tend to make the green foliage of plants look, at best, monochrome and, at worst, black, their use throughout the garden should be limited.

This can look stunning when the lights are arranged to follow the edge of a meandering path.

Installation is relatively easy in gravel paths as long as the cable is buried deeply to avoid it from becoming a trip hazard or being worn underfoot. However, fitting recessed lights in existing walls, steps, decks or patios is more difficult as holes for the lights have to chiseled out, as do recesses for the wires.

Recessed lights can be hooded to throw light either up, down or forwards on to paths and steps, or open with a frosted safety glass shield for setting into paths.

Post-mounted lights These are bollards or tall spikes fitted with a downward-facing light for illuminating paths, steps and entrances. The light they produce is practical and inviting, and they work well when placed along a path leading to a front door but risk looking municipal when placed among plants in borders. If you're after a modern, minimalist look, architectural metal bollards can be focal points in their own right, illuminating the garden at the same time.

ABOVE Recessed spotlights should be used only on parts of decking where no one is likely to tread as they may get hot to the touch.

Underwater lights The combination of electricity and water is potentially lethal so unless you are using safe low-voltage lights always get a professional to install them.

Most are simply waterproofed spotlights, which can be bolted to a stone and sunk beneath the water. For deeper ponds, it is best to use floating lamps, which can be positioned just below the surface of the water by tethering their cable to a stone, that sits on the bottom.

Pea-lights Pea or fairy lights aren't just for Christmas! Draped through the foliage of a tree or strung over an outdoor table, the light they produce is even, glare-free and very atmospheric. For winter schemes lengths of fairy lights can be wrapped around the branches of a tree to highlight its structure. Choose systems with clear white bulbs for permanent installation (coloured lights are best for parties). Pea-lights are available in nets or strings and can be used with ornamental lanterns.

Concealed lighting on decking

Concealed strip lighting can be a very effective tool on decking, provided that you follow the usual safety rules. It is a particularly useful idea if incorporated where there are changes of level or edges that might not otherwise be apparent in low light levels.

It should be used quite sparingly and positioned carefully in order to avoid it losing its effect and becoming overwhelming, and is best limited to a few areas that need to be highlighted.

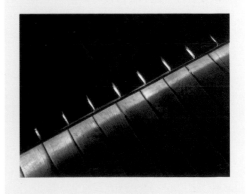

a layered pattern of shadows on the ground beneath. Choose mains-powered spots for large trees, because low-voltage lights will not be powerful enough to penetrate through dense summer foliage.

Cross-lighting Used for illuminating plants with dense foliage and for background lighting, this simply involves directing the beam of a spotlight across a lawn or border, bathing it in soft-disparate light. Although a simple technique, it is an essential one, giving shape to your garden at night and preventing more brightly lit features from

BELOW The strong central emphasis on the tree created by the paving pattern during the day is continued at night by uplighting.

CREATING EFFECTS

The lighting techniques described below will help you pick out good subjects for lighting in your garden and position the lights for the greatest effect.

The effects

Grazing Good for picking out detail, whether of brickwork, fissured bark, stone walls or paving, which can all be emphasized by shining a beam of light across their surface, to accentuate the high points and deepen the shadows between them. The closer the light is to the subject, the longer the shadows and the more Gothic the look.

ABOVE The concealed uplighters in the bed serve both to silhouette the ornamental grasses and to throw their shadows on to the wall.

Before fitting, move the light back and forth until you have found a position that picks out the subject's textural qualities to the greatest effect. Choose wall- or spike, mounted spots or recessed path/wall lights fitted with hoods to direct the beam.

Moonlighting Ideal for creating atmosphere or usable light to entertain in. Spotlights are mounted either in a tree or on a wall above a tree so that their beams shine down through the foliage, scattering the light and creating

Lighting effects

Spread lighting

Uplighting

Moonlighting

Silhouetting

Grazing

Spotlighting

the tree sunlight never reach, such as the trunk, branches and undersides of the leaves, transforming the way it looks at night.

Downlighting Low level downlighting creates functional light for picking out the treads of steps and paths without causing dazzle. It can also be used to used to 'graze' buildings and to spotlight a feature, such as a water feature, from above. Placed high, powerful mains-powered lights can be used to illuminate large areas of lawn, but glare can be a problem.

BELOW The gushing water in this contemporary water feature is made even more spectacular at night through the use of an underwater spotlight.

ABOVE The serene glow of this pond, lit from the bottom by submersible lights, compliments the Japanese feel of its surroundings.

looking as if they are floating in the darkness. It can also be used to light steps and paths, but place the light carefully to prevent the beam from dazzling. Choose spread lights and/or spotlights.

Spotlighting Position a spot or spread light to illuminate a statue, urn or fountain from above or the side. Take care when lighting statues so that dark shadows do not obscure the face or making it ghoulish and unrecognizable. If necessary, use more than

one light or cross-light from the darker side to reduce the shadows.

Silhouetting Trees with gnarled branches or plants with spiky leaves look fantastic when a light is placed behind them, outlining their silhouette and casting long shapely shadows against walls. Choose spotlights for the job.

Uplighting Use to illuminate buildings, directing the lights up the walls to accentuate the texture of the brickwork and to bounce some light back on to paths near the house to make them comfortable and safe to walk at night. Placed at the base of a tree, uplights will highlight the parts of

Lighting a pond

Garden lighting can be used either to highlight the water in a pond or emphasize brightly lit features, such as plants or ornaments around its edge, which then become mirrored on its surface. This works best where the water is still and the reflections aren't disturbed.

Use cross-lights to illuminate the shimmering water of a fountain or submersible pond lights, which can also highlight the tumbling water of a cascade. Cascades and

waterfalls look particularly magical when the light shines up through the tumbling water from below.

When using underwater lighting, take care that plant pots and pond pumps aren't caught in their beam, because this will detract from the display.

To create the illusion of depth, shine a light across the surface of the water, preventing the real base of the pond from being seen.

Shadowing

CHILDREN'S SPACES

Children's areas

Children – our own, or other people's – may use the garden more than we do, and their needs must be taken into consideration and incorporated into any garden makeover. Any attempt to ignore them and create an immaculate lawn with perfect beds may come to naught once the children start to play.

The key to planning for children is to provide what they would like rather than what the adults would like. Children are often happy with the simplest of things, such as an open space to play on and a secret place in the bushes, which they can adapt for all kinds of real and imaginary games. Structures such as climbing frames and sandpits should be designed with the child in mind rather than being selected for what will look attractive or fit in with the garden.

Young gardeners

Introduce children to the rewards of gardening by setting aside a bit of the garden especially for them. This could be a secluded corner of the vegetable patch, part of a border or simply a large windowbox. Help them to plant seeds and encourage them to water and care for their plants.

To keep children's interest, plants will need to be colourful or quick-growing. Good flowers to choose are sunflowers, sweet peas and nasturtiums (the seeds are large and easy for small fingers to handle). Herbs, such as basil and parsely, and salad vegetables are also good choices, as children then have the satisfaction of eating the plants they have grown.

LEFT Make sure that a climbing frame is positioned on a level and soft surface, in full view of the house, so that you can keep an eye on the children.

If you must have a child-free area, enclose it. One 'leg' of an L-shaped garden is ideal.

Siting
When you design the garden you need to decide if children will have free run or if their play area will be enclosed. With smaller gardens it is probably easier to let them have full run and incorporate the play things into the overall design, but in a larger garden it may be possible to set an area aside.

If the play area is enclosed it should be visible from the house or the main seating area. Picket fencing or low hedges give the children a sense of privacy while they remain in view so adults can keep a watchful eye.

Boundaries to the garden itself should be secure. This is not only to keep the children within the safe area but also to prevent unwelcome visitors from entering.

With some thinking ahead, however, the playthings you provide for the children can be turned into something else once they have outgrown them. A sandpit, for example, can be transformed into a pond. A wooden climbing frame can be clad with timber and become a shed or a summerhouse. A playhouse might become a bicycle shed.

A patio is very useful when the children need space to trundle around on trikes and bikes, but when they are older the removal of some pavers, the addition of some supports and a roof will give you a lovely,

shady arbour under which the whole family can sit for meals or lazy afternoons.

Protecting your plants
A garden with children using it means you will need to give thought to some important areas. First of all, wait until the children are older before trying to grow your specimen plants and create immaculate lawns and beds. Accidents will happen and it is far better for long-term nurturing of a love of gardening if children feel able to play without always having to be aware of damaging prize plants.

Surfaces
Surfaces such as gravel are hard to push wheeled toys through and can cause deep cuts to knees and hands. Special play surfaces are obtainable, but they are expensive. Concrete is easier to ride on but very hard. Bark chippings are popular as they create a soft area that is not out of place in a garden. It will need regular checking to make sure it is at least 5in (13cm) deep and topping up or replacing if necessary.

A utility lawn will be the choice in most cases. You can buy special blends of grass seed (fescue, agrostis and *Poa Annua* mixes) that give good green swards while being able to withstand a certain amount of wear and tear. Don't expect the lawn to escape the odd worn patch, and annual repairs will usually be necessary until the children are older.

Make sure that children learn from an early age not to try to eat things they find in the garden. No matter how sure they are that it is edible, they should never eat anything that comes from a plant. Also check you do not grow poisonous or irritating plants, and avoid those with very large thorns too as these can cause serious injury.

Steps should be built into a slope and not free-standing if you can avoid it. All raised patios should have strong rails to prevent any accidents. A row of tubs in front of the rail will help keep children away from edge. Treads on stairs should be wide and non-slip.

ABOVE This sandpit, built into the patio, can easily be converted into a pond once it has outlived its use.

BELOW A climbing frame and slide are partially obscured by young trees, giving the children the illusion of a secluded hideaway.

What you can create for the children in the garden is limitless. Jungle gyms, walkways, tunnels, sandpits, swing, dens and playhouses are all possibilities, and your choice will depend on your budget, your children and the room available. Make sure that all play equipment is secure and safe and check it regularly. Probably the best way to avoid accidents while children are very small is adequate supervision. Either ensure you can see the children at all times or place seats in the children's areas so adults can join in or relax while the children play. Doing things together will make children see the garden as an extension of the house and a safe, secure place for them to enjoy and learn to respect.

Security

In many respects the garden should be an ideal place for children to play, as it should be secure in terms both of keeping them within a defined space and in sight and also of determining what they play with. There should be gates at all access points, and the gates should be so constructed that young children can neither slip through the bars nor climb over the top. They should also have child-proof catches or locks on them.

Once the children take over in a small garden they are likely to take over the whole space. It may help to designate certain areas specifically for play, and an advantage of this is that you can use softer surfaces to prevent too may knocks and bruises. The challenge, of course, is to try to create something that the children will like.

Play apparatus

Structures for children within the garden are satisfying projects to undertake as they are certain to be appreciated. Swings and sandpits are the most built as they are not too complicated and can be designed to complement the garden's style.

ABOVE This traditional timber swing complements the stained wooden fence and the soft greens of the planting around it.

Swings

Swings are always popular and you can make your own by erecting a very strong double A-frame with supporting joists or as shown here but they need to be very securely anchored. More economical is to buy a swing from a good toymaker that conforms to the current safety regulations and erect it, closely following the manufacturer's instructions. The swing needs to be high enough for all the children to use it. Some are adjustable so can be used as the children grow.

If you have a convenient sturdy bough from a tree in a safe position you can buy specially made swings designed to hang from them. Or, if you know your knots, you can secure a tyre or wooden seat to stout rope to create a very natural swing.

A basic garden swing

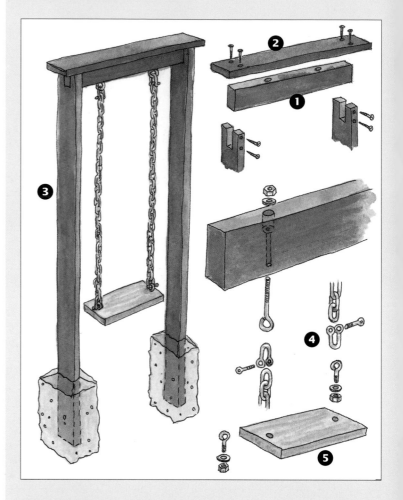

Shop-bought swings can be expensive and often come in lurid colours that may not suit the style of your garden. A simple and affordable garden swing can be constructed from two sturdy timber posts concreted into the ground with two cross-bars and a seat. The swing should be located on grass or on bark chipping to provide a soft landing in case of accidents.

Make sure you weatherproof all areas of the swing, including the seat. Regularly clean or replace chains and check joints for wear.

❶ Cross-bar: 1.15m (3ft 6in), length 100 x 50mm (4 x 2in) softwood.

❷ Capping strip: (hides tops of bolts and protects crossbar from weather): 1.45m (4ft 9in) length of 225 x 50mm (9 x 2in) softwood.

❸ Uprights: 2.75m (9ft) in length of 225 x 50mm (9 x 2in) softwood. Set about 1.05m (3ft 6in) apart in 60cm (2ft) of concrete.

❹ Chain: a welded-link galvanized chain, fitted to eye bolts top and bottom with galvanized screw-in shackles.

❺ Seat: 60cm (24in) length of 150 x 50 (6 x 2in) softwood.

Climbing frames

Children love to explore and climb. They also love taking risks. A safe way to allow them to explore and test their skills and strength is to provide a climbing frame. There are many kinds of frame available, from those made of metal tubing or wood, to modules, which fit together in several different combinations. Some incorporate bridges, walkways, tunnels and slides. Choose the size and style that suits your garden and the ages and abilities of the children using it. Always remember that there will be falls.

You can have a strong safety net fitted to the highest parts if necessary, but it is better to limit the height and skills required to negotiate the frame, while making it as interesting as possible. All frames must be sited securely on a safe surface, which, while there are no guarantees, will reduce the chances of serious injury from a fall.

In addition to climbing frames themselves, a number of interesting features for children can be made or bought. Wigwams or forts made from willow panels can be quickly put up and dismantled. These are

Constructing a swing

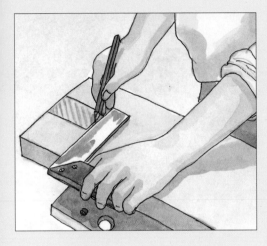

1 Mark the dimensions of the cross-beam on the end of the uprights using a try square.

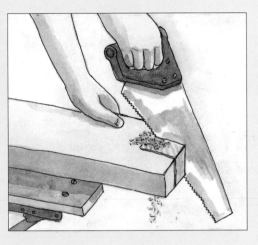

2 Saw down each side of the notches, then use a wood chisel and mallet to remove the waste wood.

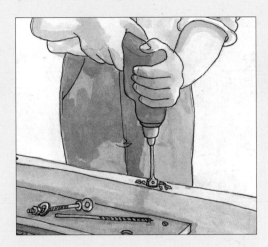

3 Drill two holes right through the cross-bar from the top edge, 30cm (12in) in from each end, to take the eye bolts. Countersink the holes on the top edge to accommodate the washers and nuts that will hold the bolts to the cross-bar. The components can now be painted or stained.

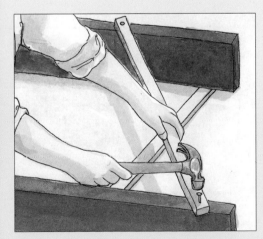

4 Use wood offcuts to brace the bottoms of the uprights at the correct distance apart while you fix the top. Cut the seat to length and drill holes 55cm (22in) apart to accept the eye bolts that will hold the chains.

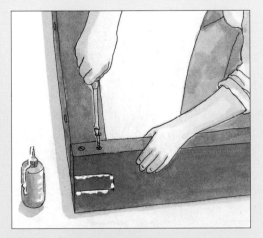

5 Affix the cross-beam into the two slots in the uprights with a strong wood glue, then drive two galvanized screws into the face of each upright to hold the cross-bar in position.

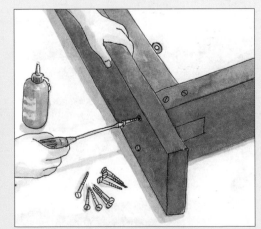

6 Fix the eye bolts to the cross-bar with washers and nuts, then saw off the projecting bolt shanks. Glue and screw the capping strip into position. Attach the chain to the eye bolts on the cross-bar and seat with galvanized shackles.

costly but provide hours of fun and can be a brilliant way to provide an instant secret area on a temporary basis for the children to play in. Pop-up tents and blow-up toys as well as portable sandpits all have their place where space is really short.

Playhouses

One of the most popular playthings for children is their own 'den'. You can create a den using willow arches or panels or by even bending saplings to create a framework. A simple den can be made using a framework of cane supports and growing fast-growing twining plants, like runner beans, along them. However, there is little to beat the ever popular 'wendy house'. Wendy houses (playhouses) are available in plastic, but these can be short lived and are not that attractive. With a bit of planning, you can build your own or adapt a small shed.

First, decide on the size of playhouse and mark out the area. Then, remove the

top soil and lay hardcore. Decking or planks over this will provide a level base. Then, cut shapes for the side panels and back. Secure these with batons. Add cross-pieces of timber for support. The front panel is made with a section removed for the door. Doors can be stable, types or open and shut types.

Add the door and front panel and cut the roof sections. Put the roof on with a central baton for support. Paint and add the finishing touches. If you want, you can cut out windows, put up curtains, include extra doors and complete the picture by placing a picket fence around the outside. The most economical way to have a playhouse that can also be useful when the children have outgrown it, is to adapt an ordinary shed. Erect a small shed but add cheerful curtains at the windows and paint it bright colours. This will be a more permanent structure, and when it has outgrown its use as a playhouse you can convert it back into a useful shed.

ABOVE Salvia and lavender screen this tiny sandpit from the patio, separating the play area from the rest of the garden.

Converting a sandpit into a pond

When planning a sandpit for your children consider the possibilities of future conversion to a pond. Build adequate foundations, using hardcore topped with compacted sand.

Place concrete slabs across the top of the sand. These can be removed when building the pond. The walls can be raised to a four-brick layer with the flexible liner being secured by a concrete top layer. Site the sandpit in an area that is suitable for both of its uses.

Soft landings

In areas where children climb or are likely to fall it is a good idea to cover the ground with bark chippings, which are relatively soft and will help cushion the fall. Anyone will be hurt if they fall from a height or fall awkwardly, but it will reduce the number of grazes and bruises. Rake it over occasionally and top it up so that there is a constant depth of no less that 5cm (2in).

1 To lay an area of bark chippings, first mark out the area and dig out the soil to a depth of about 7.5cm (3in).

2 Lay thick black polythene sheeting and pierce drainage holes in it, or use a special weed-suppressing membrane over the soil.

3 Arrange a 5cm (2in) deep layer of bark over the polythene and tread down to compact a little. Rake over and top up occasionally.

Camps

Somewhat in the same vein as a playhouse, children love to build 'camps', and if part of the garden can be put aside for this it is likely to give hours of pleasure. An area tucked out of sight, possibly at the furthest point of the garden from the house, will be best, especially if it is hidden amid a thicket of shrubs. Not much space will be required and only a few shrubs are needed. If they already exist, large rhododendrons are ideal, because they have a 'ready-built' space

BELOW An unusual children's garden consisting of sunflowers, herbs, vegetables and an unusual scarecrow.

below them. Let the children make their own camp, but it may be an idea to prune back some at least of the shrubs to create the space for them. These take several years to grow, so it may be worth thinking about creating this space well in advance so that it can be a proper feature. You may need to be prepared to replant the shrubs once the children have grown out of their space.

Sand and play pits

Sandpits never seem to be out of favour with children. Generation after generation, children spend hours building castles and knocking them down. With forethought, a sandpit can be constructed in such a way that it is turned into a garden pond once the children have grown up. If the pit is constantly supervised it is possible to have a combined sandpit and paddling pool.
It can be made of plastic, wood or stone. Site the pit in a position where it can be used for a water feature later. Portable pits do have their place, but whichever you choose, make sure they have a lid to prevent cats fouling in them.

A permanent raised sandpit will provide a ready made seat in the form of the wall. Make the pit by digging out the intended shape to a depth of 30cm (12in). Build the walls using concrete foundations and upstands 25 x 25cm (10 x 10in) wide. Put a drainage layer of stones and broken bricks 5cm (2in) deep. Lay slabs on top of the hardcore base. Put a

ABOVE One of the most popular ways of creating a playhouse is to adapt a small shed.

15cm (6in) layer of play sand over this. When you want to convert it to a pool, add a layer of compacted sand over the hardcore layer to bind the hardcore and protect the liner. Place a liner over the upstands and secure with new bricks on top sealed with mortar. Add water and some plants and you have a water feature.

TOOLS AND TECHNIQUES

Garden tools

Good basic tools are indispensable for any work in the garden. Choose them with care, selecting the right size and type for your particular needs. With proper maintenance they can last a lifetime.

Although a good spade or fork is not cheap, with care it will probably have as long a life as its owner. It is also essential to find a tool that is of the right size and model to suit your particular needs. The tool must perform the task that it is meant for efficiently, and it is also wise to take into account how frequently it is likely to be used, as this could determine the amount it is necessary to spend.

To preserve your tools it is vital to clean off any gardening dirt with an oily cloth; cutting and pruning tools should be sharpened frequently and tools that are not needed during the winter should be well oiled and kept in a dry place.

Spades

Spades are available with shafts of different lengths and blades of different sizes. The standard spade blade measures about 29 x 19cm (25 x 7½in); that of the ladies' spade 25 x 16cm (10 x 6½in); and that of the border spade 23 x 14cm (9 x 5½in). Choose whichever is most comfortable to use and bear in mind that heavy digging will probably be easier with the middle size.

The shaft of the spade should have a gentle crank to allow maximum leverage, and the strapped or tubular socket should be securely attached to the shaft. Metal treads welded to the upper edge of the blade make digging heavy soil less painful to the foot.

Spades that have stainless steel blades are far more expensive than those equipped with blades of forged steel, but they are exceptionally long lasting and penetrate the soil more easily than ordinary steel spades.
Uses An essential tool for digging and trenching, the spade is also efficient for skimming weed growth off the soil before cultivation begins.

Always hold the spade upright when cutting into the soil, so that the ground is cultivated to the full depth of the blade.

The spade is also useful for planting trees and shrubs and for mixing compost.

Forks

The fork is just as useful as the spade and is similarly manufactured. The four tines may be square in cross-section, as in the general-purpose or digging fork, or flat, as in the potato fork, which is designed to avoid tuber damage at harvesting time. The head of the digging fork measures 30 x 19cm (12 x 7½in), and that of the smaller border fork 23 x 14cm (9 x 5½in). Both stainless and forged steel types are available.
Uses A fork is easier to use than a spade for digging heavy soil, although it cannot be used to skim off weeds. It is essential for breaking down rough-dug soil and for lightly cultivating well-worked ground before seed-sowing and planting. The smaller border fork can be used to cultivate the soil among herbaceous plants

Shafts and handles

The shafts of tools can be made from different materials, including wood, metal and plastic. Wood is traditional and long lasting. Make sure that the wood of the shaft is close-grained and that the grain runs down the length of the shaft. Check that it is smooth and not likely to splinter.

Shafts made from polypropylene are lightweight yet strong, and lighter tools, such as hoes and rakes, are often equipped with tubular aluminium alloy shafts, which are coated with plastic. All three materials will offer good service if they are not ill-treated.

Spades and forks are fitted with handles in three shapes: T, D, and YD. Try all three and find the most comfortable.

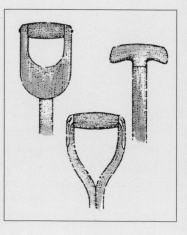

With the draw hoe the gardener must move forwards, chopping the soil and pulling it towards him or her slightly, or scraping the weeds off the surface. The draw hoe (despite its disadvantage of forcing the gardener to walk over the cultivated soil) is safer to use among closely spaced plants than a Dutch hoe. Both types of hoe can be used to draw seed drills against a taut garden line, and the draw hoe is used to earth up vegetables such as potatoes, leeks and celery.

Trowels

An invaluable planting tool, the trowel usually has a wooden or polypropylene handle, 10–15cm (4–6in) long. Longer handled versions are available but may be less comfortable to use. If possible, buy a trowel with a stainless steel rather than a forged steel blade for it will be much easier to use, less likely to bend and will not rust.
Uses The trowel may be used like a shovel or flour scoop and also as if it were a digging claw. Either method may be used, depending on the preference of the gardener. Scoop the soil out of the hole, insert the plant in the hole and refirm the soil around the roots with the hands. Use the trowel for planting bedding and herbaceous plants, vegetables and bulbs.

Wheelbarrows

In larger gardens and on the vegetable plot a wheelbarrow can save a lot of time and energy. Always check the weight distribution of a barrow before buying it – as much of the load as possible should be placed over the wheel so that the barrow, and not the operator, takes most of the weight. Barrows are available with large, inflated, ball-shaped wheels, and these are especially useful if the land to be traversed is soft. Small, two-wheeled barrows can be easier to load, unload and push than single-wheeled types. Solid tyre models are adequate where sinkage will not be a problem. Make sure that the chosen barrow is large enough without being too heavy.
Uses Compost, manure, soil, sacks of fertilizer and all manner of equipment can be moved around the garden with the aid of a barrow. Stand the barrow upright against a wall or under cover when it is not in use.

and shrubs, and the larger fork is useful for moving compost and manure. Both can be used to aerate lawns.

Hand forks

Of the same size as a trowel, the three- or four-pronged hand fork is similarly made.
Uses The hand fork is unsurpassed for transplanting seedlings, for working among tightly packed plants, such as alpines in the rock garden, and for intricate planting and weeding.

Rakes

The most popular type of garden rake has a steel head 30cm (12in) wide, which is fitted with teeth 5cm (2in) long. The shaft should be approximately 1.5m (5ft) long and smooth to allow a good backwards and forwards motion. Larger wooden rakes are useful for raking up leaves, grass and debris, which clog in steel rake teeth. However, wooden rakes wear out faster.
Uses The main use of the rake should be to level soil that has been previously broken down to a reasonable tilth with a fork. Although the rake will make the soil texture even finer, it should not be overused or the soil will be inclined to pan.

Move the rake backwards and forwards over the soil in a sweeping motion, first in one direction and then at right angles to ensure an even finish.

Hoes

There are many different types of hoe, but the two most important are the Dutch hoe and the draw hoe. Both are equipped with 1.5m (5ft) handles and forged or stainless steel blades. The head of the Dutch hoe consists of a horseshoe-shaped piece of metal, across the open end of which is attached a flat 10–12.5cm (4–5in) blade, which is designed to cut almost horizontally through the soil. The rectangular or semicircular head of the draw hoe is of a similar width but is attached at right angles to the handle. It is used with a chopping or scraping motion to cut off weeds.
Uses The Dutch hoe is perhaps the best tool for general weeding, as the gardener skims it backwards and forwards just below the surface of the soil while walking backwards. In this way the cultivated ground is not walked over and the weeds (severed from their roots) are left to dry out in the loose soil. The Dutch hoe is also used for breaking up surface pans.

Power DIY tools

There seems to be a power tool for just about every imaginable DIY task. Certainly the electric drill has become indispensable, and many other power tools are a great help in making work easier and results more accurate. Choose dedicated tools rather than just a basic drill to which lots of attachments can be added.

Tools specifically designed for the job will have the right range of speeds, and they will be well balanced and easy to use. For particular jobs, such as planing wood, you may need to hire special equipment.

Electric drill

Many power drills have a hammer action, which enables them to penetrate dense masonry, timber and softer metals. The action is one of pumping the drill bit back and forth to increase the bite. It can be engaged or disengaged as necessary.

Simple drills are commonly geared to provide two speeds at the chuck, but the important feature to look out for is a variable-speed facility, usually operated by the trigger. As you squeeze the trigger in and out the speed alters progressively between dead slow (important when starting a hole) and the maximum (which can be variably set on some models).

Another common option is a reverse gear, which is most useful for screwdriving. It enables you to withdraw screws as well as drive them in. As well as screwdriver blades, other useful drill options include circular sanding discs and wire brushes for cleaning and removing rust.

Safety

As a safety precaution when using any mains-operated power tools, fit an RCCB (residual current circuit breaker). This device will cut off the power supply in microseconds in the event of a fault or accident involving a leakage of electricity to earth. After the fault is repaired, resetting the device is easy.

Electro-pneumatic drills, incorporating powerful hammer actions, are for tough masonry jobs, but they are large, single speed and expensive. They are best hired for those occasions when they are needed. Cordless drills offer convenience and are easy and safe to use outdoors. But note that they are considerably less powerful than a mains-powered tool.

Power drill kit

❶ Power drill

❷ Rotary sanding attachment with glasspaper grades and polishing disc

❸ Wire brush attachment for scraping off rust from tarnished metal

❹ Masonry bit

❺ Twist drill bits

❻ Cordless drill/screwdriver

❼ Screwdriver bits and extension

❽ Countersink attachment

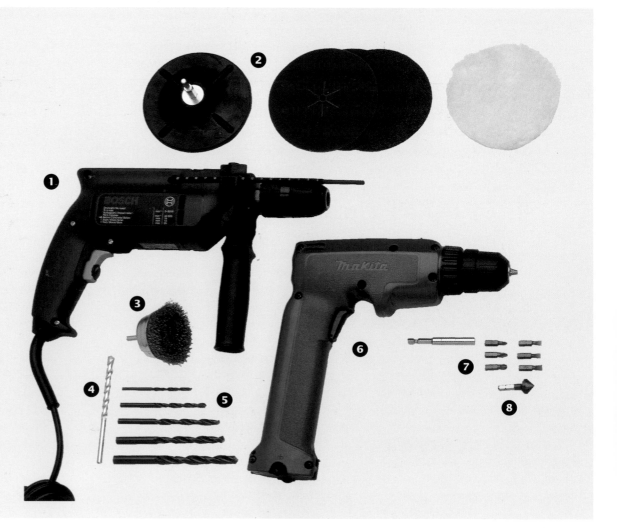

Electric saws

Jigsaws are invaluable for general cutting of timber and sheet materials. The best jigsaw will have a reciprocal blade and blowing action to clear the cutting line. Scroll action is another refinement, enabling you to make tight curved cuts by turning the blade and not the whole tool. Circular saws are useful for cutting sheet materials and timber in a straight line. These are not as versatile as jigsaws – and they are considerably less safe to use. Different blades are available for cutting a variety of materials.

Electric sander

Rotary sanders are simple attachments for power drills. Glasspaper is fitted to a simple sanding disc or, for a better finish, a foam drum sander.

An orbital sander, on the other hand, is a dedicated power tool. It drives a rectangular pad to which the sandpaper is fixed, in small, rapid orbits. Use gentle pressure (always with both hands on the tool) to produce a smooth finish in quick time.

Jig saw

A hand-held power tool used for curved work.

Circular saw

Shown here as a cordless version of the popular hand-held circular saw.

Multisaw

A reciprocating saw, also used as a detail sander.

Hot air stripper

This is a convenient alternative to a blowlamp for softening and stripping old paint, particularly useful when renovating old garden furniture. The heat of the blown air is still great enough to cause scorching, however, so you need to exercise caution.

Orbital sander

A flat half-sheet sander that has been largely superseded by the random orbital sander.

Random orbital sander

A sanding machine that does not leave scuff marks in the finished work.

Belt sander

A sander capable of removing a great deal of material very quickly.

Electric fret saw

Has very fine blades and is used to cut curves.

Special equipment

Many garden DIY jobs can be made much easier with professional equipment, which you can hire, based on the length of time you borrow the item. Charges for delivery and collection – which may be unavoidable for heavy equipment – need to be taken into consideration, too.

For large projects of long duration, it may make better sense to buy special equipment, such as a cement mixer or platform tower. Compare retail prices with hire rates. Bear in mind that you can always sell equipment in good condition after you have finished.

If you have never used an item of equipment before, get as much advice as possible before starting work – especially on safety aspects.

Detail sander

Used for sanding into small awkward corners.

Power plane

A hand-held power plane used for planing narrow components.

Hot air stripper with scraper attachment

A safer alternative to a blowlamp for stripping paint off wood.

Woodworking tools

The right tools for the job greatly simplify the task in hand and ensure the best possible results. Some tools are expensive, but you must weigh their cost against the savings you will make by not paying someone else to do the work for you. Always buy the best tools you can afford; good, well-cared-for tools will last a lifetime.

For general use, do not buy a made-up tool kit. These often include a number of tools you will never use. Be selective and choose good quality tools according to the work you plan to do. A soft hold-all is best for transporting tools. Wooden, metal or plastic tool boxes are cumbersome.

Tool directory

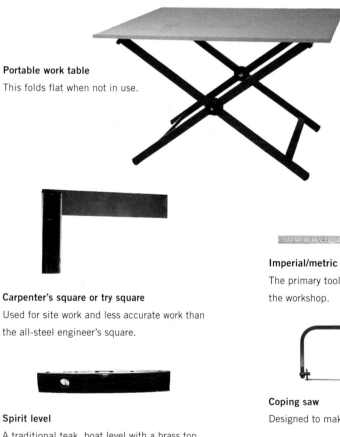

Portable work table
This folds flat when not in use.

Carpenter's square or try square
Used for site work and less accurate work than the all-steel engineer's square.

Spirit level
A traditional teak, boat level with a brass top plate. Commonly made from aluminium.

Tenon saw
Usually 30cm (12in) in length; used for larger scale joinery work.

Be safe

- Any cut should be made away from the body. Wherever possible, clamp work to free both hands to hold the tool correctly.
- Always unplug power tools when they are not in use, and store them out of reach of children. Wear protective clothing where recommended.

Panel saw
The shortest of the bench saws used for small-scale joinery work.

Ripsaw
Mostly used for ripping solid wood down the grain.

Crosscut saw
A slightly longer saw used in solid hardwood and sheet material.

Imperial/metric steel rule
The primary tool for measuring accurate work in the workshop.

Coping saw
Designed to make curved cuts in wood.

Claw hammer
The most common carpenter's or joiner's hammer, used to drive nails and designed with a claw for removing nails.

Club hammer
A useful tool when assembling structures. Can be used for a chisel or for knocking glue out of a joint.

White rubber mallet
Useful when assembling more delicate garden furniture.

Pin hammer
Very popular hammer that is used for all pinning and light work.

Cabinet screwdriver

So-called because it is widely used by cabinetmakers for driving in screws.

Awls

Two patterns of awl here: the bradawl, with a smooth circular blade, and the birdcage awl, with a four-sided blade. The latter is most useful for positioning screws when hingeing.

Bevel-edged chisel

A general-purpose and widely used bench chisel.

Pump-action screwdriver

Drives screws by pumping the handle in and out.

Large mortise chisel

A heavy patterned chisel, with a leather washer and steel ferrule on the top of the handle; for use with a heavy mallet.

Bench knives

Useful for cutting material, scoring and craft work.

Electric glue gun

Distributes hot melted glue in a continuous bead; very useful for mock-up and temporary holding purposes.

Cabinet rasp

Used for filing and shaping curved surfaces.

Cordless electric drill

Widely used for drilling and as a power screwdriver. An essential part of any tool kit.

Jack plane

General-purpose bench plane. If you can afford only one plane, this is the one to go for.

Miniature rasps and files

Used for shaping and fine filing.

Carpenter's brace

Used with lip-and-spur (Jennings) pattern bits for boring holes in timber by hand.

Smoothing plane

This is used for final finishing of already flat surfaces.

G-clamp

Capable of applying considerable pressure during assembly to bring components together.

Tool care

Clean tools immediately after use. A wipe with an oily rag ensures metal surfaces stay free from rust. Never let sharp tools rub against each other – this is the most common cause of blunted cutting edges.

Wheel brace

Small hand-held brace used with jobber's drill bits.

Digital readout callipers

Used for measuring and checking the thickness of components.

Working with wood

In many respects wood is the ideal for garden projects. In appearance it is very much in keeping with the natural qualities of a garden; it is a sympathetic material. Wood is an easy material with which to work and can be worked with a few simple tools. It is surprisingly strong and can be shaped. Finally, it is relatively cheap and readily available.

Choosing the right wood

Wood can be broken down into several different categories, and the one you choose will influence the outcome of the project, both in terms of its final appearance and durability. Your choice will also greatly influence the cost of the project. A few rustic poles from a local woodcutter may cost little more than glass of beer, but top grade hardwood could cost a small fortune. Costs can be cut by using second-hand timber, but be careful: money saved on the wood may be lost by having to replace tools that have been ruined by hitting hidden nails or other fixings in the old wood.

Another aspect of your choice of wood is going to be the use to which the wood is put. Permanent decking is going to require a better quality of timber than, say, boards around a compost bin, which can be easily and cheaply replaced if they rot. Similarly, poles for a rustic arch need not be as perfect looking as those for a more formal structure.

If you are unsure of the types of wood available, wander around both a garden centre and a wood yard or timber merchant's to see what there is and roughly what each type costs before you proceed too far with the planning of the project.

Check the wood thoroughly before buying. Look for any splits at the edges of the wood and make sure the wood is not bowed or twisted in any way. Knots are unavoidable and can make for an attractive feature, but avoid dead knots (those with a black ring around them) as these may fall out and weaken the wood.

Rustic poles

Rustic poles have limitations in a garden as they always look like rustic poles. Their uneven shape make them difficult to use where you want something to look reasonably formal. A slightly twisted rustic pole holding up a piece of trellis, for example, may add an unwanted lean to the panel. However where a rustic or even Gothic appearance is required, they are essential as it is very difficult to distress a piece of regular timber to look as if it is a natural piece of wood. The big advantage of working with rustic poles is that from a visual point of view it does not matter if your woodworking skills are not that good, because the occasional imperfect joint will not look inappropriate.

When working with rustic poles it is always best to remove the bark. They may look better with the bark on, but water and insects will soon collect below the bark and start to attack the wood inside. Normal wood-working joints can be used. Galvanized nails are usually better for fixings than screws.

Softwoods

The softwoods have a different cellular structure from that of hardwoods. (Softwoods are not necessarily softer than hardwood; balsa, for example, is a hardwood.) They are quicker growing and cheaper to buy, but they also tend to decay faster. They are easy to work, and for many garden projects, such as sheds, summerhouses, arbours, pergolas and arches, they are likely to be the preferred wood. They are also more generally available; the majority of timbers carried in pole or plank form by garden centres, timber yards and DIY stores is likely to be softwood.

Softwood comes in two forms: 'planed' or 'prepared', and 'sawn'. Sawn is in its rough state with the saw marks visible and with a rough surface. It does not have the

Softwood

Larch
Larix decidua

A wonderful timber for outdoor use, it not only grows to great height but produces really wide boards. Often seen in the form of fencing, garden sheds and even flooring in outdoor and indoor buildings. Unlike the pines and spruces which are evergreen, this species loses its leaves in winter.

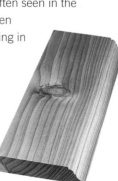

Douglas fir
Pseudotsuga taxifolio

A giant of a tree, often growing in excess of 85ft (280m). Generally reddish in colour, the sectional sizes available are enormous, thus its use is vast, from large wooden structures to interior usages. It is not only very tough but also water resistant.

Scots pine
Pinus sylvestris

In Western Europe this species abounds as household furniture and structural members in house building. Prone to movement, its wide summer growth is quite soft, making the harder winter growth pronounced. It changes colour with ultraviolet light, which can be unattractive if the exposure is uneven.

finished look of prepared wood and the rough surface can cause splinters if rubbed. Planed or prepared timber has been put through a planer and has a smooth finish to the surface. It is easier and more pleasant to work with, but it is also more expensive. Where surfaces are not seen or touched, such as the framework or rafters of a shed perhaps, then sawn is preferable; elsewhere go for planed. When timber is cut it is sawn to precise size, when it is planed this size is reduced a little. So 50mm 'sawn' will be 50mm, but 50mm 'prepared' may only be 46mm or even less, so check before you buy if dimensions are critical.

Hardwoods

Hardwoods are less frequently used in the garden, partly because they are more expensive but partly they are not really necessary. For durability and good looks hardwood wins hands down, but the costs are usually prohibitive. The type of structure where they may be used is decking, especially if it is likely to be used by people with bare feet as hardwood is less likely to splinter than many softwoods. However such extensive use is expensive and hardwood is more often used for items such as furniture, which undoubtedly look better and will last longer if made from, say, oak or one of the more exotic hardwoods.

Sheet woods

Wood is not only required for poles and posts, it is sometime needed as cladding. This may come in the form of planks or sheets. Planks for cladding sheds, summerhouses or fences is usually 'feather-edged' – that is, the wood tapers across its width so that one side fades away to virtually nothing. The advantage of this is that the planks can be overlapped without increasing the thickness of the cladding. Such planking is usually laid horizontally on shed walls and vertically on fencing.

The other form of cladding is in sheets. Such sheets are always artificial

Hardwood

Jarrah
Eucalyptus marginata

A fair percentage of Western Australia is built of jarrah: it is used in bridges, railway sleepers, flooring and many areas where its strength and suitability for outdoor use prevail. Used for internal cabinet work, it is a very even red colour, but often lacks the character of beautiful grain.

Wenge
Millettia laurentii

When planed, wenge changes in ultraviolet light from straw colour to almost black. Open pored but, with a good grain filler, it replaces rosewood admirably. Very straight grained and has a wonderful grain distinction. Brittle and very splintery.

English oak
Quercus robur

The English oak has a majesty all of its own and, of all the oaks, is the most magnificent for furniture-making.

Teak
Tectona grandis

A timber which exudes a natural oil from its pores, enabling it to withstand exceptional conditions. Very difficult to de-grease for gluing purposes, but still a joy to work despite its calcium pockets and grit particles blunting your tools. A species to experience, and excellent for furniture.

British elm
Ulmus procera

What a pity it is so prone to Dutch elm disease. When available this species provides all that one could desire in terms of durability, size, depth of beauty and wonderfully exotic figure.

American white oak
Quercus alba

This oak is regarded by many as adequate in that it is durable and tough, has good sectional sizes and length, but is prone to having sapwood included in sawn boards. It is, however, dull and must rank as a functional oak rather than a character oak.

in that they are made up of layers of wood – plywood or made up of compressed and glued chips or sawdust – chipboard or sterling board. Usually such board is used only in interiors (as floors to summerhouses, for example) or roofs over which a layer of felt is placed as a protection. If it is used as an exterior wall or roof where it is exposed to the weather then it is important to use an exterior grade or it will very quickly decompose.

Man-made boards

Man-made boards can be a cheap alternative to natural wood particularly for furniture or panelling. Despite their vulnerability to exposure, you may wish to use these materials in a summerhouse or playhouse, or as furniture in covered outdoor living areas. There are five main types.

Blockboard – consisting of a softwood core with veneer surfaces. The inner cores are generally 20mm (⅞in) wide. It is a robust board, but can suffer from telegraphing (soft core showing through to the veneer).

Chipboard – made from wood chips mixed with synthetic resin and placed in a heated press. Different levels of thickness are available, but some chipboards sag under their own weight. Edging the board with plastic, metal or wood is advisable because without this it is unsightly and vulnerable to chipping.

Hardboard – made from pulped softwood compressed into dense, thin sheets, hardboard is vulnerable to buckling.

Medium-density fibreboard (MDF) – a relatively new board, which is extremely adaptable. It is made from compressed wood fibre and is the popular alternative to hardboard and plywood. It is essential to use a good dust mask when machining MDF, as the dust is harmful if breathed in over a period of time.

Plywood – made by bonding a number of sheet veneers together. The use of veneer leaves that have been poorly dried means the board is susceptible to distortion. Finding undistorted boards is a time-consuming business so many DIY enthusiasts opt for MDF instead.

Working with board materials

Where you see defects in a board's face, try not to use fillers. These shrink in time and show below the surface. Always use the actual veneer material, such as birch for birch ply, gaboon for gaboon ply, MDF for repairs to MDF and so on.

Cutting a joint

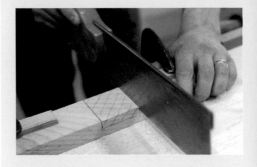

❶ Make vertical cuts with a saw to the depth of the joint. On wider joints make several cuts, each to the width of the chisel.

❷ Chisel out the waste down to the pre-marked gauge line. Work from either side of the cross-halving, paring slightly upward.

Types of joints

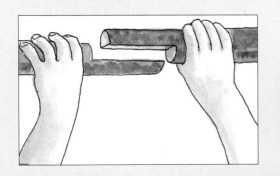

Scarf joint
The simplest practice is to join lengths of wood with a simple scarf joint, if possible arranging it so that the joint coincides with a post.

Half joint
Use a simple half joint where two pieces of wood cross: each joint is cut to the width of the opposing pieces of wood and to half of its own depth. Half joints can also be used for joining at corners and sides. Again, each joint is cut to the width of the opposing pieces of wood and to half its own depth.

Mortise and tenon
The mortise and tenon is a strong joint used primarily in frame construction. It consists of a rectangular hole in the edge of one component, called a mortise. On the end of the component that joins it a tenon is cut by removing material so that the remaining projection fits the mortise precisely.

Nailing

1 To make it easier when hammering nails into a pole, place a weight, such as a heavy hammer, opposite the nail to absorb the impact.

2 When a nail is inserted through the end of a piece of wood there is the likelihood of it splitting. Drill a pilot hole first.

Screwing

A pilot hole for the screws should be countersunk to take the head of the screw.

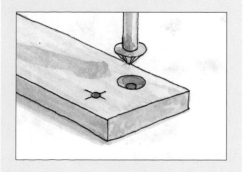

Joining wood

When working with timber in the garden, keep all joints as simple as possible, unless you are making furniture out of expensive hardwoods when it is worth spending a bit more time and effort. The same joints can be used for either round (i.e. poles or posts) or flat wood. All screws or nails should be rust-proof. Make certain that all cut surfaces are flat and marry tightly together with no gaps.

Sometimes it is necessary to use stronger joints when joining two pieces of wood, such as when making gates and a mortise and tenon joint should be used.

Fixings

There is a wide range of fixing available from DIY stores. Since any fixings are likely to be exposed to the weather it makes sense to choose materials that will not corrode. Galvanized steel or stainless steel are two obvious choices. The most common fixings are nails and screws, but bolts are best for joining heavy timbers. Ship's chandlers are a wonderful source of out-of-the-ordinary types of rust-proof fixings that may be needed in the garden from time to time.

Cutting and shaping

Wood is usually cut with a saw, either by hand or using power. Make certain that the wood is firmly placed on a bench or trestles and preferably held in place by clamps. Mark where the cut is to be with a pencil; don't guess. Cut just on the outside of the line. Joints are cut with the combination of a saw and a chisel. Keep all tools sharp. If the wood is rough or needs thinning down slightly use a plane, either a hand or power one.

Shedding water

Water can sink into the end-grain of exposed upright posts and rot it. Cut the tops so that water is shed (1). Alternatively cap the posts with wood or lead (2).

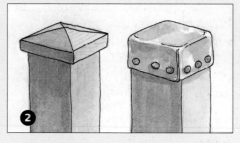

Preserving posts

All exposed timber should be treated with preservative to prevent decay and attack from insects. Avoid using creosote as this can affect nearby plants. It is easy to paint the exposed pieces of timber with preservative but it is impossible to do this below ground. It is the junction between the ground and the air where posts are most likely to rot. Drill a 1cm (⅜in) sloping hole into the post and fashion a wooden plug to fit the entrance of the hole. Once a year, remove the plug and fill the hole with preservative and then replace the plug. This will slowly seep into the wood, protecting it from decay.

Painting and staining

A basic knowledge of different paints and stains is essential for anyone wishing to make or transform garden ornaments, or indeed pursue any other form of painting and decorating.

Specialist paints

A variety of specialist paints will prove useful for finishing garden furniture, ornaments and accessories. Some are formulated for use with particular metals, others for glass or ceramics. Red oxide, the prescribed paint for rust-proofing iron and steel has recently been superseded by a number of extremely effective proprietary iron primers, some requiring their own solvent.

ABOVE A bench and outdoor table have been matched by a pastel blue matt emulsion, which will need protection from an exterior grade varnish.

LEFT A blue-stained wooden fence makes the perfect contrast to an ingenious display of plants in modern terracotta pots.

Paints

Commercially available paints are generally either water based or spirit based. There are various other paints that are made from milk or linseed oil, using earth or other pigments, and a mention should be made of limewashes and distempers, which are still available from some specialist paint and decorator's shops and are well worth experimenting with for their soft, subtle, chalky effect. They are particularly suited for use on substrates that need to breathe.

Water-based paints

Water-based paints are easy to use. Modern paint technology has produced water-based gloss paints, which have obvious advantages, and their manufacturers claim that their strength, longevity and resistance to fade are equal to that of oil-based paints. Another commonly used water-based paint is acrylic combined primer/undercoat – again very useful and quick drying.

The most useful water-based paints are the modern acrylic emulsion paints, available in literally thousand of colours. In matt or silk (semi-gloss) finish, either off the shelf or mixed to match, these paints are a boon to the modern decorator. Although not recommended by their manufacturers for outside use, if properly protected with an exterior-grade varnish, emulsion paints can be used for most outside purposes.

Modern oil-based paints are generally obtainable in gloss or satin (semi-gloss) finishes, although a limited selection of matt (or flat) finishes can also be purchased. White spirit, turpentine or turpentine substitute are necessary for brush cleaning, as well as for any spillage or drips. For convenience, many of these paints are now sold in a non-drip form. The colours available are almost as many as for emulsion paints and, although slower drying than water-based paints, the semi-gloss paints can dry surprisingly quickly. Oil-based paints should generally be applied over an appropriate undercoat.

LEFT Hardwood chairs will need to be sanded down to the base wood before applying the stain as any remaining varnish will reject the stain.

Stains

Stains can be divided into three categories: fence stains or paints, transparent stains and opaque stains. Whichever type of stain you use, be sure it has been formulated specifically for use on exterior timber. Many exterior stains will contain a timber preservative.

Fence stains come in a limited number of colours. Largely designed to emulate the natural colours of timber, together with a few other popular shades, they are usually water based and easy to use.

Transparent stains are either water or spirit based. Water-based stains are most useful for rough-sawn or planed timber, but have a tendency to raise the grain on planed timber. To achieve maximum penetration and an even finish, water-based stains must be applied to dry timber. Spirit-based stains tend to penetrate wood better, give a more solid colour and dry extremely quickly. Care should be taken, however, to apply the stain evenly or an uneven finish will result.

A recent development in stains has been the introduction of new opaque water- and spirit-based wood stains. These stains can be mixed to almost any imaginable shade and are very easy to use. Particularly useful for planed timber, they are made in interior and outdoor formulations and offer excellent cover and colour saturation.

Safety precautions

Before using stains and varnishes on large areas of wood, such as decking, carefully read the manufacturer's instructions on the tin or the accompanying leaflet. Many of these products are highly volatile and give off unpleasant or potentially dangerous fumes. Do not smoke, drink or eat while using them. If you are working in a summerhouse or other enclosed area make sure it is well ventilated, and if you are particularly sensitive wear a face mask and some form of eye protection, such as goggles or glasses. Do not apply stains or varnishes if you have any kind of breathing difficulties.

Keep these products away from exposed skin and make sure the containers are out of the reach of inquisitive children.

It is best to apply stains and varnishes during the day so that you can keep the windows open. Daylight is also best for judging the effects you are creating.

Ageing techniques

The colour and patina that ancient materials develop over time is quite lovely and the same look can be artificially recreated. Old painted wood that has been exposed to the elements develops a tone and texture that bears little resemblance to its original state. Stone, tiles, clay bricks and terracotta pots attract moss and lichen and over time discolour with exposure to the elements.

New trellis and fencing can look harsh, but a simple wash will create a soft, unobtrusive tone. The wash is easy to make, but you should have plenty of timber scraps on which to test the colour. When dry, the wash will give a more solid colour than is apparent when first applied.

Half-fill a plastic bucket with water. Ideally, add a concentrated colourless wood preservative to the water, then add a small quantity of white emulsion paint and mix thoroughly. Add a little black emulsion paint and a smaller quantity of blue. Mix again until the paint is completely dissolved. The wash should be a very watery gray colour and, when applied to bare wood, should not change its surface colour to any great extent. The effect of the wash when dry is to reduce the brashness of bare cut timber and to transform it to a soft gray weathered appearance, which will further mellow as the wood changes colour with time.

A similar technique can also be used on new terracotta, whether pots or tiles, to give a softer, weathered effect. You will get a more realistic look if you mix up a white wash and a dark gray wash separately and apply the white first, leave it to dry, then apply the gray sparingly over the top. This will give an attractive mottled appearance.

Installing electricity

Electricity can transform a garden both in terms of how it looks and how it is used. Aesthetically, an electrical supply will drive pond pumps for fountains, cascades and waterfalls creating movement, sound and focal points, while outdoor lighting highlights views and features that go unnoticed in the day and enables alfresco summer parties to go on long after sunset.

Fitting an outdoor electrical supply is practical too, providing power for pond filters, security lights, greenhouse heaters and propagators as well as lifestyle accessories, such as heated spas and pools. When connected to outdoor power points, electrical appliances such as lawn mowers, leaf blowers and hedge cutters make tasks quicker and easier. More importantly, the job is safer when run from a conveniently placed outdoor socket than from an extension cable trailed across the garden from the house.

Outdoor power points also come in handy for DIY jobs allowing extra work space and keeping the dust from jigsaws and sanders away from carpets and curtains.

Types of electricity supply

There are three types of garden electrical supply – mains, low voltage and solar.

Solar power works by capturing the energy produced by the sun in photo-cells and turning it into low voltage electricity. Both small pond pumps and garden lights are available – the lights working at night using energy caught and stored in a battery during the day. Solar technology is improving all the time but is still relatively new and expensive, and in temperate countries where the weather can be temperamental, solar-powered equipment is often less than reliable particularly in winter. However, it is completely free to run and by far the easiest electrical supply to install requiring nothing more than a place in the sun.

Low voltage electricity

Low voltage pond pumps and garden lights connect to the mains via a transformer that steps down the mains voltage to 12 volts before it goes out into the garden. Installation is straightforward, the transformer being plugged into a 13 amp power socket in the house, shed or garage and low voltage cables leading outside to lights or a pond pump.

Cables do not need to be buried and can run along the surface of the soil. Do not position across paths where they could create a trip hazard or over solid surfaces, such as rocks or paving where the cable will get damaged if stepped on.

Low voltage pond pumps are available in sizes from small 400 litre per hour pumps for gurgle fountains and pebble ponds to 9,000 litre per hour pumps for large fountains. They are all submersible, and should be positioned below water level allowing extra cable to prevent the joints becoming stretched and fatigued if the pump moves during use.

Low voltage lighting systems come in a wide range of styles, from bollards for illuminating paths and flights of steps, to submersible spot lamps for ponds. They are versatile, easy and cheap to install and can be used to great effect. Their one drawback is that they lose power the further they are positioned from the transformer – (a maximum working distance of 30m/100 ft is average) and with the greater the number of light fittings on each run of cable. For this reason, multiple transformers may be necessary to light a garden effectively.

Installing an outdoor power socket

There are two ways in which outdoor sockets can be wired: to an existing ring or radial circuit in the house/garage or on their own separate garden circuit.

Connection to a radial/ring circuit is via a spur from an existing power point. When power is spurred off an existing circuit in this way, the socket should be positioned near to the existing circuit to limit the length of the extension and should also be protected by a residual current device (RCD). This can either be integral to the socket or fitted in the circuit near the consumer unit. **Do not attempt any wiring unless you are sure that you know what you are doing.** If you do fit your own outdoor sockets get them checked by an electrician before connection.

For power sockets positioned away from the house or a series of sockets in a garden, they should be connected on their own separate garden circuit. Installation is best left to an electrician but you can save money by digging your own trenches. (See preparing for garden cables, right)

All outdoor connections and sockets should be weather-proof with a sprung flap to prevent moisture entering the socket when it is not in use.

Fit to walls or wooden posts ensuring that they are well above ground level to avoid rain splash and damage from wheelbarrows.

Preparing a garden for cables

The best time to lay the cables for a mains electrical supply is before a garden is built as the trenches required to carry them invariably need to cross borders and paths. Where they do pass under hard surfaces, the cable should run through plastic pipe conduit so that it can be removed or replaced in case of faults.

When mains electricity is being installed to an existing garden, cables can be fixed to walls and fences to avoid digging up patios. Any electric cable that runs above ground should either be armoured or enclosed within impact resistant plastic conduit.

Always keep an accurate plan noting the location of cables in case repairs are needed and to pass on to new owners of the house.

❶ Mark out a 30cm (12in) wide trench route connecting the point where the cable enters the house to the location of power points/lights/pumps etc. Where possible, position them next to paths and drives or along the bottom of a fence, keeping them away from areas that are regularly cultivated.

❷ Dig out the trench to a depth of 50cm (20in) and line the base with sharp sand for the cable to lie on.

❸ Lay the cable in the trench, looping it up where light fittings and junction boxes for pond pumps are needed. Secure in place with saddle or buckle clips ready for wiring by a qualified electrician.

❹ When wiring is completed, any cable that runs beneath borders should be given extra protection by laying tiles or flat stones over its top before back-filling with soil. As an extra precaution, black and yellow warning tape can be laid over the tiles as a warning in case the tiles are dug up at a later date.

Cable types

Three types of electrical cable can be used in the garden – armoured, mineral insulated copper sheathed (MICS) and PVC insulated cable. Which one you choose depends on how the cable is run.

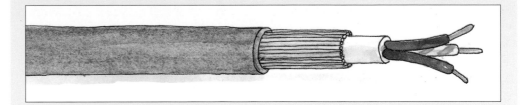

Armoured cable (above) is ordinary insulated two or three core cable, protected inside a steel wire sheath which in turn is protected by PVC insulation. It needs no extra protection when buried under ground but is expensive and requires extra junction boxes at each end to connect it to ordinary PVC insulated cable.

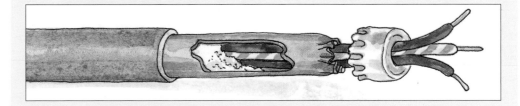

Mineral insulated copper sheathed cable (above) is similar to steel armoured cable except that its armour is made of tightly packed magnesium-oxide powder held in place by a sheath of copper. It can be buried in the soil without extra protection but needs special junction boxes to connect it to ordinary PVC cable and it is expensive.

PVC insulated cable is the most economical way to take power out into a garden. Because it has no armour of its own it should be protected within a sheath of impact resistant plastic conduit. The conduit comes in interlocking sections and can be concreted below paths and run up walls and fences to lights and outdoor power sockets. The cable inside the conduit is continuous. When burying the cable and conduit beneath borders or anywhere that is regularly cultivated, place tiles or flat stones over the cable before back-filling with soil.

Mains electricity

Mains electricity is the most versatile and can be used to power everything from outdoor sockets, lights, irrigation systems and jacuzzis. It is also the most expensive to install requiring its own permanent circuit of cables in the garden and a separate switching unit from the consumer unit in the house, incorporating its own fuse and residual current device (RCD) with a minimum trip rating of 30 milliamps. RCDs are an essential safety device that automatically switch off the power supply if any change in the current is detected – before anyone operating a faulty piece of equipment receives an electric shock.

Installing a permanent outdoor electricity supply should be carried out only by a qualified electrician. However, you can save money by preparing trenches for electrical cables to run through and filling them in yourself after the electrical supply has been connected (see box Preparing a garden for cables) and by planning for everything you want both now and in the future, so saving money on electricians' fees and time digging out new trenches later on.

Plumbing

An outside tap can make watering the garden, filling the pond or cleaning the car so much easier than if the hose is connected to the kitchen tap and run out of the window, and you don't need a knowledge of brazing or soldering to fit one.

Outside taps are connected to 'the rising main' – a 15mm (⅜in) copper pipe that carries water from the mains to the water tank in the loft and directly to the cold tap in the kitchen. For convenience, the position of an outdoor tap should be as close to the rising main or the pipe that feeds the kitchen tap as possible and it should also be situated above the mains stop cock so that it can be shut off with the rest of the water supply to the house.

All outdoor taps must by law have a double seal non-return valve fitted into their plumbing to prevent the possibility of water from the garden entering the mains and polluting it. It is also advisable to fit a 'drain cock' which allows the water in the tap and outside pipe-work to be drained to prevent any frost damage in winter.

Joining copper pipes using compression fittings

Compression joints enable lengths of copper pipe to be connected to fittings such as stop cocks, taps, tee pieces, drain cocks and 90° bends without the need for soldering, all the things you need to install your own outdoor tap. At each point where the copper pipe connects to a fitting there is a 'cap nut' that as it is tightened on to the fitting squeezes a ring of soft metal (called an olive) around the copper pipe creating a watertight seal. They are easy to fit even for a novice.

Note: If your house is old and the plumbing is made of lead, you'll need to get a plumber to connect up the pipe-work.

Fitting a water butt to a drain pipe

Water is a precious resource and increasingly, as the water we use in the garden is metered, it makes sense both financially and environmentally to save as much rainwater as possible. The simplest way is by collecting the

Weather watch

As water freezes it expands and in extremely cold weather, there is a risk that water trapped inside taps, plastic and copper pipes will freeze and puncture their sides. To prevent this, turn off the stop cock outside and turn the taps on to drain water from them, also draining water from hosepipes. Any pipe-work above soil level or in unheated garden buildings should be insulated with lagging.

Fitting a diverter

❶ Mark the pipe leading from the gutter to the drain at the same height as the hole for the inlet on the water butt.

❷ Cut the pipe in half at this point and insert the diverter.

❸ Fix hose between the water butt and the diverter and replace the pipe leading to the drain.

Assembling compression joints

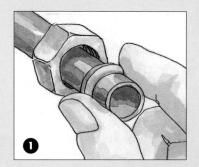
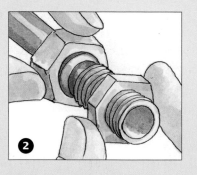
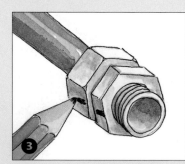
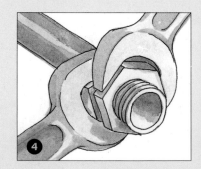

❶ Cut the copper pipe squarely and remove the burr with a file. Undo the cap nut and slide over the end of the copper pipe. Remove the olive and slide this over the end of the copper pipe too. (If one side is longer than the other, the long side should face away from the nut.)

❷ Push the copper pipe firmly into the joint twisting gently to ensure that it goes fully home. Slide the olive up to the body of the joint and tighten nut the by hand.

❸ Mark the position of the nut with a pencil.

❹ Then, holding the body of the joint with one spanner and the cap nut with another, make one complete revolution using the pencil mark as your guide. If, when the water is turned back on, the nut appears to be weeping tighten the nut by approximately a quarter turn.

Note: If, the nut is over tightened there is a risk of the joint leaking. If this happens drain the pipe and dismantle the joint, cutting the olive from the pipe with a junior hacksaw. Check the fitting for damage and if there is none fit a new olive and re-tighten. If the problem seems to be an irregularity in the pipe where it contacts with the inside face of the fitting, wrap three or four turns of PTFE tape over the olive before tightening.

Fitting an outside tap

1 Turn off the main stop cock and drain the water from the pipe through the drain cock (usually situated above the stop cock on the rising main) and by turning on the kitchen tap.

2 Mark the position for the new tap on both the inside and outside wall, making sure that no other services (e.g. electricity, drainpipes or gas) will obstruct the pipe-work.

3 Drill through the wall just above the position of the new tap and push a length of plastic pipe (available from plumbers' merchants) cut to the width of the wall into the hole. This acts as a conduit, carrying the copper pipe through the wall and aiding fast detection of leaks while preventing water soaking into the masonry.

4 Fit a tee piece in the rising main connected to a 10cm (4in) length of pipe leading towards the position of the tap.

5 Fit a stop cock on the pipe so that the outside tap can be isolated and another short length of pipe after it.

6 Fit the non-return valve next and another short length of pipe followed by the drain cock.

7 Run the pipe through the wall. Screw the base plate fitting of the tap in position and fit the pipe to it.

8 Wrap PTFE tape (fine plastic tape used for water sealing metal joints) around the screw thread of the tap before screwing to the base plate.

9 Turn the water on and check for leaks.

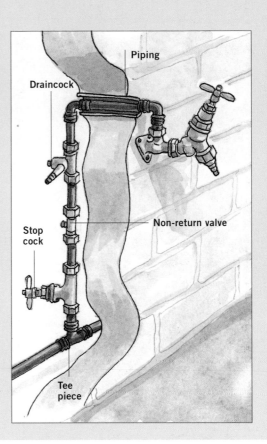

Piping

Draincock

Non-return valve

Stop cock

Tee piece

ABOVE This novelty squirrel-shaped tap handle adds a small, but quaint and rustic feel to a cottage garden.

rainwater that falls onto the roof of the house or greenhouse in a water butt attached to the gutter. Water butts should have a tap and a lid to keep out insects and should be placed on a solid stack of bricks to make the tap high enough for a watering can to get beneath it. It is a mistake to cut the pipe leading from the gutter and run it straight into the water butt, as there is a risk that when the butt is full, that water will overflow down the sides of the house, potentially causing damp. To prevent this, either buy a water butt fitted with a 'diverter' which redirects water back to the drain or fit one in the gutter pipe itself.

Gravity system

If your greenhouse is situated a long way from the outside tap, a gravity-fed irrigation system could save you the expense of fitting an outside tap and a considerable amount of time dragging a hose to and from the greenhouse.

The system involves a water butt, connected to a hose that runs into the greenhouse. Providing that the base of the water butt is at least 60 cm (24in) above the height of the greenhouse floor, water will always flow from the butt to the greenhouse to give crops grown in the borders a drink or fill a watering can to irrigate plants on the greenhouse bench. To stop the flow, simply hook the end of the hose to the side of the greenhouse frame in a position above the water level in the butt.

The beauty of this system is that it is very simple to install. The water butt can either be connected to the gutter of the greenhouse, or to the gutter of the house, with the hose running the length of the garden hidden at the base of a hedge or fence. If you are prepared to keep the butt topped up, it can be placed anywhere in the garden, even concealed among the foliage of a hedge. If the greenhouse is at the bottom of a slope and the butt is by the house, fix a tap to the end of the hosepipe so that the flow can be stopped when you have finished watering.

Rainwatering

Collected rainwater is the best for many pot-grown plants such as azaleas, camellias, and ericaceous heathers as it is has less lime in it than tap water. However, collected water also contains fungal spores which can attack and kill seedlings, so it should not be used until plants have grown their first true leaves.

Glossary

Aggregate Pieces of crushed stone or gravel used in making concrete or as a base material.

Arbour Garden structure that usually incorporates a seat and plants (typically climbers) into its design.

Arris rail Angled rail that runs horizontally along the middle of a fence. Intended to provide support and divert rainwater away from fence panels.

Bolster chisel A type of chisel with a broad blade that is splayed outwards toward the cutting edge. Used to cut masonry.

Butyl Rubber-like material that can be used as a pond liner. Durable but relatively expensive.

Cloche A glass or polythene cover used for propagation or for protecting early crops raised in open ground, or to warm the soil before planting.

Club hammer A heavy hammer often used with a chisel.

Cold Frame An unheated structure made from wood, brick or glass, with a hinged glass or clear plastic lid, used to protect plants from cold weather.

Compression joints Used in plumbing to connect lengths of pipe to various fittings. The joint seals by screwing home its nut, which in turn compresses an olive onto the pipe or fitting.

Consumer unit A domestic electricity fuse box.

Coping Cast concrete pieces, bevelled wooden strips or masonry used to deflect rainwater from the face of a wall or fence.

Crazy paving Consists of broken pieces of paving slab laid on wet mortar to produce a complex decorative pattern.

Datum peg A wooden peg set at a particular position, forming the point from which measurements are taken.

Decking Timber platform constructed at either high or low level for use in the garden. An increasingly popular alternative to the patio.

Double digging A cultivation technique in which the soil is worked over to a depth of two spade blades.

Double leaf (of a wall) Having two layers of bricks.

Drainage The passage of excess water through the soil, or systems of drainage which are used to remove excess water from a building or structure.

Duckboards Wooden slats supported by timber bearers. A versatile alternative to decking.

Flexible liner Can be made from PVC or butyl rubber and can be used to line a pond of any shape.

Float Tool with a flat, usually steel, rectangular face, which is used to apply plaster to walls.

Footing A narrow concrete foundation for a wall or the base of garden steps.

Gazebo A garden pavilion or summerhouse.

Hardcore Broken bricks, concrete or stones used as a base beneath foundations, paving and other garden structures.

Hawk A small square board with a handle beneath, which is used for carrying mortar.

Header A brick or stone laid across a wall so that its end is flush with the outer surface.

Humus The organic residue of decayed vegetable matter in soil.

Joist Timber or metal beam used to support a structure, for example a deck.

Loam This is normally soil of medium texture, easily worked, that contains more or less equal parts of sand, silt and clay and is usually rich in humus.

Mastic Waterproof filler and sealant.

MDF (Medium-density fibreboard) Versatile and inexpensive board that has a plethora of DIY uses.

Mitre The method of cutting two pieces of timber at complementary angles so that they can be joined.

Mulch A layer of organic or other material applied to the soil surface.

Nosing The front edge of a step, often protruding from a riser.

Olive Soft metal ring that fits around a pipe to form part of a compression joint as used in plumbing.

Padsaw A small narrow saw used for cutting curves.

Perennial A plant that lives for at least three growing seasons.

Pergola A trellis or framework supported on posts that carries climbing plants.

Pesticide A chemical substance used for killing pests.

Pier Thick column of brickwork that buttresses a wall.

Plasticizer Added to mortar to aid the workability and flexibility of the mix. Lime was traditionally used for this purpose, but nowadays chemicals are more commonly employed.

Profile boards Narrow wooden crosspieces nailed to uprights used to mark out foundations for walls.

Raised beds Elevated flowerbeds frequently made from brick. Used to increase the space available for planting. Can be used on paved areas.

Residual current device (RCD) A device used to protect against accidental shock. Recommended for use whenever mains cabling is taken across the garden. The RCD automatically shuts off the power supply if any change in current is detected.

Rigid liners Pre-formed, usually fibreglass, liners for ponds.

Riser The vertical part of a step.

Scree A slope comprising rock fragments, simulated in gardens as scree beds, in which drainage is particularly good.

Screed A thin layer of mortar applied to give a smooth surface on which to build brick or block walls, or as a finish for concrete.

Skim The final layer of fine plaster that is applied to a wall or structure.

Soakaway A pit filled with rubble, into which water drains and percolates to earth.

Spirit level A tool with a bubble vial which is used for checking horizontal levels.

Spotboard A panel of chipboard or plywood with a handle beneath that is used to hold mortar.

Stretcher A brick or stone laid horizontally with its length parallel to the length of a wall.

Subsoil The layer of soil below the topsoil which is lighter in colour and lacking in organic matter, soil life and nutrients.

Tamping To ram down an area of sand, hardcore or similar base material using a timber post.

Tesserae Small square blocks used to create mosaics, for example broken china and tiles.

Topography A description, map or diagram of the natural and artificial features of an outside area.

Tread The horizontal section of a step.

Trellis Usually a latticework of narrow wooden or plastic slats, forming open squares.

Index

Page numbers in *italics* refer to illustrations.

Acknowledgments

Acknowledgements

Jacket credits:

Harpur Garden Library/Pershore College, RHS Chelsea Show Front Cover bottom left.

S & O Mathews Front Cover top centre.

Octopus Publishing Group Ltd. /Polly Wreford Back Cover centre left, Back cover right, Back Cover top left, Back Cover bottom left, Back Cover bottom right, /Mel Yates Front Cover top left, Front Cover top right, Back Cover bottom right.

B & B Photographs 146 Centre Right.

Eric Crichton/Daily Telegraph RHS Chelsea 92/ Design: Elizabeth Bank Associates 181 Top, /Mrs Una Carr, Avon National Garden Scheme 29 Top Right, /Neil Collett Esq, Warwickshire National Garden Scheme 22 Bottom Left, /Mrs Daphne Foulsham, I/C of National Garden Scheme, Surrey 158, /RHS Hampton Court 2000/ Design: Gabrielle Pape & Isabelle Van Groeningen 'Go Organic' 59, /Chiffchaffs – Mr & Mrs KR Potts, Dorset National Garden Scheme 55 Top Right, /Private Garden 13 Bottom Right, 32 Top Right, 56 Top Left, 62 right, 134 Bottom Left, 176 Top, 200–201, /RHS Chelsea '89 196, /RHS Chelsea '92 164, /RHS Chelsea '93 (small gardens) 17 Bottom Right, /RHS Chelsea '97 125, /RHS Hampton Court '94 122 Bottom Left, /RHS Chelsea '99/ Design: Alan Sargent 'Deckscapes' 49, /Sissinghurst National Trust 114 Top Right, /Barnsley House, Rosemary Verey 129 Bottom Right.

DIY Photo Library 36 Top, 53 Bottom Centre, 53 Bottom Right, 141, 142 Bottom Left, 142 Bottom Centre.

Garden Picture Library/David Askham 81, /Lynne Brotchie 137, /Brian Carter 217, /Bob Challinor 72, /Eric Crichton 86–87, /John Glover 85, 130 left, /Juliet Greene/ Chris Gregory: 'Where Lovers Meet', Chelsea Flower Show, 1999 74, /Juliet Greene/ Design: Pamela Woods 116, /Juliet Greene/ Design: Robin Williams 'Sights, Sounds & Senses Gdn' Hampton Court 1997 128 Top Right, /Marijke Heuff/ Priona Gardens 140 Top Right, /Michael Howes 144 Bottom Left, 214, /Ann Kelley 194, /Lamontagne 47, /Gary Rogers 182 Top, 184–185, /Alec Scaresbrook 35, /Alec Scaresbrook/ Ironhorse Studios 160 Top, /Ron Sutherland 146 Bottom Left, 178, /Ron Sutherland/ Anne Mollo Garden 108, /Ron Sutherland/ Design: Anthony Paul 190 Bottom Right, /Ron Sutherland/ Design: Duane Paul Design Team 52, /Ron Sutherland/ Design: Murray Collins 45 Top, /Ron Sutherland/ Mike Paul's Garden 156–157, /Brigitte Thomas 107 Bottom Left, /Brigitte Thomas/ Design: Chevalier & Frinault 159 Top, /Juliette Wade 128 Bottom Left, 138 Top Left, 175 Top.

John Glover 4, 42, 54, 159 Bottom Right, 168 left, 171, 183, /Design: Julian Dowle 166

/Design: Chris Jacobson 28–29 Bottom Centre, /Janis Ridley 175 Bottom Right, /Design: Peter Styles 172, /Chelsea 2000/ Design: Robin Templat Williams 106 Top Right, /Design: Alan Titchmarsh 199 right, /Design: Mark Walker 129 left, /Design: Claire Whitehouse 58 Top, /Design: Jane Fearnley-Wittingstall 143, /Wollerton Old Hall 16.

Octopus Publishing Group Ltd. 30 Bottom Left, 37 Top, 71, 92 left, 106 Bottom Left, /Paul Barker 45 Bottom Right, /Mark Bolton 10 left, 10 Centre, 13 left, 31 Bottom Left, 33 Bottom Left, 38, 51 Bottom Left, 51 Bottom Centre, 51 Bottom Right, 94, 147 Bottom Left, 147 Bottom Centre Left, 147 Bottom Centre Right, 147 Bottom Right, 148 Centre Left, 148 Centre Right, 148 Bottom Centre, 148 Bottom Right, 160 Bottom Left, 188 right, 191 Bottom Right, 202 left, 202 right, 202 Centre, 203 left, 203 right, 203 Centre, /Design: Cannington College 79, 84 Bottom Centre, /Design: Naila Green, Pecorama, Devon 40 right, 55 Bottom Right, 60, 61, 76, /Design: Ellie Hawkins 33 Bottom Centre, 176 Bottom, /Design: John Labrum 33 Bottom Right, 58 Bottom, /Lady Farm, Somerset 62 left, /Design: Jane Reeves 188 Top Left, /Design: Jo Singleton, Sailmakers Cottage, Devon 95, /Colin Bowling/ Paul Forrester 205, 206, 207, 208, 209, 210, /Paul Forrester 204, /Jerry Harpur/ Bob Flowerdew 89 Bottom Left, /Neil Holmes 63, /Di Lewis 99 Top Centre, 99 Top Right, 99 Bottom Right, 120, 121 Top Centre, /Clive Nichols 90, /Malcolm Robertson 69, /Stephen Robson 57 Top Left, /Mark Winwood 24 Bottom Left, 32 Bottom Right, 92 right, 119 Top Right, /Steve Wooster 17 Top Left, 25 Bottom Left, 55 Bottom Left, 84 Bottom Left, 96, 97 Top, 134 Top Right, /Polly Wreford 97 Bottom Left, 121 Bottom, 129 Top Right, 129 Centre Right, /Mel Yates 1, 97 Bottom Right, 98 Top Centre, 98 Top Right, 98 Centre, 100 Top Centre, 100 Top Right, 100 Centre, 101 Top Centre, 101 Centre, 101 Centre Right, 101 Bottom Left, 102 Centre Left, 102 Centre, 102 Bottom, 103 Top Left, 103 Top Right, 103 Centre Left, 103 Centre Right, 103 Bottom Right, 104, 109 Bottom, 112, 118 Top, 118 Bottom Left, 118 Bottom Centre, 118 Bottom Right, 119 Bottom Left, 119 Bottom Right, 121 Top Right, 151 Top Right, 151 Centre Right, 151 Bottom Right, 152 left, 152 right, 152 Centre, 153 Top Left, 153 Bottom Left, 153 Bottom Right, 154, 155, 179 Top Centre, 179 Top Right, 179 Centre Right, 179 Bottom Right, 212 Bottom Left, 213 Top Left, 213 Bottom Centre, 213 Bottom Right.

Harpur Garden Library 111, /Barnsley House, Glo 15 Top Left, /Design: Mary Effron, California 22 Top Right, /Design: Simon Fraser, London 162, /Design: Edwina Von Gal, NYC, USA 192–193, /Design: Sonny Garcia, San Francisco, USA 186, /Design: Luciano Giubbilei, Kensington 50, 53 Top, /Design: Bunny Guinness/ RHS Chelsea 1997 110, /Marcus Harpur, Barnardos, Essex 31 Top Right, /Marcus Harpur/ Design: Jean M. Clark, Suffolk 167, /Marcus Harpur/ Design: Marney Hall, RHS Chelsea 1998 182 Bottom, /Iden Croft, Staplehurst, Kent 33 Top Right, /Design: Deborah Kellany, Norfolk 66 Top Right, /Lambeth Palace, London 24 Top Right,

/Design: Arabella Lennox-Boyd, London 28 Bottom Left, /Design: Steve Lorton, Seattle, WA 26–27, /Design: Christopher Masson, London 3, /Design: Jim Matsuo, LA, CA, USA 41, 122–123 Top Centre, /Design: Keeyla Meadows, Berkeley, California 30 Top Right, /Design: Ryl Nowell, Sussex 198, /Park Farm, Essex 138 Bottom Right, /Design: Jason Payne, London 117, /Design: Roger Platts, RHS Chelsea Show 20 Bottom, /Design: Lisette Pleasance, London 14, /Design: John Plummer 67, /RHS Chelsea Show 48, /Design: Mark Rios, LA, CA, USA 109 Top, /Design: Judith Sharpe, London 8–9, /Sun House, Suffolk 177, /Design: Barbara Thomas, Seattle, WA 25 Top Right, /Design: J Tripp & P Masson, New Zealand 132, /Cary Wolinsky, Norwell, Mass. 140 left, /Design: Peter Wooster, USA 150.

Andrew Lawson 15 Bottom Right, 40 left, 56 Bottom Centre, 64–65, 68, 82, 88, 89 Top Right, 91, 142 Top Right, 168 right, /Arrow Cottage, Hereford 174, /Design: Jonathan Baillie 66 Centre Left, /RHS Chelsea Flower Show 2000. Berkshire College of Agriculture 191 Top, /Bosvigo House, Cornwall 20 Top, /RHS Chelsea 1999. The Very Interesting Landscape Co. Design: Paul Dyer 173, /Hampton Court Flower Show 2000 32 Top Left, /Design: Penelope Hobhouse 6, 107, 126–127, /Design: Margot Knox 75, /Design: Ryl Nowell, Wilderness Farm 44, /Old Rectory, Sudborough 29 Top Left, /Sticky Wicket, Dorchester, Dorset 135, /Hampton Court Flower Show 1999. Still Water & Dreams. Design: Jane Sweetser 114 Centre Left, /Wollerton Old Hall, Shropshire 181 Bottom.

Marshalls (www.marshalls.co.uk) 37 Centre, 37 Centre Right, 37 Bottom Centre, 37 Bottom Right.

S & O Mathews 133.

Clive Nichols Photography/Design: Jonathan Baillie 140 Centre Right, /Design: Rachel Fletcher 120 Top Left, /Lighting by Garden and Security Lighting 189 Top, 189 Bottom /Design: Bunny Guinness, DGAA Homelife Garden, Chelsea 97 153 Top Right, /The Nichols Garden, Reading 130 right, 144 Top Right, /Save the Children Garden, Chelsea 1991 195 Top, /Design: Paul Thompson &Trevyn McDowell 190 left.

Derek St Romaine/Design: Barbara Segall 195 Bottom, /Design: David Stevens, Hampton Court 1998 199 left.

Design Maritn Topping
Picture Research Zoe Holterman
Additional Text Susan Stephenson
      Toby Buckland
      Richard Bird
New Illustrations Jane Hughes
Index Alan Thatcher